The
Promise

Book #3 in the
Comes the End series by
William Creed

ISBN 978-1-9393060-7-4

Library of Congress Control Number: 2013944788

© 2014 William S. Creed
All Rights Reserved

Printed in the United States of America
Published by 23 House Publishing
SAN 299-8084
www.23house.com

visit www.williamcreed.com

First, I want to thank my wonderful wife, Sharon, for all her support. I could not have done it without her. I want to thank the many readers who have sent me notes of support. Receiving such notes and letters brings me great joy. The life of writing is a solitary one, and rarely do I get the opportunity to hear from readers once the manuscript leaves my hands. Lastly, I want to thank those who helped me in refining the manuscript. I want to mention a few names, and apologize if I have left anyone out. My thanks to: Zack C., Monique C., Mari B., Mary W., Col. Tom G., Kaye S. and Mike C.

Table of Contents

Chapter 1 1
Chapter 2 12
Chapter 3 26
Chapter 4 38
Chapter 5 56
Chapter 6 65
Chapter 7 77
Chapter 8 85
Chapter 9 96
Chapter 10 104
Chapter 11 115
Chapter 12 128
Chapter 13 136
Chapter 14 150
Chapter 15 163
Chapter 16 171
Chapter 17 182
Chapter 18 194
Chapter 19 204
Chapter 20 216
Chapter 21 227
Chapter 22 239
Chapter 23 248
Chapter 24 258
Chapter 25 270
Chapter 26 278
Chapter 27 287
Chapter 28 300

The Story Continues...

In *The Gathering*, the second book in the *Comes the End* series, Andy Moore and Stephanie Collins are fleeing from the Ancestral Brothers and their human henchman, the Goonies. They find their way to an abandoned Christian camp at the top of a mountain secluded by clouds. Camp Noah, as it was called in its day, becomes a refuge for Christians on the run, and believers began to arrive.

As they start to organize the daily operations of the camp and the constant stream of arrivals, Andy and Stephanie realize that their love is destined for the next level – marriage. They find a pastor in the underground network of a nearby city who performs the ceremony and joins the couple in matrimony.

The camp attracts a number of interesting individuals, including a mysterious, old hermit living in a nearby cave who appears at just the right time to offer council to Andy. It is clear to many people that Andy has been chosen by God for a leadership role, and they begin calling him the Prophet. Another recruit to the camp is an Army Major named Frost who has deserted the military because of his Christian beliefs; Frost is given a position to lead the ground security for the camp. It turns out that he is a spy for the Brothers, however, who is reporting on the activities of the Christians.

On a mission to protect the camp, Stephanie is shot through the heart by the traitor Major Frost, and is killed instantly. Her body is brought back to camp, where Andy collapses. The Hermit reminded him that God gave believers the power to heal the sick and raise the dead. With the prayers of all the Christians in the camp, led by Andy, God restores Stephanie's life.

The Promise begins shortly after the miracle, with the Goonies beginning to close in on the Christians' camp.

For in the time of trouble he shall hide me in his pavilion: in the secret of his tabernacle shall he hide me; he shall set me up upon a rock.

– Psalm 27:5

Chapter 1

Tim was scared, and for good reason. He was not a good thief – just a necessary one. He knew bad thieves were eventually caught; and then, what would the children do? That was the worry. Since he was only seventeen and an inexperienced thief, he recognized that the probability of his getting caught was very high. Perhaps he had not thought of everything this time – perhaps this time, he would fail.

Slowly, he shook his head, trying to rid himself of such doubts. Then, after carefully reviewing everything, he assured himself that he had every angle covered. He had the seven-year-old twins, Alison and Katie, watching the road to the north. Mickey, the twelve-year-old, was watching to the South.

Tim closed his eyes. Who would have thought he would be leading a gang of child thieves? Yet, what was the alternative? Was he to take the children back, and have them taken into custody by the Ancestral Brothers – those supposed ancient ancestors of humans? As far as he was concerned, they were just a bunch of murderers. Tim was sure they had already rewarded the Goonies for the attack at his church. He would like to know how much they had paid per body for killing his parents, along with the hundred or so other members. No, he would rather his little family live like animals than live among them.

Wiping his nose on his sleeve, he gave a final look at both the store and the deserted Highway 276. He knew it was time.

Suddenly, the two-way crackled in his hand and a cow's

1

moo came out. Tim jumped at the unexpected sound. Then, lifting his walkie-talkie, hissed, "Quiet! How many times do I have to tell you?" He was sure it was Alison. Kids.

The radio fell silent again.

Tim waited a moment, regaining his composure. "Alison, how's it looking?"

"All clear," was the muffled response, obviously trying not to laugh. Tim clicked over the lever. "Mickey – how about you?"

"Nothing. Haven't seen anything for a long time."

"Okay. I'm going in, keep me posted – and be quiet!"

"Did you say a prayer, Tim?" It was sweet Katie, Alison's twin sister.

"No honey. Why don't you say one?" He then quickly added, "Say it to yourself." He was in no mood to have God hanging around, and messing things up.

Slowly, Tim stood and looked around. There had been no movement around the combination gas station and country store since the clerk shut off the lights and drove away two hours ago. In fact, at this late hour, there was little traffic at all on the narrow asphalt mountain road. Truth was, now days, there was almost no traffic at all, regardless of the hour, anywhere. Especially, since the Goonies were running around stopping cars and killing Christians.

His vantage point was on a ridge about fifteen feet above the store and running in a semi-circle from the side of the store around to the back. Moving to the south side of the wooded ridge gave him a view of the side, back, and the pumps in front of the store. Giving one last look around, Tim carefully made the trip down from the ridge to the store's level. With a practiced casual walk, he made his way toward the back of the store. The rear door, an old wooden, windowless pine, did not appear substantial. Carefully, he looked at the door's edges while running his fingers along them, inspecting for telltale signs of a burglar alarm. He neither saw nor felt any. Nudging the door gave some indication it was locked. Backing up, Tim took a deep breath, and ran at it. He expected the door to offer stiff resistance, but to his surprise, it did not. There was a loud crack as the hinges ripped away from the old wood, and he burst through. His momentum exceeded his steps, and with a thump, he fell on his face.

Quickly jumping to his feet, he looked around the darkened, deserted interior for any sign of life. Beams from the outside light pole poured through the front window giving sharp corners to the aisles inside. The only other light was a beer sign, illuminating the store's far corner where the coolers were located. The interior was heavy with a dead silence, interrupted only by the steady ticking of an antique-style wall clock behind the register, to his left. Listening, but hearing nothing else, Tim was satisfied the age-worn store was deserted.

He pulled out a laundry bag and a pair of gloves from underneath his shirt and prepared to go shopping. First, he put on the gloves for no reason other than it made him feel better. The cereals were first, followed by bread, some hotdogs, three cartons of orange juice, and two gallons of milk – must not forget that. He would make sure they drank these first before they went bad. He continued to fill the bag. When the bag was full, he reached under his shirt and pulled out two smaller bags.

Near the front of the store, he found a counter with children's T-shirts on it. Most looked too small, but he found a few with the NC State logo he thought were about right. On another shelf, he spied some coloring books and crayons and added them to his loot. He wished he had help – he would love to take more – they needed everything he could bring. For a moment, he considered calling Mickey, but there wasn't time. Lastly, he went to the cash register in search of money, but there was none. There never was. No need of money anymore as everyone was using those ID cards the Ancestral Brothers, or Visitors – or whatever they called themselves now – were issuing. He knew some of these country stores still accepted cash, but apparently not this one.

Looking under the counter, he spotted something under some paper towels. Lifting the towels revealed a gun looking dark and ominous. Cautiously he picked it up and examined it closely. It looked to be a forty-five caliber – not that he was an expert, but he had seen them in the movies and someone told him they were 'forty-fives'. Turning the gun upside down, he saw an inserted clip. With some fiddling, he was able to eject it, and found it held bullets. He put the clip in his pocket and stuffed the gun in his waistband.

The radio crackled and Mickey's excited voice blurted through, "Tim – watch it! There's a cop car coming!"

Grabbing the walkie-talkie Tim said, "Okay – got it. Hold still, let's see what happens." He ran to the back door, and grabbed it. He raised it up and attempted to fit it back into the doorframe. Since he had broken the hinges, it would not stay up. Tim spotted the inside bolt and he quickly threw it. That did the trick. He ran to the front window and saw the approaching police car turn into the store's drive. As it did, the spotlight flashed on and began scanning the store. Reaching the front of the store, the police cruiser drew to a stop while the spotlight continued to play on the front window.

Instinctively, Tim drew back. Even though he was certain the police could not see him behind the groceries, he felt his heart trying to escape his body. Peeking from behind the cereal boxes, he saw a police officer get out of the car, and approach the store.

Looking frantically around to see if all appeared right, Tim spotted the three bags on the floor where he had dropped them, in full view of the window. He ran around the cereal aisle, so that he would not pass in front of the window. He dove toward the end of the racks, reached out and grabbed the bags. Quickly he pulled them back behind the rack, out of view from the window.

A large shadow floated across the room as the officer held his face to the window. Tim kept low, now peering between the loaves of bread. The officer brought out his flashlight and began scanning the store. Finally, satisfied that all was normal, he turned and began walking back to the car. The searchlight went out and Tim watched as the patrol car pulled back onto the highway and continued in a southerly direction.

Pulling out his radio, he shouted, "Alison! Watch out! Cop car coming!"

Alison's voice came back, and she was surprisingly calm "I see him, Timmy. I see him."

After giving a quick look around, he threw the bags over his shoulder and exited the rear of the store. The building was located at the bottom of a small hollow in the Carolina hillside, which meant he had to climb up the steep embankment. With an effort, he worked his way to the top, half carrying, half dragging his loot, until he was next to their bicycles and overlooking the store. Still breathing deeply, Tim called the children to join him.

"Did you get some Honey Roasted Flakes?" asked Mickey the moment he arrived.

Tim nodded and sighed. "When are you gonna try something else? I can't get those things all the time – and stay outta that stuff. We have a long way to go, and I don't wanna see you kids pickin' at the bags."

The small troop made their way into the forest, sometimes riding, and sometimes pushing their bikes. They followed the power lines for an hour, until they hit the creek; then, north for another half-hour, walking in the creek's cool water to hide any evidence of their being there. Finally, reaching a small rock outcropping, they scrambled out of the creek, hid their bikes and climbed up the hill, pulling and pushing their bags of loot to the small opening of the cave they called home. They pushed and pulled the bags through the cave entrance. It would have been easier to follow the narrow path that ran around the tall and rocky cliff, but Mickey was afraid of heights. The result was they walked up the wide, though steep and rocky face of the tall hill.

Before following the three children inside the twenty-foot hole in the Carolina hillside, Tim gave a cautionary look around.

For several moments, all were silent as they rested from the trip. Finally, Mickey broke the silence.

"Timmy, it's too far – it's getting' too far, Timmy," he said, still gasping for air.

The twins murmured their agreement.

Tim nodded. It was too far – time to move again. Besides the distance, they had hit so many stores around this camp that Tim wondered why they had not already been caught. He was certain the extra care the cop had taken to look in the store was due to the reported burglaries.

Tim nodded, "Yeah, okay. We'll scout out a new location tomorrow." Tim had been thinking about moving and recalled his parents talking about a place in the mountains of North Carolina. It was run by a man everyone called the Prophet. Trouble was – Tim did not know exactly where the place was, or how to get there. They only had their bikes and he doubted they could peddle that far – especially the twins. At any rate, the kids were right. It was time to move.

"I want my own bedroom. Can I have my own bedroom, Tim?" asked Katie.

Mickey laughed, the motion making his hair wave. The dirtier his hair got, the further it stuck out from his head, and the more it weaved back and forth as he walked. "Me too, I want my own bedroom," he said, followed by, "Where can we go? Know of any place?" He paused for a second then blurted out, "We should move into a house with a big-screen TV."

"We think we should go back to Perkins, Ohio," announced Alison, a note of resolution in her voice, as she remembered the tree-lined streets, and the old Perkins Mansion. Her mother was born in Perkins. When she saw something she didn't like, she would evoke the name of the 1798 town founder by saying, "Old man Quincy would turn over in his grave if he knew..." and then fill in whatever unsightly thing may have caught her attention. She loved Perkins, "This is where a family can sink in some roots and raise a family," is what she used to say.

Katie nodded and then sniffed, "How do we know that Mommy and Daddy are dead?" She said, her voice cracking while her face crinkled, allowing a tear to escape.

"Now girls," began Tim; this was not the first time he had heard this. His voice was soft as he tried to comfort the girls. "Let's not talk silly. We can't go back, you know that. I'd wish we could– remember the soap box derby?" he asked with a smile.

"I remember," chimed in Mickey. "I was in the one two years ago. I'd a won if that wheel hadn't come off," he added with a note of displeasure.

"But girls," said Tim, "I've told you so many times, no one's alive except us. I would give anything if someone was there for us – you know that; but I saw what they were doing. No one else survived."

"Tim, what did happen?" asked Mickey. "You always say that no one survived, but you never tell us exactly what happened."

"Yeah, what happened, tell us," chimed Katie and Alison in unison.

Tim sighed deeply, and was quiet for a moment. "Well, this is hard," he said. "Remember, my parents died, too. I just

7

don't like to talk about it."

The three children remained quiet as Tim gathered himself.

"I heard the soldiers come in. I was downstairs in the kitchen. All the parents were upstairs singing up a storm. Then, I heard a big commotion – I guess that's when the soldiers busted in. Next, I heard the soldiers yelling for everybody to get down. All of a sudden there was lots of gunfire and there was lots of screaming." Tim paused for a moment allowing the emotion of the memory to pass.

"Yeah," said Mickey, "I remember the screaming. Mrs. Gotlier shoved us through that secret door in the closet downstairs."

"I heard them take her away – she was crying," said Alison. "I think I heard her scream later. It sure sounded like Mrs. Gotlier."

Tim nodded. "I peaked around the corner and saw them dragging her up the stairs. There were four of them. I recognized one – he was the mailman."

"Mr. Bower?" asked Alison in astonishment. "I thought he was a nice man. I used to get the mail from him on Saturday when we were there for Girl Scouts."

"So, then what?" asked Mickey.

"Well, I could hear all this screaming, and gunshots. It went on for maybe fifteen minutes. I also could hear the..." Tim stopped.

"Hear what?" asked Mickey

Tim could feel his throat closing as he fought back the tears. He coughed to clear his throat before continuing. "–hear the hacking. I could hear the hacking." He stopped again, this time putting his hand over his eyes, but the sounds of the victims being Handed remained. It was the new way of collecting rewards for killing Christians. No longer did one have to lug bodies into cars and trucks; now, just bring in the right hand that showed no mark, and the reward was paid. All the children were quiet, except for Alison sniffing her tears back.

"I waited 'til I heard them leave," continued Tim finally, "then I sneaked upstairs." He paused.

"So Timmy, what did you see?" Mickey asked softly.

Tim looked up, brushing the tears from his eyes and sniffed. Taking a deep breath, he continued. "They were all dead. Everyone was dead. There was blood everywhere and…and all their right hands were gone. The Goonies had Handed them all."

"Stop!" shouted Katie. "I don't wanna hear anymore!"

"You said you wanted to know! Every day you say you want me to tell you – now I'm telling you!" He paused, looking down. "So now you know."

"I heard stories they did that," said Mickey in a subdued voice. "They get some money for every right hand they turn in that doesn't have that stupid Mark on it."

Tim nodded silently.

"So, did you see our parents?" asked Alison. "Where were our parents?"

Tim was silent for a moment. "I didn't go to each body; there were almost a hundred of them. But I did see your father, Alison. Believe me – they were all dead. Everyone was dead! My single thought was to get us out of there to some place where we could all be safe. We are the only survivors. Now, I don't wanna talk about it anymore."

Alison was quiet. Her twin sister, Katie, sat with silent tears running down her checks.

Tim scooted over and put his arm around her shoulder. "Now Katie honey, they are in a better place now. They are with the Lord, and someday you'll see them again." Tim paused and looked around at the small group. He didn't believe anymore that the Lord cared much one way or the other.

However, talking about God seemed to have a calming effect on the kids.

"I don't think mama is dead," whimpered Alison.

Katie remained silent, detached.

Tim did not respond. Perhaps it was better that they had some hope.

Without warning, the ground moved. A tremor came through as the Earth shuddered from a distant quake. They waited it out in silence. Such things were becoming more and more common. A couple of months ago a similar thing would have struck fear in the hearts of all the children, with even a possible scream from one of the twins. Now, it drew no comment from any of them.

After a few seconds, the rolling sensation ceased.

"I think if we follow Route 276 north we should be able to locate something," said Tim.

Mickey nodded. "But won't that put us further into the mountains? That's a real long way to go on our bicycles. I don't think I can peddle uphill like that. I don't think they have a lot of stores up there."

Tim knew Mickey was right, but he also heard you could find safety. Word was, the Goonies didn't go into the mountains. If that was true, they could be safe there, at least for a while. "Maybe," responded Tim, "but I think we need to disappear for awhile. I get the feeling something is coming, and I just think the mountains would be the best place. If we need to, we can always move again. Besides, maybe in the hills we can find a deserted cabin."

Mickey grinned. "Yeah, maybe one with a big-screen TV."

"Why can't we go home and see if Mama is still there? You said once we could look for her," said Katie.

Tim sighed; why had he promised that? Why wouldn't she forget he had said that – that was three months ago. "We can't go back, Katie." He looked at Mickey and shook his head,

"And Mickey, there won't be any big-screen TV. Look, we have to start being realistic. We have to make do with what we have and what comes along." Tim smiled at the children, "Let's not get our hopes up – safety is the main thing we got to worry about." Seeking to break the mood, he clapped his hands together. "Okay, tell you what we do, I threw some candy in one of those bags, and there's also a couple bags of already-popped popcorn. We'll take one out and we each can have two handfuls of popcorn, plus one candy bar. Then, we have to hit the sack. We've got a long day ahead tomorrow," said Tim, "and I want to get as far as we can toward the mountains."

Everyone brightened up at the mention of candy and popcorn – rare treats these days.

The stars watched over a quiet, tired group that night, each lost in their own thoughts – except Mickey, who was savoring his Baby Ruth candy bar. With care he licked the chocolate off, and then nibbled at the peanuts – it was the only real way to eat a Baby Ruth. Yes, for the moment, life was good.

Chapter 2

The morning sun chased the last vestiges of night, devouring its darkness as Tim awoke. He went to each of the three children making sure they were awake. Today promised to be long – and maybe dangerous. Having broken into several stores to the east, Tim was somewhat familiar with the territory for about ten miles, but was unsure of the land beyond, and that concerned him.

Digging through his knapsack, he dragged out the United States Atlas he had stolen a few weeks earlier. Its pages were dog-eared from their journey from Ohio southward toward North Carolina. Locating North Carolina on the map, Tim searched for a route that would take them off main roads, yet allow them to move steadily eastward. He thought of the rumor that there were some people, including one they called the Prophet, who lived in the hills. They could possibly provide shelter for the children.

First, they would have to get a car. All this travel was too much – especially for the twins. He retrieved the gun from the knapsack, and again put it in his belt, before calling to the others. It might become useful if they were to get a car.

"Okay, let's get up and get going. We have lots of ground to cover. Here, I got some breakfast bars last night – everybody take one, and don't complain to me about the flavor."

Silently they devoured the bars before they carefully packed their gear on their bikes. They then wheeled their bikes down into the cold waters of the stream. After a mile, Tim led them into the forest, with which they had all become familiar over the past few weeks. Within the woods was a shallow ravine running parallel with the highway for about three miles. As the highway went further north, the ravine began to deepen, and at various points they were unable to see the road. From time to time, Tim would climb up until he could spot the road through the trees. Finally, as the sun was well past noon, he signaled them to stop. The children collapsed where they were without a sound. Tim let everyone rest for thirty minutes, before getting them up again, but not without protests.

"I'm tired, Timmy," whined Katie.

"Yeah, what's the hurry?" chimed in Mickey.

"Okay. Done complaining?" asked Tim with an edge to his voice. "We have a long way to go. Later I wanna get us a car."

"Okay, now you're talking – let's get a sporty one!" said Mickey enthusiastically.

"Let's get one of those big ones where they got a TV in them and some place we can sleep," added Alison.

Tim smiled. "I think we'll get what we can, and that's it."

The troop set off again, alternating between pushing and riding their bikes. As the sun approached late afternoon, Tim called a halt.

"Okay, we'll stop here," he said, carefully laying down his bike so not to disturb its cargo. The others followed suit. Tim looked at the deserted highway. During the entire day, only one car had passed and he regretted not rushing out to stop it. It was obvious their traveling by bike wasn't the best way, especially for the young twin girls. At first, he considered all four of them waiting by the side of the road for another car, but decided four of them might discourage people from stopping. Instead, he decided the twins would look cute.

"You girls will come up with me to the road. When we get there we'll flag down the first car that comes along," he said, then looking at the twins, "be sure you're smiling when he stops."

He felt in his belt for the forty-five he had gotten from the store, then retrieved the clip from his pocket and re-inserted it. Finally, putting it in his waistband, he pulled his shirt over it. The cold metal of the gun against his skin was not the only thing he felt – there was a knot of fear too. This would be his first attempt at armed robbery. Things could get crazy when people see a gun; at least it did in the movies. Leaving Mickey in the ditch with their gear, he and the twins climbed up to the highway. The rest of the afternoon went without any traffic at all. Then, nearing five o'clock, Tim saw a van approaching from the south.

"Okay girls, wave."

The girls began waving frantically while Tim stepped out holding out his hand with the palm in a 'stop' motion. To his surprise, the van slowed and stopped, just short of their position. Tim smiled as he approached the van with the girls following, also smiling, as instructed. Reaching the driver's window, Tim pulled out the gun and held it only inches from the driver's face.

"Stop right there!" he shouted, feeling his heart pounding his temples.

The silver-haired driver did not respond, but studied Tim for a moment, then turned and looked at the girls, who were still smiling.

The van driver had an old and crevassed face evidencing long years; his sharp eyes had the look of intelligence, and he wore a bemused smile. Slowly, he turned back and looked at Tim holding the wobbling gun. "Now son, what are you doing?" he asked with slow voice.

"Shut up and get out of the car!"

"You forgot to add that if I don't, you're gonna shoot me."

"Yes – yes, I will! And this forty-five makes a big hole!"

Mickey ran up and joined the group. He stood panting beside the girls – now, all three were smiling.

"Young man, I've faced many people who wanted to do me in during my seventy-five years here on Earth. I ran up the beach on D-Day, been robbed three times in New York, was in the civil rights marches, nearly died in a car accident and I got these alien buggers chasing me. Now you show up and wanna shoot me too. Well, I am tired of it. You go ahead and pull that trigger. However, let me warn you. This here van is a touchy animal. She will do a good job for you if you keep her oil up to snuff – and watch the right rear tire, it tends to lose air. And by the way, that isn't a forty-five, that's a twenty-two. Why, you'd most likely run outta bullets before you do any real damage."

Tim stood silent for a second. The driver looked at him with an expression that betrayed neither fear nor anger as he waited for Tim's response. He seemed patient, almost bored. At last he asked, "Well, you gonna shoot?"

Tim nodded, but without conviction. "It's a forty-five."

"No, it's a twenty-two. Now give it to me before somebody gets hurt."

"Lemme see your right hand," challenged Tim.

"Only if you show me yours."

Slowly, both extended their hands revealing no mark had been placed on either.

Tim found himself giving over his gun.

"What'd ya do that for!" shouted Mickey. "Now what we gonna do?"

"Shut up," said Tim.

"Okay," continued the stranger, as he opened the door and got out. "My name is Jed Drexton," he said, extending his hand. "What's yours?"

"Tim. Tim Barter."

"And who are your companions?"

"This is Katie and Alison Myers – they're twins; and this here," he said pointing, "is Mickey Streeter. He's twelve and sorta the second-in-command."

Drexton smiled. "So now, I don't think we should take much more time here. Someone we don't want to meet could come along. You all hop in, and we'll find a place where we can have a little talk."

"We got some stuff back there along with our bikes."

"Well, get it, but don't take too long."

Tim opened the van's sliding side door, noting the interior was in some disarray. It took only a few minutes to retrieve their supplies and bikes, then each of the kids climbed in and Tim slid the door shut before climbing up front next to the driver.

The group rode in silence, giving Tim the opportunity to sneak some looks at their benefactor. He was obviously up in years. He did not appear to be a bad man, but not all did. Now and then, he would start to hum a tune, but then stop – after a few minutes start again. It was annoying. The group road in semi-silence for a while until Drexton braked, and turned down a narrow gravel side road where he continued for five minutes before finding an area where he could pull off.

The van protested with squeaks and groans as he drove off the road into a field, behind a small grove of trees.

"Okay, I think we'll be fine here. If you kids will bring that cooler there between the seats I've got some food for lunch."

Testing the cooler's weight, Tim lifted it out of the van, then, with Mickey's help, the two boys brought it over to where Drexton waited.

"Don't get your hopes up about there being anything cold in there – there's not. Can't get ice anywhere." Drexton reached down and pulled the lid open to reveal a dozen bottles of water. "Nothing like good water, warm or cold, I say."

Tim nodded in agreement. Water was wonderful and he had often wished they had some when riding their bikes, but it was too heavy to carry. He gladly accepted the offered bottle, passing it on to Alison before accepting another from Drexton.

"So, why don't you tell me about your little group here?" Drexton said, smiling.

"Not much to tell. We were at church when the Goonies

16

broke in, killed our parents, then handed them," he said, referring to the practice of cutting off the right hand of Christians for bounty. "We've been on the run ever since – about three weeks now. I think it's about three weeks, I sorta lost track of the days," said Tim.

Suddenly, Drexton held up his hand. A moment later they felt the Earth, beneath them, roll as though someone ran a rolling pin under them. They waited a moment, before resuming. Such quakes were becoming almost commonplace now. The Visitors said it was a sign that the end of this Earth was near.

After waiting, Drexton spoke. "Musta been tough seeing your parents and everyone else murdered like that."

Tim was silent for a moment, then nodded.

"I don't wanna pry, son, but I know something about seeing stuff like that, and what it can do to you. I was in the Big War back in '44. I saw a lot of things I didn't wanna see. It does something to you. You aren't the same. Am I right?"

Tim looked at Drexton then nodded again.

"Sooner or later you're gonna have to deal with it. It took me a long time – almost ruined my life but I came to face it. There was a big empty void in my life for a long time. Like, before I ran up that beachhead, I knew the order of things in my life. I knew where God was, where I was, my family, my girlfriend, my dog – everyone was in their little cubbyhole inside of me. There was right and wrong and there was God and the Devil. But after – after I saw men dying, heard their screams, saw Germans with fear in their eyes before I shot them; well, everything just got mixed up in me."

"So, what did you do?"

Drexton took a drink and watched as Tim ran his fingers through the grass.

"For a long time," he continued, "there was this empty space inside of me – a darkness I didn't want to go near. I sorta

17

built some walls around it and then closed and locked the door. Friends wanted me to talk about it, to tell them of the action, the glory, the victory. I couldn't talk about it. I didn't even want to think about it. I wanted my life back where everything was in order – where everything made sense – where there was Good and Evil – and where Good was winning and God was in control – where the good people were blessed and the bad people cursed – where mercy and love were bestowed upon the faithful – and all prayers were heard by God."

"I think God hears prayers," said Alison in a small voice.

Drexton smiled, "You bet He does, honey. I tell you what, why don't you, Katie, and Mickey put everything back in the van? We're gonna leave soon." He waited until the three were cleaning up before continuing.

"I'm telling you these things, 'cause I been through it. Don't let that blank space lie too long inside you. Sooner or later you gotta open that door and deal with what's inside, or it will eat you up." Drexton smiled. "Sorry if I sound like I'm preaching. It's just I know what it can do to you, and to your life. Don't give up on God – He won't on you."

Tim remained quiet. He had no response.

"So, what's your plan," asked Drexton. "Just keep running?"

Tim shook his head slowly, "No, I heard there were some people in the mountains that we might be able to hook up with – some say a prophet lives up there."

"Well, today is your blessed day – that's exactly where I'm headed."

"Really!" exclaimed Tim. "Can we go there with you?"

"I don't see why not. I used to know the Prophet."

"You did?" said Mickey, who was close enough to hear. "What's he like – can he really do miracles? I heard he can make it rain anytime he wants, and if he looks at you real hard, you die!"

"Oh Mickey, stop it. That's just stupid!" said Tim.

Mickey sunk his head into his shoulders and stared at the ground muttering, "Well, that's what I heard."

Drexton smiled. "I knew him before he was called "the Prophet." I used to be editor at a newspaper in DC, called the *Washington Post*, and the Prophet, back then, was known as Andy Moore. He was a reporter with the *Washington Dispatch*, our chief rival."

"I didn't know him well, but I knew he was a very good reporter." Drexton paused. "Then I heard he ran into some personal problems and, well, sorta fell outta sight. Then, a few years later, he pops up as the Prophet." Drexton shook his head. "Life sure has gotten strange. Anyway, I hope he remembers me and invites me to stay with his group. Maybe you kids can stay too."

Tim nodded. "Yeah, I think the children need something stable – a home they can come to every night and maybe get some normal things back in their life."

"And you? What about you?"

Tim shrugged his shoulders. "I think I would like to have a home too – at least someplace where I could call my own. But mostly I wanna kill Goonies. I don't think that's what this Prophet guy does, so I'll probably move on."

"Must have been pretty tough seeing everyone dead," said Drexton. "Let me ask the big question, 'cause I understand the Prophet is big on religion. Are you a Christian?"

"My parents were big time."

"What about you?"

"I used to be, but I don't know now. I don't get it anymore. Why does everybody have to die – why doesn't God step in and say 'enough'? Shouldn't He stick up for his people? Where was God when they came and killed our folks?"

For a moment Drexton was silent, and then sighed. "Mystery, mystery, and more mysteries," he began. "I'd like to tell you that as you grow older the mysteries get solved, but they don't. I don't think people, even with as many wrinkles as I have, suddenly discover the facts that solve those mysteries. Sometimes I wish we did and could then pass it on to young folks like you. I guess that's what faith is all about. I guess every man and woman has to discover truths for themselves. I think, over time, we come to our personal settlements with God in which we just agree to let God be God. That's what I hope you do."

"So you just give up finding the truth?"

"No – not at all. When we give up trying to prove God, when we stop trying to discover the facts that reveal God – ah, behold, we then find Him – discovered through the mystery of faith. It's a personal discovery. I see Him differently than others through my private portal. I could tell you of many, many times when I have seen God act in my life – you wouldn't believe any of them. That's because I have such a personal relationship with God that only I recognize His presence in my everyday life, as do others in their lives. It's not only a commonly-shared belief in God that brings Christians together; it's also our personal, private, and individual relationships with God that bind us together. We all start with God's Word. We meet there in a communion of mutual worship. We constantly refine this mutual, yet personal relationship, through our private experiences. It is a shared, yet private relationship, through which we rejoice in the mystery of the ages – faith."

Tim was quiet for a few moments as he tried to digest what the older man was saying. Finally, he looked up at Drexton. "I just don't get it. They say God is love – I'm not seeing it. There's just too much ugly crap going on for me to believe that God even cares. Sorry."

"Oh, don't apologize to me. We all come to discover God in our own way and own time. Some might not discover Him until the next life, but I believe all will eventually."

"So, will your Prophet allow us to stay? Will he allow me to stay if I'm not a Jesus Freak? Does he know you are coming?"

"Oh, I think he'll welcome all of you. Yes, he knows I'm coming. I got word to his group about three weeks ago."

"How did you let him know – did you call him?"

Drexton smiled, "No, I didn't call him. I got word to him through a network I stumbled on back in Washington."

"A 'network'? You mean on the computer?"

"Someday I'll tell you more about it."

"I think, for sure, this Prophet guy will allow the kids to stay," said Tim with some optimism, "they all used to go to church every week, you know."

"We were in the Children's Choir too!" added Katie.

Drexton chuckled. "Oh I'd be surprised if he didn't let someone as cute as you stay."

* * * * *

Andy Moore lifted his hoe and let it fall back to the red dry Carolina soil. Though it had not rained for a while, the clods of dirt broke apart readily as the limp hoe bit into them. His gardening always followed the same routine. He arrived at the garden and enthusiastically began smashing the soil with the hoe. It always ended with him slowly lifting the hoe, and letting it fall back down while thinking it might be time to go. He really did need to start an exercise program, but was convinced gardening shouldn't be it.

Next to him, Stephanie stopped and rested her head on her worn wooden handle, bleached almost white by the Carolina sun. Using her kerchief to wipe her brow, she watched her husband work the field. She enjoyed watching Andy work the earth, feeling there was something primal about it. Of all

Andy's talents, she loved those that were the simplest, the best. Then he was not a leader or Prophet or even her husband; he was a man in an ageless contest to wrestle a bit of sustenance from the Earth's reluctant bosom. Of course, seeing the slow and limp work of the hoe, it appeared the earth was winning.

Andy looked up and caught her watching him. "So, what are you looking at?" he smiled. "Watching the rugged guy I am?"

Stephanie smiled in return. "I wouldn't say rugged."

Andy wiped his forehead and took a deep breath, letting it run out slowly. "Whew, give me my office job back!"

"How much longer, Andy?"

"How much longer?" he asked and then wrinkled his face, "Oh, you mean 'how much longer till...' I don't know. I DON'T know – haven't got a clue. It's a dark, mystery to me – get a brush and paint me stupid. I'm surprised you even keep asking me that question. How many times have I said that God hasn't told me? Maybe I'm no prophet, after all."

"Yes, you are. Sarah said you were."

Andy threw his hoe down. "Sarah, Sarah, Sarah. Look, I know she certainly was a prophet. That doesn't mean she was a hundred percent right about everything she said and did. How many times I gotta tell you, God doesn't talk to me, ever."

"But an Angel did. I was there."

"Well, he talked to you too, so you must be a prophet also, or is it prophetess?"

Andy walked over to an old tree stump near Stephanie. The stump had been worn smooth over the years and its bark had long ago disappeared. Sitting on it, he could view the camp below with all of the cabins. He could see the peaceful lake that the cabins bordered – he could even see, on a clear day, the highway almost a mile away. He loved their camp, which he knew was a gift from God to His people in their time of trouble. He sat down.

"Can we just drop the subject – I mean forever? I'm tired of it. The only reason I let everyone call me 'Prophet' is 'cause I can't stop them. I think they got the idea from you. I look at it like a nickname."

"I didn't start it – don't blame me. I think it just got started on its own. They see something in you that you don't."

"Well, I wish they would stop 'seeing', really. You know when I get to heaven, God's gonna be mad – probably send me to hell for impersonating a prophet. But it's not my fault, and I'm gonna tell Him that too. I'll tell him to talk to you – it's all your fault. How about that?" he smiled.

Stephanie came over, dragging her hoe behind her, and sat next to her husband. Leaning over, she was about to give him a kiss when over his shoulder she saw Sergeant Larry Evans, of Camp Security, running toward them. He was out of breath when he reached them, and took a moment to regain it.

"The Goonies have set up a road block on Highway 62," he said. "I think they will stop our guest's arrival if he gets here today."

"Check it out," replied Andy with an edge to his voice.

"I'll go, too. Where is Major Frost? " asked Stephanie, referring to the Head of Camp Security, both here and at the other three new camps.

"I don't know – said he was doing some recon this morning. Should be back soon," answered Evans before heading off toward the camp to alert the Ready Squad to check out the roadblock.

Stephanie watched him leave and then turned to Andy. "We've got to stop these intercepts," she said, referring to the number of Christians who had been attacked coming to the camp. "The Goonies seem to know when someone is coming. Major Frost and I have talked about how they are doing it, but we can't figure it out."

Andy sighed. "Yes, something is not right. I think what we

have to do is start by examining the security in our line of information custody, which begins with us. As we hear of people coming, say through one of our informants, we keep the information private – just you and I."

"Well there are others that are going to know. Whoever is working the radio will know, and Major Frost has to know, and he's gonna want a few men to provide some security, so they would know too," said Stephanie.

Slowly Andy nodded. "Yes, already we have too many. Let's think on it a bit, and see if we can come up with some solution."

Stephanie nodded. "Okay, but we need to come up with an answer soon." She was about to leave when Andy put his hand on her shoulder.

"Be careful," he said without a smile.

Suddenly, the ground began to move. It seemed to move back and forth beneath their feet while, at the same time, seeming to rise and fall. Andy grabbed onto Stephanie, holding her for the few seconds until the tremor ceased.

They both stood silently waiting to see if it was over. Finally, Andy kissed his wife on the forehead. "See," he said smiling, "all gone."

"Andy, how long is this going to go on? Some say that eventually Camp Noah is going to go up in smoke. I worry that we are living on top of a volcano. Sometimes I wonder if we should all move."

"I don't know. I really don't," replied Andy softly. "But, until He comes and knocks me in the head, and tells me to get out, well, I'm just staying here. Here is where He put me, and here is where I'm gonna stay."

Stephanie smiled, "I'll always be with you." Without waiting for a reply, she began running after Sergeant Evans.

Andy slowly shook his head as he watched her leave. Lifting his hoe, he intended to let it fall; instead, he rested it on his shoulder. Perhaps he had done enough gardening for the day.

For he shall give his angels charge over thee, to keep thee in all thy ways.

Chapter 3

Sergeant Harkins navigated his Humvee through the streets of Asheville, now littered with rubble from buildings broken away during the tremors. The rubble and garbage lay in piles at the curbsides. Harkins found it easier to navigate the streets in a military vehicle. The pedestrians were more respectful, or maybe more afraid. They waved him past, rather than walk in front of his vehicle and force him to stop or to hit them.

Finding a side street near his destination, he parked the Humvee in one of the many vacant spaces. He made sure to park in different locations each time he came to Asheville. He did not want to establish a pattern. It was such patterns that the intelligence boys loved to see. He then walked to the intersection, turned left on Biltmore, walking west until he arrived at Randy's Thrift Shop. He stopped and casually looked around while he stood in front of the window. Then, peering through the window, he saw the Reverend standing by a counter. McDee smiled at him. Harkins opened the door and walked inside.

Reverend McDee met him halfway, extending his hand. "Hey there young fellow, good to see you again!" he said enthusiastically.

Harkins shook his hand, smiling. "Looks to me like you've had a few good meals since I last saw you," he chided.

Reverend McDee laughed, "Yes, I think you're right. So, what's up?" he asked as they walked to the back of the store where an office was once located.

Harkins brought out the order that he had copied and handed it to McDee. The Reverend sat down heavily in the wooden swivel chair behind an equally old and dirty wooden desk.

"So, there's a new Commander coming. What's Syme got to say about that?"

"I think he's been expecting it. I thought you folks ought to know about it. This new guy is gonna come in breathing fire, I think. I wouldn't be surprised if Camp Noah is going to be near the top of his list – if for no other reason than to impress the brass."

Reverend McDee nodded. "Probably right. I think the Prophet has been expecting it. He has been acting a little strange lately. Maybe he knew about this before you or I did."

"Is it true, Reverend McDee, that he can see the future?"

"Oh, I don't think in the way you mean. He gets ideas or feelings about things and sometimes he knows they are right and sometimes wrong. I don't know exactly how, but I believe God does speak to him."

"You mean he hears voices – I mean, The Voice?"

McDee smiled, "No, I don't think so. I think a lot of time it is just that he feels things. We Christians call it 'knowing by faith'. It's not something you can explain easily to someone like yourself, who doesn't subscribe to Christ's Divinity," said McDee. "Now, about this new Commander, when do you expect him in?"

"Don't know – maybe in a month, maybe tomorrow."

"I'll let the Prophet know, and thank you, Scott, I really appreciate you helping us out."

Harkins nodded with a smile.

"You know, young man, you are taking a big risk doing this, and you not even a Christian. Why? Why are you doing it?"

"It just doesn't sit right with me, Reverend. Something's

wrong about all of it. I hear all the time about how this group of Christians or that one has been wiped out and all because we are suppose to be going to the stars? Doesn't really make sense. I don't get it."

McDee smiled, "Well, I think Christ is working on your soul, and one day you'll just pop out – a brand new Christian," he smiled.

Harkins laughed, "Who knows, Preacher, who knows."

The two parted company, and Harkins carefully found his way back to the car. He couldn't help thinking about what McDee had said – yet, really – become a Christian? He doubted it.

* * * * *

The North Carolina hills had a blue cast to them as the van approached from the West. The twins, along with Mickey, had drifted off to sleep, while Tim sat next to Jed Drexton. He wondered if he'd made the right decision in handing the gun over. Drexton seemed like a nice man, but appearances can be deceiving – especially now. Your next-door neighbor could be your friend, then turn around and collect a bounty by turning you in to the Goonies. These were bad times for good people.

"So," asked Drexton, "what was the plan for yourself and the kids back there – before meeting up with me?"

Tim was silent for a moment. "I guess, find a place to hole up till we have to move on – just like we've been doing."

"I don't mean to be critical, but son, that isn't much of a plan."

"Well, I sorta figure stuff out as I go along."

The conversation died as the van began climbing into the hills. The climb uphill wasn't hard and the van handled the slow lazy curves running upward through the hills with ease until, eventually, they felt their ears pop.

"How much longer?" asked Alison, yawning from the back seat.

"Not too much longer," answered Tim. He had no idea how far they had to go, but the question was one often asked by Alison, and that was his auto-response.

Tim found himself drifting off; lured toward sleep by the low hum of the tires, and the warm sun through the van's windows.

"Uh oh," Drexton softly said, taking his foot off the pedal.

"What's up," asked Tim, rubbing his eyes.

"Up ahead," said Drexton in a flat tone, "Goonies."

Tim sat up quickly. He could see, some hundred yards down the slowly curving highway, a pickup truck parked horizontal in the road. Three men stood in front of the pickup holding rifles. He also could see another pickup parked behind with at least two or three additional heads behind the truck, and all were paying close attention to this van.

For a moment, Drexton sat silently contemplating. "We can try to turn and run, but I don't hold out much hope for that. This old van isn't going to outrun that pickup, especially on these curving roads; or, you kids can get out now and head up the embankment. It looks to me like there are some heavy woods up there. You could hide there."

"Any other choices?" asked Tim.

"Well, we could charge ahead and see if we could make it through," said Drexton. "But I don't think that is a good choice."

Tim looked back at the children, then up ahead. "Well sir, we've lived in the woods all we can stand, and if there's even a chance we can make it to that camp, I say we go for it."

Up ahead, there was movement as the men took the van's hesitation as a sign warranting their investigation. Two of the men, began running to the second truck parked in back.

Drexton knew it was now or never. "Hold on tight kids,"

he said, as he shifted the van into first gear.

Tim looked in back and motioned the three children to keep low, while he tightened his seat belt. Drexton handed Tim the pistol he'd taken from him, then punched the accelerator.

With a jerk, the van leaped forward, its tired tires squealing slightly. Drexton kept the accelerator floored as they approached the roadblock. Carefully, he aimed the van for an opening to the left of the pickup truck that was blocking the highway, judging there was just enough room to squeeze the van between the truck, the edge of the road, and the drop-off not far beyond.

If he steered too far left, he would be in danger of running off the highway and down the embankment that ran down a hundred yards before leveling off again. Both he and Tim scrunched down as they neared the men, now holding raised weapons and taking aim.

The sound of gunfire seemed to erupt from all the rifles at once. Tim could hear the bullets striking the van. The windshield suddenly exploded as some of the bullets found their mark. Almost at the same time, he heard Drexton groan and fall to his left causing the van to veer left. For a second, Tim felt the van loose contact with the ground as they vaulted off the edge of the highway toward the valley below.

"Hang on!" screamed Tim as he reached desperately and vainly for the wheel. The van landed with a hard thump, but with its wheels still beneath it. Grabbing the wheel, Tim tried steering the van in a straight line. The angle of the hill propelled the van, until it hit something that jerked the front wheels sideways. Tim felt the steering wheel tear out of his grip as the van jolted to the right. Instantly they began to roll. His seat belt held him in place, but as he reached for the children, he saw Alison hit against the top of the van, and Katie fall on top of her. The van rolled twice before sliding to a halt on its side.

For several moments the only sounds Tim heard were papers and cans inside the van settling down. That done, there was absolute silence. He struggled to undo his seat belt while yelling, "Is everyone alright?"

Mickey was the first to stir, and Katie began a frightened whimpering.

"I think we're okay, Tim," said Mickey, his voice shaking.

Tim leaned over Drexton, whose eyes were staring into a void. He nudged Drexton while listening to his silent heart. There was a nasty entry wound in his neck, along with a large amount of blood on his shoulder. Tim looked over the front seat at the three children in the back. Mickey was helping Alison, while Katie struggled to exit out the door, now above her head.

"Quick! We have to get out of here!" Tim shouted. With the van lying on its side, it required Tim to stand in order to peak out of the smashed windshield. He could see five or six men beginning to make their way down the hillside toward them.

"Hurry!" he shouted. First Alison pushed open her door and climbed out, followed by Katie, with the assistance of Mickey. Tim squeezed through the window in time to help Mickey exit the van. "This way!" he shouted, and they began running from the pursuing gunman, now halfway down the embankment.

Alison fell, and Tim scooped her up, running with her as best he could. The ground was covered in some kind of plant life that came up to his chest. A quick glance back revealed the men were gaining. He saw one of the men stop and raise his rifle.

"Get down!" shouted a voice in front of him. Suddenly, ahead of them, several men stood with their own guns, shoulder high, and fired. Tim dove for the ground, as did the children, rifles exploded over their heads. Again and again the guns thundered. Tim could hear Katie crying, joined quickly by Alison.

Finally, the gunfire ceased. The children stayed down, as did Tim, until he felt someone poke him in the back, "You can get up now, young man," said the voice. Tim got up slowly, helping Alison as he did so. Mickey was doing the same with Katie. As he stood, Tim could see men walking toward their fallen pursuers, their guns at the ready.

"Who are you?" asked Tim in a not-too-confident tone, while looking up at a tall man dressed in a worn uniform.

"My name is Captain Charles Essex," he said, smiling. "And who are you?" His voice was kind and his smile relaxed. Instead of a uniform cap, he had a Chicago White Sox baseball cap that tried, unsuccessfully, to hide his hair.

"Tim Barter is my name."

"Here, follow me, Tim Barter, and we'll get you to our camp. You all will be safe there," he smiled. "Is anyone else with you? We were supposed to meet a man here. I think his name was Drexdon or Dresdan."

"Drexton," volunteered Tim. "His last name was Drexton. I think he said his first name was Jed. He's dead," said Tim pointing toward the van lying on its side.

Essex motioned a couple of the men toward the van. "Check it out. Drexton is up there with the truck – he may be dead." The two men nodded and began making their way toward the van.

Essex turned his attention back to Tim. "There's someone I want you to meet."

They walked ahead; the children accompanied by two other men trailing by some twenty feet back. At the tree line, a woman, and two more men met them.

"This here is Stephanie Moore. She's in charge of camp security, and she's married to the Prophet," added Essex.

"You're married to the Prophet? The same one

32

everybody's talking about?" asked Mickey, his tone betraying his excitement.

Stephanie nodded while kneeling down to Mickey. "Yes, the same one. Now, tell me your name."

Mickey introduced himself and each of the others, informing her that Tim was in charge, but that he was second in charge.

Rising up, Stephanie shook Tim's hand and asked him to follow her back to a truck, hidden in a grove of trees. Essex got in behind the driver's seat, while Tim and Stephanie took the passenger seat. The kids climbed into the bed of the truck and they began the trip back to camp. On the way, Tim filled Stephanie in on their journey.

"So what are your plans now?' asked Stephanie.

"Well, I'm hoping the children can stay here."

"And you?"

"I wanna kill Goonies," answered Tim resolutely. "Figure I'll stay to make sure the kids are all settled in, and then head east and hook up with some others who wanna do the same thing."

Stephanie nodded silently, as they pulled into the road leading to the camp. Finally, she sighed, "Well, I think you may have come to the right place. I think maybe you should talk to my husband."

"The Prophet?"

"Yes. Maybe he has some ideas for you."

"Well, Ms. Stephanie, I don't mean to be disrespectful or anything, but I don't know if your husband is gonna let me stay. You see, I'm not a God guy anymore – no disrespect intended."

Stephanie smiled. She had heard it before.

The truck slowed as it neared camp. These days the camp was a very busy place; in fact, vehicles were no longer allowed on the Grand Circle Drive. There were so many people in camp that the Drive was usually crowded with people. Instead, Essex parked the truck near the Communications Shack.

Standing at the corner of The Grand Circle Drive and Camp Noah Drive was an elderly man nicely dressed and holding a Bible in his hand. He smiled as Stephanie passed and did a short bow.

"That's Elmer Dorby," said Captain Essex. "He's sorta the camp character. A nice old guy, we all love him, but he's a little on the weird side."

"Now, don't say that!" snapped Stephanie. "I think Elmer is a fine senior citizen of the camp. I think we would do well to listen to him a little more. I'm sure there are people who say the same thing about Andy when he spouts off."

"Elmer Dorby," explained Essex to Tim, "is a little on the unusual side. He just turned seventy-one, and some think he suffers from dementia. Others say Mr. Dorby is a smart old bird, and think we would do well to listen to some of what he says."

"What's he say?" asked Tim

"Well," said Stephanie, searching for the right words, "He says that he knew the Aliens were coming here long before they came. And I think I believe him," said Stephanie. "Then, shortly after coming to the camp, he predicted earthquakes were coming, and sure enough they did. Those are the points in his favor. On the other side, he also thought that Democrats were demons, until that Republican, Jerry 'The Happy Singer' Carson ran for president. Then he was convinced the demons switched parties, and we are all were doomed."

Stephanie gave a wave to Elmer as she exited the truck. She asked Tim, and the children, to stay in the truck while she went into the Communications House. She and Captain Essex disappeared into the small one story building.

A knock on the truck's rear window drew Tim's attention. Turning, he saw Alison motioning him from the truck's bed to open the rear-sliding window. "Are you guys okay?" he asked, after sliding the window open.

"Timmy," said Alison's excitedly, "this place looks great! Can we stay here? Can we get one of them cabins?"

"Do they have TV?" chimed in Mickey. "Did you see all the swings they have?" he asked, pointing to the swing sets in the distance, next to a very large octagonal building.

Tim smiled his answer.

Captain Essex emerged from the house and headed across the street to the truck. "Well, I've got some things I have to do, so I won't see you for awhile. Glad you are here," he said, and started to leave, but Alison caught his attention.

"Those swings over there, can anybody play on them?" asked Alison.

"Sure can – and, I'll bet you'll be going down to the lake to swim too."

"Really, a lake?" gasped Mickey. "Do they have fish?"

"Sure do. We got big ones too! Are you a fisherman?"

"Well, I went with my dad once – but I sure would like to fish some more!"

"Well, you can certainly do that. I gotta go now – good to have you folks with us," he smiled.

Tim thanked him and they watched him walk down the street.

Moments later, Stephanie came out and motioned for Tim and the children to follow her.

"My husband is at the Great House – probably sneaking watermelon again." she smiled. "That man can sure gobble watermelon." The twins snickered at the word, 'gobble'. Stephanie led the children down the street, then across the lawn bordering the Great House.

Without speaking, Tim nudged Alison, pointing to the large swing sets, and gave her a silent 'thumbs up.' Alison smiled and nodded.

Stephanie led them inside the large octagonal house, which proved to be packed. They found people engaged in all sorts of activities; some were seated playing cards, or just having coffee; others were busy eating sandwiches made from an assortment of meats on a center table. At one table, some women looked like they were knitting, while in the corner, a group was huddled around a television mounted on the wall. A few waved at Stephanie as she entered, leading the children through the main dining, then through double doors into the kitchen area.

"Uh oh," Stephanie said as they entered the kitchen. Two men stood bent over examining the dishwasher. A third slightly overweight man, with hands on his hips, stood watching them. He looked up as Stephanie spoke, and smiled. "Hi honey, bad news here – dishwasher's busted," he said.

"Can we fix it?"

From inside the lower level of the dishwasher they heard a voice. "Yeah, think I can."

"Who's that?" asked Stephanie

The man withdrew from the washer, "Just me," said Roy Kegler, smiling. "See, the impeller sheared off. This model does that every so often. I can fashion a new one in the workshop."

"So," said Andy, "Who are your guests here?"

Quickly, Stephanie introduced each one and filled Andy in on what had happened.

"I knew Jed Drexton," he said to Stephanie. "Not well, but from the impression I had, he was a decent man. I'm sorry to hear he didn't make it." He looked at Tim. "So, you're the leader of this group?"

"Yes, sir."

"Well, I think your folks would be very proud of you. They did a good job in raising you, son."

"Andy," said Stephanie, "I was thinking, could we use one

36

of the Batch cabins for them?" she asked, referring to one of the two Bachelor cabins, commonly reserved for single men. "We don't get as many new men arriving as we used to. I think just one Batch cabin would do, don't you? I know we are real tight for cabins now, and most of the new arrivals are put up in the tents, but I hate to have the children out there."

Andy nodded. "Oh, you don't have to sell me. Roy, could you ask a few of the men to take a look at Batch One and see what we can do to convert it into a cabin layout for these kids?"

Roy smiled and nodded. He extended his hand to Tim, "Great to have you folks part of the group. I'm sure you'll enjoy your stay here."

Tim smiled, and then frowned, "Excuse me sir, but living here, would it mean I have to go to church?"

Chapter 4

Having unloaded his share of the gathered firewood from Kegler's cart, Tim smiled and waved goodbye. Roy accelerated the G-bus, the camp's name for the Golf Carts used to get around, and headed for his own cabin.

Tim made his way into their newly-remodeled cabin. For the first time, in a very long time, he felt something like optimism. He didn't have to worry about where, or if, there would be food. He knew every night where they were going to sleep and felt safe enough not to sleep with his pistol under his pillow – though he still did, on occasion. In addition, they had wood for the fireplace. Kegler said the Prophet had granted the camp's households permission to use fireplaces, now that the Goonies knew the camp was occupied.

Tim gently kicked open the door and entered the half-finished cabin, his arms full of wood. Although his bedroom still needed insulation, and the kitchen wall wasn't quite finished, still it was home. It was, in fact, the best home they had since all the trouble began. After laying the wood next to the large stone fireplace, he closed the front door. The fall air had begun to get a little cool.

Suddenly, he tensed, hearing a noise from the rear of the cabin. Cautiously looking down the narrow hallway toward the bedrooms, he tried to make out the figure he saw in the dark hallway, but could not. "Who's that!" he challenged.

"Oh, don't worry young man. It's just me."

Andy came forward so that Tim could see him clearly. Andy was a big man, over six feet tall, with a body in the mid 200's. His nose was a little crooked, from a scuffle in the distant past, and he had a full mustache, which drooped at the ends, framing his mouth. A first impression of him was someone you would not like to meet in a dark place – like this

– but then, Andy would smile, transforming his face and demeanor to that of a friendly, slightly overweight bear.

"Oh, it's you," said Tim. "Hello, Mr. Prophet."

Andy extended his hand and Tim shook it – or rather, it shook Tim, as Andy's large hand swallowed Tim's.

"Haven't had a chance to really talk to you since you arrived," said Andy, smiling and looking around at the living room. "Looks like they're making real progress in getting this cabin set up for you."

"Yes, sir," smiled Tim. "We all are very happy here – I can't tell you how much I appreciate your letting us stay here."

Andy nodded. "My wife, Stephanie, was telling me how you and the kids came to be here. You've been through some trouble haven't you, son?" he asked, but did not wait for a response. "A lot of the folks here have similar stories, and in time, I assure you, some of the pain will ease. My wife also tells me you're a little upset with God."

"If you don't mind, sir, I don't wanna talk about it," replied Tim.

Andy nodded. "I understand. Now, I see you've been helping around camp, and I appreciate that. Everybody here sorta has his own jobs. Helps get everything done that needs getting done. Now that you're settled in, we'll have to find some steady work for you."

"I would like to join the Guard here at the camp."

"How old are you?"

"Seventeen, almost eighteen."

Andy nodded. "Well, we have a rule you gotta be eighteen to get into the Guard, and have that as your primary job. Of course, in times of emergency, everyone 16 and older is used to defend the camp. You'll be in the reserve guard, for sure."

Tim nodded.

"Now, until you can get into some kind of full time job, I was thinking you could help me out with something. We got a couple of gardens up on the ridge, and my wife and I started one of them. However, lately, we're so busy, we just don't have time to care for it. I'd consider it a real favor if you would care for my garden for a little while until we can catch up and they find you a permanent job."

"Garden? I don't know anything about gardening."

"Oh, we have people that can help you with that. It's just pulling weeds, mostly."

"Sure," said Tim without enthusiasm, "I could do that."

Andy turned toward the door and started to leave.

"So," said Tim, "are you a real prophet?"

"What's a real prophet?"

"Well, talks to God."

"What else?"

"Prays all the time, you know, talks to angels and stuff."

"Well, I guess that makes me a prophet – but then, I think a lot of people in camp must be prophets too." Andy smiled. "Look, son, in hard times we all talk to God a lot, and sometimes we see Him in our lives, even hear His voice speaking to us from within. And, some of us even get mad at God – real mad – just like you. Doesn't make us bad or good in God's eyes – we're His children, and He loves us no matter what. I know you don't wanna talk about it, but just let me tell you as one prophet to another, God loves you, and He's waiting." Andy smiled as he opened the door. "Hope you'll go up to that garden soon, those weeds are growing every day."

Tim watched Andy as he walked down the short path to the road and then toward the Great House. Tim thought he had better watch out for that old man – he was not sure he liked, or even trusted him. Calling himself a prophet – huckster, would be more like it.

* * * * *

40

Andy continued down the path until it met up with Grand Circle Drive, then up to the Great House. He had heard a disturbing rumor there was going to be an announcement on the state-run television this morning, and he didn't want to miss it.

Entering the Great House, he saw many more faces than he expected. Apparently, many were as curious as he was about the announcement.

Andy saw Stephanie standing next to Roy Kegler at the back of the room. Roy was leaning against the wall, with his arms folded. He nodded as he saw Andy approach.

"Do you know what the announcement is, Andy?" asked Roy.

Andy shook his head.

The TV sound was off, as it generally was, unless it was something deemed worth hearing. The scene changed to the view of a podium. One of the viewers in the house turned up the sound.

Approaching the microphone was a mousy looking man who cleared his throat before beginning. The sound could have remained off for all the importance of what he said – who was there, who to thank, to whom to pay tribute, and then much about the wonderful days ahead with the Brothers. Finally, after clearing his throat again, he introduced the main speaker, Arthur Ramon. He was slimmer than the last time Andy remembered seeing him. His face was almost skeletal, with the expression of an old man with an unhappy thought. His seventy plus years were obviously weighing heavily upon him, engraving deep circles beneath his eyes, while feasting upon his hair, devouring it one strand by one.

Ramon began with what some might interpret as a smile, but looked more like an inconvenient arrangement of wrinkles. "My friends," he began, "I come to announce something our Ancestral Brothers, our Visitors, as you like to call them, have

41

given us today – a piece of our history, long hidden from us, until now. It is a scientific revelation, which people who follow a so-called god will find disturbing.'

"In ancient times there were creatures upon the Earth, we have said lived long before our Brothers visited here. Our ancestors came, as you recall, establishing a camp for the punishment of their own. Abdon, our wonderful leader, was forced to punish some who had committed crimes against their perfect, eternal order. He could not bear to kill them, as was called for in the law, so he placed them here on this planet to die a natural death. Here, they were isolated and could no longer contaminate the Brothers' kingdom. However, they did not die, did they? No, they lived. As you know now, we are their descendants.

"We know there were other creatures upon the Earth when the Ancient Brothers arrived. We found their bones, called them animals and gave them a number of names: Brontosaurus, Iguanodon, Trachodon, Diplodocus and Camptosaurus, among others. Moreover, while many existed millions of year ago, others evolved. One that did, though many did not know it, was the beautiful Tyrannosaurus Rex. Some say the first T-Rex creature existed sixty million or more years ago. Indeed, some did – but their descendants existed even more recently, and, in fact, were here when the Brothers brought their captives to Earth. At that time, when the Brothers came, T-Rex was a much different animal than when he first existed. No longer was he the fierce animal of years past." Ramon smiled, and it was obvious he was delighting in delaying whatever knowledge he intended to share.

"You see, all things evolve, and so did T-Rex. From the fierce animal of sixty million years ago, he was now a smaller, almost gentle creature."

Suddenly, behind Ramon, the screen displayed a picture of a Tyrannosaurus Rex. However, while earlier descriptions put the animal at over forty feet long and fifteen feet tall, this image showed measurements less than twelve feet tall with a length of about fifteen feet.

"Our scientists for many years have found what we think are the eggs which gave birth to these creatures. We struggled to extract from these eggs and other fossils any kind of deoxyribonucleic acid, or DNA, that we could. We have not been successful. We've even tried using almost 'reverse engineering' by taking today's egg of a chicken and trying to regress it through its evolutionary journey."

"Though our efforts have lately been partially successful, we have not been able to rescue the entire genetic string. That is, until now and this is the wonderful news: Our Ancestral Brothers have given us some of the DNA from those ancient years. Along with this ancient DNA, they have bestowed to us a method that will restore what once was dead. Using this DNA we have given birth to a T-Rex!" These last words he shouted with such enthusiasm that his voice broke. Instantly, the screen behind him showed a picture of an animal remarkably close to the popular concept of a T-Rex.

The size was smaller – the head, face, small upper arms, overly large feet and gigantic tail were all identical to the images of a T-Rex. On his side appeared to be a large scar as though at some time it had been cut. The creature had a few pointed teeth protruding from its upper lip, giving the animal the appearance of smiling. The eyes seemed small for the body, but they were not piercing, fearsome eyes; rather, looked kinder with a brown cast that made them look soft, almost intelligent.

The small upper limbs did not seem to fit the massive body. They were shorter than one might expect, appearing almost spindly. Unexpectedly, while looking around, the animal raised one of its arms and scratched its neck, bringing a titter from the viewers. The creature seemed quite content to sit on it massive rear legs, using its large tail as a chair to balance his weight.

"Let me introduce you to Abby," said Ramon, trying to smile. "The scientists named the creature in honor of our leader, Abdon."

There was a smattering of applause from those in his audience. The applause grew until Ramon held up his hands. "Now comes, an even bigger surprise. Let me introduce you to Sharon Miller," said Ramon. Immediately to his left, a middle-aged woman, her hair in a tight bun with dark-rimmed glasses rooted in it, approached the dais. "For the past six months Ms. Miller has been working with Abby. You see, my friends, we have learned that Abby can speak!"

Immediately there was a large stirring within the audience.

Even in the Great House, there were gasps.

Ramon nodded, "Yes, she speaks. That was one of the greatest surprises. All this time we assumed such creatures, being the fierce looking animals they were, would growl, grunt, or bark – but not speak. We saw no indication of this in any of the fossils. I'll let Ms. Miller tell you about this remarkable discovery."

Miller stepped to the microphone, clearly nervous. First, giving a quick, but unconvincing smile, she then referred to her notes. "Yes, I have been working with Abby every day. I was called in when the caretakers heard Abby trying to communicate with them. They made some initial progress by treating Abby as though she were a dog, or chimp, trying to learn a new trick. However, and I don't mean to denigrate the efforts of these well-intentioned people, but such a tactic must have been insulting to Abby. How could they know this creature was capable of an intelligence at least as well developed as our own, possibly even greater?"

Again, there was a murmur throughout the gathered crowd, including those at the camp.

"I began working with Abby, and it immediately became apparent to me, that the sounds she was attempting to communicate with me were patterned in such a way as to resemble some kind of speech. I decided, rather than me teaching her how to speak our language, I would allow her to teach me hers, and she has," smiled Miller.

Ramon stepped forward, "Why don't you give us a demonstration, Ms. Miller?"

Miller flashed a smile, and then faced the large TV screen. She began speaking in a guttural, choppy way. It was not at all pleasant sounding, but from the expression on the T-Rex face, she seemed to comprehend. After Miller finished speaking, the T-Rex was silent for a moment then, to the astonishment of everyone, began growling back at Miller. Her pattern of sounds clearly indicated she was forming some kind of words. Suddenly she stopped.

"I asked Abby if she was happy to have this attention," said Miller. "She replied that she likes talking with me, and would like to talk with others, and asked me if she could have a treat," smiled Miller.

There was a chuckling among the assembled audience.

Elmer Dorby stepped forward. "Shut the television off!" he commanded.

"But we wanna hear some more about this," protested one woman, sitting at one of the tables. Others murmured their agreement.

Elmer Dorby held up his hands. "You are watching an unholy event!" he shouted. "This is an unholy thing we are seeing! Have you not read in the Word about this beast, told to us so long ago, but only now revealed? It's here in the Bible," he said, holding up his copy. He began thumbing through the pages. "Here, in the eightieth chapter of Ezekiel, it talks about 'abominable beasts' locked up in a room filled with evil iniquities." Dorby looked around for support, but the room was silent. "Don't you understand? All have thought the 'abominable beasts' was imagery for sins but they were not. They were, in fact, real beasts who Satan has put upon this Earth in the image of himself!"

There was a growing murmur around the room until Andy held up his hand for silence. Andy cleared his throat. "Let Elmer speak," he said softly.

"Here, in Revelation, it says, 'and one of his heads as slain to death, and his wound of death had been healed: and the whole Earth wondered after the beast.' This is that beast," said Dorby. "Did you see the wound it had?"

Dorby paused, putting the Bible down. "We are in those last days, and now those words we have read all these centuries are bearing fruit. However, they are words meant for faithful ears. Don't allow your human logic to deceive your soul. What we have seen today is a magnificent, but unholy, display. We see, therefore, we believe. Remember the saying, 'don't believe everything you see.' We should heed that warning. Faith is our doorway to heaven, not human logic.

"Did Peter walk upon the water because it was logical? Did Christ turn the water into wine with a written formula? Were the lepers healed with a prescription? No, of course not – faith was their answer, and it remains our answer. Do not be deceived by the wondrous creations of the mind. Satan, in the beginning, through Eve discovered that logic was the backdoor to our souls. It was his clever use of logic that deceived Eve, and his tactics have not changed.

"What we see today is just another, in a long list of deceptions, used to lure us from our faith into worshipping our own logic. I see now that this thing, this beast, they have created will be thrust forward as something to be admired, revered and, yes, worshiped."

Dorby stopped and the room remained silent. For once, everyone was listening intently to what the old man was saying.

Slowly eyes around the room turned upon Andy.

"Is what Dorby says true or not?" Andy asked the crowd. "I don't know. My guess is that I think Mr. Dorby is close to the truth. I think, in the hereafter, we will learn many truths that will astound us. Dinosaurs? Personally, when I see this animal, my soul is reviled – why? I don't know. I have my own opinions, but do they represent God's truth?" Perhaps it's best to keep them to myself. Maybe I just don't like the creature's looks. However, it's not dinosaurs we need concern ourselves about now. We live in the last days of this world. I say, be vigilant. The end is near. Let's not be deceived by the wonders of these last days. Believe me when I say that we shall not see another winter."

* * * * *

"Mister, are you head of the soldiers?" asked Mickey.

Frost looked down at the boy standing beside the path. "Yes, young man, I am."

"Well, sir, I'd like to join," said Mickey puffing out his chest and coming to attention.

"And what's your name?"

"Mickey Streeter. And you're Major Frost."

"How old are you?"

"Sixteen."

Frost squinted down, "You don't look like you're sixteen. What year were you born?"

"Year? Ah, let me see..."

"Now, let's start again, how old are you, ten?"

"I'm not ten! I'm twelve!"

"You have to be eighteen to join the Guard, young man," said Frost. Then, putting his hand to his chin said, "Let me see..." his voice trailing off as he thought. "I tell you what, why don't you be my secret spy?"

"A spy? Sure, I could do that. What do I do?"

"Hmm. How about you keep your eyes open, and if you see anything suspicious you come and tell me."

Mickey came to attention. "Yes sir, I'll do that."

"Now, you can't tell anyone you're a spy or it won't be a secret spy anymore."

"Yes, sir – do spies salute?"

"No."

"What's my rank?"

"Uh, spies don't have rank. Now, I have to go. You keep your eyes open."

"Yes sir," said Mickey, resisting the urge to salute. It really sucked that spies didn't salute or didn't have rank. He watched as the Major walked down Grand Circle Drive. Turning, Mickey ran toward the cabin that Tim was fixing up for them. He couldn't wait to tell Tim he was a spy. Suddenly, he came to a halt. The Colonel told him not to tell anyone. Mickey frowned, surely, he could tell Tim – he wouldn't tell anyone else.

Mickey resumed running and came upon Tim walking down Bachelor's Way road.

"Timmy, Timmy!" shouted Mickey. He was out of breath by the time he reached Tim, and it took a few moments to stop panting long enough to speak. "Spy," he gasped. "Spy."

"Where?" asked Tim.

Mickey leaned forward, "Me. I'm a spy," he gasped.

"What are you talking about?"

Mickey related his conversation with the Major. "Now, you can't tell anyone – I mean *anyone* – okay?"

Tim resumed walking. "You can count on me."

"Where you going?" asked Mickey.

"Oh, up to a garden – the Prophet wants me to keep the weeds out – say, why don't you come with me. I could show you how to do it."

"Can't – I promised Mrs. Kegler I would help out with cleaning at the Great House. Now, you won't tell anyone I'm a spy?"

"Count on me – hey, remember, I want you back at our cabin by five o'clock."

Mickey gave him the thumbs up, then pressing his finger against his lips, raised his brows, before running off toward the Great House.

Resuming his walk, Tim saw a young woman ahead who was looking at him. She was standing at the point where Bachelor's Way Road met Grand Circle Drive. Tim judged her to be about his age, and from the way she was looking at him, she definitely was waiting for him.

As Tim approached, she smiled. "Your name is Tim?"

"That's right," he responded as he neared. "How did you know?"

"I heard."

"So what's your name?"

"Mary. How old are you?" she asked.

"Seventeen."

" I'm eighteen," replied Mary with a little attitude.

"I'll be eighteen in a few weeks," retorted Tim, a little annoyed. He then smiled again, "What do you do around camp?"

"I work fixing meals, sometimes I work at the day care center or the phone center."

Tim was reluctantly impressed with Mary. She was pretty. She was an inch or so shorter than he, with brown hair, bleached here and there by the sun giving her blond strands. Her hair was combed into pigtails that reached just below her shoulders. Her light brown eyes complemented her brown-blond hair. She was, as the boys would say, a nice package. She had a pretty smile, in fact, a very pretty smile. "I'm going up to the Prophet's garden, you wanna come?" asked Tim.

Mary smiled, "Can't. I gotta make it over to the phone center – I answer the phones some days, but I'll walk as far as the phone cabin with you. My last name is Kegler, she said extending her hand.

Tim grasped it in his own taking care not to squeeze too hard.

"Where do you live?"

"My mother and father have a cabin right on Grand Circle, number 101. We had that cabin long before the Prophet arrived." Quickly Mary told Tim a short history of the camp and how once it was deserted, but now was serving as a safe haven for Christians.

"So," said Tim. "I suppose you are a Christian."

"Sure," replied Mary with a smile, "aren't you?"

"I used to be, but not so much now."

"Really? I just assumed you were a Christian – you taking care of the children as you do. I was very impressed when I heard how you cared for them."

"Well, they're kids. They are my family now. I don't think that has anything to do with God."

"So, you don't believe in God?"

"Oh sure, I just think He doesn't believe in us anymore."

"What if I told you Jesus healed me? That I was blind and He made me see again?" said Mary as she stopped at the entry to the telephone cabin.

"Really? You were blind?" asked Tim and then narrowed his eyes. "You're putting me on, aren't you?"

Mary shook her head, "No – not at all. Ask anyone in camp, and they'll tell you I was blind and Jesus healed me."

Tim thought for a moment. "I don't know. I mean, maybe it was something else – you know – just a freak moment, when whatever caused your blindness was gone – a natural thing."

Mary shook her head slowly, "Tim Barter, you have a lot

to learn – a lot to learn." Mary turned on her heels and started to walk toward the telephone station.

"Wait," said Tim. "I hope I didn't offend you, Mary. I'd like to talk to you again – you know, maybe you can convert me, or somethin'?"

Mary glanced back and smiled.

"So, how do I get in touch with you?" asked Tim.

"I told you where I live," she said still smiling and then turned and continued toward the telephone cabin.

Tim watched her go. Now why was he interested in talking to her again, he wondered. She was obviously a Jesus Freak. On the other hand, she was pretty – actually, very pretty. Turning, he resumed walking toward the garden. Maybe, on the other hand, he could get her to talk about something else – maybe movies or sports – no, not sports – maybe travel. After all, he thought, she was very pretty.

Stopping to get some directions, Tim arrived at the garden twenty minutes later, and a little out of breath. A make-do shack had been erected and, as promised, he found gardening implements inside. He picked out a hoe and made his way over to a spot of land with a homemade sign, saying "The Prophet's." The garden was a little overrun with weeds, but not bad. Starting at one corner, he began patiently pulling the weeds.

"You don't garden too much, right?" said a voice from behind.

Tim jumped at the unexpected sound. Turning, he saw an old man, not much over four feet tall, perhaps even less. He was bent over and leaning on a crooked staff. If Tim were to estimate his age it would be somewhere between ninety and a hundred-fifty. There were deep grooves worn in that area of his face not overgrown by a scraggly white beard that dripped past his shoulders. His head was crowned with long silver strands that joined his beard and cascaded over his shoulders.

51

Tim jumped to his feet. "Who are you!" he demanded. He did not like people who sneaked up on him.

"Oh, folks around here call me Hermit. I come and go – go and come – that's me. I like it up here – nice fresh air. I have been keeping the garden over there for a long time. I keep it so the folks down in the camp have fresh veggies – it's important to have fresh veggies, don't you agree?"

"Why are you sneaking up on me?"

"Oh, sorry – didn't mean to alarm you. I just saw you tending to the Prophet's garden and thought I'd come over. So, you don't garden too often, am I right?"

"So what?"

"Well, you're doing a good job of pulling the green onions and leaving the weeds."

Tim held up the stalks. "These are onions?"

The Hermit smiled. "Yep, some college guy named them Allium Fistulosum Parade, but I think Green Onions is a better name, don't you? Now, see the straggly things on the bottom of 'em? Those are the roots."

"So, these over here are the weeds?" asked Tim as he fingered the green leaves he had been leaving.

"Yep, that's them."

Tim sat down and began pulling the weeds. "So, where do you live?"

"I stay on the other side of the mountain – don't like folks to know exactly where – they keep trying to visit. If I wanted visitors I'd live down with you folks."

"So, this is your garden?"

"Well, not this one. This one belongs to the Prophet. He comes up here now and then to care for it. Not so much lately – guess he's a lot busier now. No, the garden I started is over there – the big one."

"You did all that yourself?" marveled Tim. The garden the Hermit indicated covered a large area, perhaps several acres. It seemed bursting with so many varied plants.

"Well, there are a bunch of people who come up and care for it now, and they get all the veggies for the camp. I just plant some more when they leave, keeps me busy."

The two fell into a momentary silence. The Hermit pointed with his cane to a few weeds Tim had missed. Tim looked up at him with a little annoyance. It seemed to Tim that if this old coot had enough energy to plant all this stuff, he should have enough to help him weed.

"You know," began the Hermit after a few minutes, "I know about you. I heard the story."

Tim stopped and looked up. "You heard about me? What did you hear – and who's been talking about me? I don't like people talking about me behind my back." He emphasized his displeasure by yanking the next weed with some anger.

"Oh, now don't get all in a bundle. I heard some very nice things about you. Mostly, how you took care of the children – kept them safe, fed them and brought them here. Yes, you did a very nice thing. Be assured God knows about it, too."

"Humph, God," said Tim. "You keep Him. I don't have a use for Him anymore."

"Oh, but He does you."

"Well, He's gotta do whatever He's gonna do, without me. I'm not gonna be part of His game anymore. No thanks, I take care of me and mine by myself. I've seen what praying day and night about stuff gets you. He didn't help those folks in Africa when they were dying from diseases, or the Jews when they were killed by the millions. He didn't help my parents when they were killed like dogs while praying. Nope. God is a fraud, if you ask me."

The Hermit was quiet for a moment. Then clearing his throat, said: "Let me tell you a little story."

"Is this a God story? If it is, I don't wanna hear it," said Tim.

53

"Well, it's just a little God story."

Tim didn't reply but simply moved a little further down the row to work on a new batch of weeds.

To his annoyance, the Hermit moved too. Then, taking a deep breath began, "There was this Christian man who died and went to heaven. He'd led a good life, not a perfect one, mind you, but a respectable Christian life. He went to college, got a decent job, married his sweetheart had two wonderful children, and they all loved the Lord. He was a member of the local church and went fairly often – and always on every Christian holiday. He had a blessed life, and he wanted to thank Jesus now that he was in heaven, so he got in the 'Talk-To-Jesus-Line'.

Slowly moving along in the line, he looked down toward hell. He saw millions of souls who had committed every kind of evil imaginable. They were being tormented and were in great agony. Their screams brought tears to his eyes as they begged for mercy.

The line kept moving, and soon he saw millions upon millions of babies, lying silent, yearning to give a first smile. Their silence was deafening to his soul and it brought more tears to his eyes, and now some anger to his heart.

Further along, he saw more millions who had never heard of the Lord and they were in great distress and weeping at the loss. Again, anger filled him as he wondered why Jesus hadn't done something to save them.

He found, as the line neared Jesus, he was filled more with anger than gratitude. Finally, it was his turn. "Lord," he challenged with some anger in his voice, "why didn't you send someone to save all those unborn children, why didn't you do something to save all those who fell to the deception of Satan – or something to save all those who never even heard your name?"

Jesus leaned forward and replied, "I did do something. I

sent you."

For a moment, Tim was silent. Finally, he asked, "The point is?"

"There is a lot of injustice that goes on in the world, but you can help correct some of it. I think a lot of that is your job and mine too. God did His part – He sent you to represent Him. We can be the fingers of Christ, the loving hearts of God. Just think, if everyone had just done one small thing to defend and uphold the name of the Lord and His Word – what a different world we would have today."

"Well, I'm gonna do my part. I'm gonna kill as many Goonies as I can."

"Oh, stop with the killing talk. You already have done a lot to help correct some of the injustices – you brought the children here. Do you think you were able to keep them safe and guide them here on your own? Of course not, God was there to guide and protect."

"Now, if you are waiting until you can answer all the 'whys' of the world before giving Jesus your heart, you will be waiting a long, long time. Questions with 'why', 'when', and 'how' are God's business. You need to decide soon to let God be God. Our journey here is not about deeds, but about faith. Deeds are the fruits of our faith. Concentrate on faith and deeds and blessings will follow. I tell you this Tim Barter, you haven't seen the end of injustice and its sorrow, but you also haven't seen the end of God's grace and mercy. Keep in mind, the game doesn't end when you die – that's only half-time."

"You're a Jesus Freak, aren't you?"

The Hermit smiled, "Yes, I am. I certainly am."

For with what judgment ye judge, ye shall be judged: and with what measure ye mete it, it shall be measured to you again.

– Matthew 7:2

Chapter 5

Reaching across the desk, he picked up the triangular nameplate, and then turned it around. He stared at the gold lettering engraved into the mahogany: Lt. Col Donald Syme. He couldn't guess how many times he'd imagined what it would look like with the rank of General on it. He let the nameplate slip from his grasp and bounce once on his desk. That was all gone now, and he knew it. It was only a matter of time now. Today, tomorrow, or maybe next week his phone extension would ring and he would be told the Visitors were here to see him.

He stared at the closed office door, and barked out, "Harkins! Harkins!"

Within a minute, the door opened and Sergeant Harkins entered. He didn't normally come to attention when his boss called – it wasn't necessary – however, today he did.

"Don't give me that formal crap," said Syme. "Here," he said kicking a chair, "sit down for a minute."

"Yes sir," replied Harkins.

"I guess I haven't been the easiest man to work for, right?" asked Syme.

"Oh, sir, I wouldn't…"

"Cut the bull, boy. I know I haven't been, and so do you. I should have promoted you long ago. I wish I had, son – you've done a good job. I'm just an ornery old man, and I wish I hadn't been. But I'm getting mine now, eh?" smiled Syme, ruefully.

Harkins remained silent, afraid to match the smile Syme

56

flashed at him.

Syme got up from his desk, and came around the side. He perched on top of his desk, while allowing one foot to rest on the carpet. "I got a question to ask you, Harkins. I suppose it's the reason I never promoted you. Should have asked you long ago – are you one of those Jesus Freaks?"

The question shocked Harkins for a second. "No sir, I'm not."

Syme nodded silently for a second. "Don't know why I thought you might be. Thought maybe you were some kinda informant," he smiled. "You know why?" he asked, but did not wait for an answer, "Because you're too nice. Yep, that was it. You were just a goody-goody boy, so I thought you might be one of them. You know how they go around with all their goody-goody talk?" he snorted. "Well, as I said, I'm getting mine now, so you can take some comfort in that."

"Sir, I would not do that."

Syme stood up and raised his hand "Don't give me that, Harkins. I want you to know, though, that I've put in a recommendation that you be immediately promoted. I don't know if it will carry any weight, but I thought I would try to make it right before I left."

"Thank you, sir," said Harkins.

For a moment, Syme didn't move or say anything, as he stared at Harkins. Then suddenly, he stuck out his hand. "It's been good knowing you Scott," he said.

Harkins stood up and shook Syme's hand, suddenly feeling sorry for the man. "Thank you sir, I wish you luck in your new assignment, whatever that might be."

Syme nodded, "Okay, now get outta here, I got some stuff I need to get done," he said, turning his back on Harkins. He walked back behind his desk.

Harkins left quietly, closing the door behind him.

Syme sat down behind his desk. Saying those things to

Harkins felt good. It was the right thing to do. Of course, the Visitors might think differently.

Syme let a rueful smirk cross his face. Visitors – that's what they called them now. First, it was Aliens, then Ancestral Brothers and now, Visitors. Slowly he rose from his desk, taking a few moments to straighten his uniform coat, making sure the tie was exactly right. It was important to be at his best.

It was quiet, no one called him, and no one knocked on the door. He knew Harkins and the other men in his office were just sitting at their desk, not talking – just waiting too. They knew. Everyone knew. Soon the phone would ring and the boys would answer, "Yes sir, he is here; yes, he is waiting." Then, they all would wait for the Brothers to arrive. Syme wasn't new to this. He had been on the other end a few times when accompanying the Visitors to remove someone else.

Syme breathed a sigh as he looked out his office window while tapping nervously on the sill. How could it have gone so wrong? There was a time when he was on the path to that General's star. What happened? Okay, so there had been a few set-backs. The motor pool soldiers got away. Then there was that debacle of his men charging up the hill, only to turn tail and run. However, he thought he had covered himself on that by executing their Commanding Officers.

The phone rang, Syme jumped at the sudden sound. Slowly, he turned toward the desk. The phone rang again, but he was in no hurry. Finally, he lifted the receiver just as it began to ring a third time.

"This is Lt. Col Syme." He said softly. "Yes," he said. He would be here. "Yes," he replied. He was expecting them. They then hung up. Slowly, Syme replaced the receiver on the hook, resting his hand on top for a minute or two. Finally, straightening his uniform once again, he decided it was time to say goodbye to the other men outside.

Opening his office door brought the heads of his men

around, revealing somber faces. They knew. Syme cleared his throat, "Well, gentlemen my time here is about to come to an end. I want to thank you for your service. I'm sure whoever replaces me will be very fortunate to have you assisting him." For a moment, he glanced around the quiet room. He didn't know what else should be said, and apparently, neither did they.

Slowly, he turned around and went back into his office. He quietly closed the door behind him.

Sergeant Harkins stared at the closed door for a moment. He was a career soldier, wearing the stripes of a Staff Sergeant. Harkins knew, if he had been working for someone else, he would have at least two more stripes. Still, he was determined to see out his twenty years, though working for Syme had made him doubt his commitment more than a few times. He wasn't sorry Syme was going – that was certain; however, his little talk with Syme had left him shaken. He found himself feeling sorry for the man. Nevertheless, overall, the guy was a jerk. Funny how jerks always had regrets, but no foresight.

Turning back around he realized the other men were watching him. Without changing his stern expression, he winked. A couple had to cover their mouths for fear of laughing. No, Syme would not be missed.

BAM!

The gunshot caught them by surprise. Harkins jumped to his feet and was about to rush to the door, but stopped. Slowly turning, he returned to his seat and sat down. Sergeant Harkins was a busy man, with a lot of work to do. He, followed by the others, pulled worksheets from their in-boxes and quietly resumed their tasks.

* * * * *

The rap on the door was almost too light to be heard, but

Betty Jo, working in the kitchen, heard it and answered the door.

"Well, hello there," she said to Tim. "What a pleasant surprise – what can I do for you?"

"Well, Mrs. Kegler, I was wondering if Mary was home."

"Mary? Well, uh – yes, let me tell her you're here."

Quickly Betty Jo went to Mary's room and found her daughter listening to music with earphones. Motioning to Mary's ears, she waited for her daughter removed the earphones.

"That boy, Tim, is here to see you."

Mary smiled, "Really."

"Now listen to me, Mary, I don't think it's a good idea for you to go seeing this young man. He seems nice, but he has real problems."

"I know Mama. I'm not running away with him for heaven's sake, he probably just wants to have a cola or something."

Betty Jo gave her daughter a look. "Young men don't come calling on young women because they're thirsty."

Mary smiled, and went to the front door.

"Hi," smiled Tim. "I – well – I thought maybe you might wanna go to the Grand House and have something to drink or eat. I heard the Prophet was handing out watermelon," said Tim, feeling quite uncomfortable, and showing it.

Mary smiled, "Sure, but don't count on getting a lot of watermelon. If the Prophet got there before we did, chances of eating that melon are slim," she smiled. "He says watermelon helps him lose weight."

"Yeah, he asked me if I thought he was overweight – I didn't know what to say."

"Well, it's not that he's fat, it's just the choices he gives you are strange. I think he asks everybody he meets," laughed Mary.

For a few moments, they walked in silence as Tim tried hard to think of a topic to discuss, "It's getting colder," he said finally.

"It never really gets terribly cold here. My father says it's because of the ground being so warm and radiating heat. The lake stays pretty warm too, unless there is a lot of snow and then the cold streams coming into the lake, cool it off – but I've never seen it freeze."

For a minute, silence hung in the air, until Mary broke it. "Wanna see a trick?" she asked.

Tim smiled, "Sure."

"Do you have a driver's license?"

"A license? Sure."

"Let me see it," said Mary.

Tim fished in his back pocket for his thin, very undernourished wallet. In one of the slots was his old Ohio license. Pulling it out, he gave it to Mary. She looked at it briefly and gave it back.

"Now, ask me what the numbers were on your license. You can ask me now, or tomorrow, or next week and I'll be able to tell you what they are."

"Really?"

Mary smiled, "Yes, it's just a trick memory I have. I remember names and numbers real good."

"Like a photographic memory?"

"My mother doesn't think so, 'cause there's some stuff I can't remember – but numbers and names I can – for some reason or other."

Tim held the license up. "So, what were the numbers?"

Mary thought for a second. "C630887777086"

"Wow. I'm impressed. I'll ask you tomorrow and see how you do. Course, that means you need to go out with me tomorrow, so I can check to see if you still remember."

Mary smiled. "Well, we'll see. Maybe."

"I'll be eighteen next month," said Tim flatly.

"Uh-huh, you told me that before."

"Oh, well, I didn't know if I mentioned it. It's just that we'll be the same age and all."

Mary smiled "Yes, that's true."

"Do you fish?" asked Tim.

"Fish? Oh, heavens no, I barely like to eat them."

"Do you play baseball, or tennis, or anything?"

"Reading. Since I have my eyes now, I read all the time. I just can't get enough of it. The thing I like about reading is how the words make pictures in my mind."

Tim held open the door to the Great Hall for Mary. "Yes, I can understand that would be something wonderful for you."

Tim saw a small round table in the corner and pointed it out to Mary. Once Mary was seated, he went to the counter where some snack food was laid out – apples, carrots, two different ugly cakes, some cookies – and true to the rumor – watermelon. There were several pieces still left and he took two plus two glasses of lemonade. Balancing them carefully, he arrived back at their table without incident.

Mary was looking at the television mounted in the corner opposite them.

"Did you hear that?" she asked as Tim sat down.

"Hear what?"

"The new pyramid, everyone's been waiting for, and that was suppose to land down south, is now going to be settling down near Jerusalem!"

"Uh-huh, so?"

"Don't you know anything about prophecy? It says that in the last days the Antichrist is going to set up his kingdom in Israel."

"So, then setting up their headquarters there means the Antichrist has come?"

"I think so. I mean, I don't really know for sure what it

means – but, believe me, it's not good news. I'll ask my father what it means, or maybe the Prophet, if we see him."

After several nervous small sips during the ensuing silence, Tim cleared his throat. "So, do you have a boyfriend?" he said, hoping he sounded casual.

Mary smiled. "Oh, not right now." She paused for a moment, then, "Actually," she laughed, "I've never had a boyfriend."

"Really? Never?"

Mary shook her head slowly. "No, I didn't really ever think I would. You know, being blind. I just figured boys want girls who can see. You know, just like you asked – about baseball, tennis, and stuff like that – that's what people do, but I couldn't. I prayed that when I got older, someone would love me though. My mother kept telling me not to worry, that God would provide someone, someday."

Tim was quiet.

Mary smiled, "How about you?"

"Well, I've been around a little – there was Janice," said Tim, trying to impress yet not sound too worldly.

"Who was Janice?"

"Oh, just a girl I met. She was okay, but I didn't love her or anything," said Tim. He remembered Janice – she was nine and so was he. She liked to practice kissing. Girls! Every stinking time they played King and Princess, Janice said they had to kiss. He didn't like to play King and Princess but she wouldn't pitch at baseball for the rest of the week if he wouldn't be King.

"So where is Janice now?"

"Now? Oh, I don't know – it wasn't a serious thing." Tim ate a bite of his watermelon.

"Do you think I'm pretty?" asked Mary suddenly.

"Pretty? Well, sure I do," stammered Tim, unprepared for such directness. He paused for a moment. "Actually Mary, I think you are more than pretty. I think you are beautiful. I can't understand why every guy in camp isn't pounding on your door." Tim stopped; suddenly he was out of breath. Was he nuts? He couldn't say stuff like that just because she's having watermelon with him. What was he thinking? Now, she probably thinks he's a jerk.

"Really?" said Mary, with a slow smile.

Tim felt his face starting to burn.

Mary looked up at the clock on the House wall. "Well, I've got to get to work. I'm helping out at the telephone shack again."

"Okay. I'll clean this up. Thanks for spending some time," said Tim.

"Until next time," said Mary smiling and waving goodbye.

Tim watched her leave the House. Through the window, he watched her walk down to Grand Circle Drive, his mind racing – until next time – how about that? Until next time. A big smile brightened Tim's face as his brain whirled. What did that mean – until next time? Until next time – what? Until next time – nothing? Until next time – when they were old? Until next time, would they ever see each other again? Hmmm, until next time.

Chapter 6

A practiced, crisp knock came at the door. Eppinger impatiently opened the door and snapped, "About time!"

"Yes, sir," replied one of the two young soldiers. "You're transportation is here, sir."

Without another word, Eppinger motioned toward his packed bags, which were waiting next to his bed. Leaving the soldiers to their duties, he preceded them to his waiting transportation. This whole trip he found to be annoying. His last duty post was one of the best he had ever had: southern California as Regional Director for the Blue Brigade. He had worked hard to get that command, its perfect weather, and glorious home. It had taken him two years to get everything in order there: the soldiers, the civilians, the Jesus Freaks working, but finally he had accomplished his goal. It was his turn to take it easy, relax with his wife, and enjoy the good life. Now, suddenly he was transferred to Asheville, North Carolina as Regional Commander of the Red Brigade... the worst-run region in the U.S.

His mood did not improve when he learned his flight was delayed an hour because of weather. Disgusted by the whole mess, he made his way to the bar, but found it closed. Everything seemed closed these days – no worker bees. It was a stupid policy killing all the Christians. Who did they think would pump their gas, clean their offices, baby-sit their brats, or pour the stupid drinks! Turning, he made his way to the main hub of the terminal, where he found a bar open – self serve, of course. A young girl was at the cash register, and none too happy about it.

"Two," said Eppinger to her, and paid the money. He was drinking too much lately and having just two today would be an improvement. He could pour himself more drinks than what he paid for, like so many of the others were doing, but he wouldn't. What did they expect the others would do, be honest? The country was now filled with thieves, liars, robbers, and murderers. He decided to pour a third drink – screw 'em.

Finally, feeling better after this fourth drink, he made his way to the appropriate gate, and boarded his plane bound for Buenos Aires; from there he would change planes for the final leg of the journey to the Pyramids. That was another thing, he complained to himself, why did they have to locate the stupid pyramids so far south, and in such cold conditions? The silly Christians said it was because it was foretold in the Bible. They thought the location 6 degrees west, and 66 degrees south fulfilled some kind of prophecy. No wonder they were killing them off – such stupidity had to be weaned from the genetic pool forever. Still, why such a cold and desolate location?

The flight was long enough for him to have a couple more drinks and a nap. When Eppinger woke, he actually felt pretty good. Finishing a quick cup of coffee – self-serve, of course, he found the plane was circling the three gigantic pyramids. It had been a year since he had been here, and the sheer beauty took him by surprise – just as it had before.

The three triangular shaped structures were immense in size rising out of the sea. Each one could comfortably contain a large city. The setting sun reflected off them, giving gold glimmers, mixed with the light blue glass sides and ice blue of the water. It really was breath taking. Surrounding and connected to the inner pyramids was a large wide area, which served as both landing strips and docks for the many ships waiting to unload goods and passengers. In the center of the immense structure was a large open area of water. It was said this was reserved for the final pyramid, which would come one day – when all was ready for the people of the Earth to visit their homeland, their true ancestral home.

Circling once, the plane landed on the runway, then slowly

taxied up to its assigned terminal. Eppinger made quick work of deplaning. His Colonel wings were finally of some use, now that he was back on military ground. They helped him again in immediately securing transportation that would take him to the Officer's Quarters. From his previous visits he knew the procedure, and what to expect. This resulted in his being checked into his room in record time. They said his bags would be delivered later, but he was not concerned.

The room was for Senior Officers. There was a reasonably large bedroom located to his left as he entered. Beyond the bedroom door, a small kitchen was to his right, which had a serving bar that opened to a small dining area. Immediately to the left, and at the end of the hall, was a large living area. An immense picture window measuring eight feet by twenty feet allowed him a clear view. Being on the 170th floor, gave him a wide view of the ships and docking area below. He reached out to touch the window, but felt no glass. It always amazed him how they could make the glass disappear. He could feel something solid, but certainly could not see any evidence of it. A narrow balcony was outside the window and could be accessed from a door located in the dining area.

Despite his irritation at having to make this long journey, now that he was here, he was glad. He had forgotten how impressive this structure was – how the very presence of it made him feel. It seemed as if it connected him to the universe, and made him feel a part of human history never dreamed of by his ancestors. He, Hans Eppinger III was not only a colonel, but would soon be traveling to a wonderful land with a life that would last forever. He thought about his Uncle, and namesake, Hans Eppinger. He had died in disgrace, hung as a war criminal after World War II. Not many knew that fact, he certainly did not advertise it, but it gave him some satisfaction that he was able to bring his family's name from the gallows of Europe to the stars.

His appointment with General Powell was for the next morning, and he was happy about that. It meant he could quickly conclude his business and be on his way. This meeting was only a formality at best. He knew what they wanted, and they knew he knew. Best to get the show over with so he could make his way to Asheville, and begin being miserable as soon as possible.

True to his expectation, his bags were delivered a short time later. After unpacking, he spent most of the afternoon lounging around on the sofa. The refrigerator was stocked with his favorites, as it always was when he visited. Yet, for dinner, he decided to dine at one of the many restaurants available in each of the pyramids. Whatever he desired was available in a number of varied venues. After some thought, he chose French. It was not a hard choice since he had been there before. The French Chicken brought him back to this restaurant. It reminded him of his visit to Paris back in 1975 where he met Lorraine. Lorraine made French Chicken for him. He could not remember all that she did except she cut up some apples and oranges and an onion and dumped them into the belly of the chicken. The only other thing he remembered was she sprinkled flour all over the chicken before putting it in the oven. Whatever her recipe, it tasted good... or maybe it just tasted good because Lorraine made it. Either way, he enjoyed the memory of the chicken and Lorraine whenever he ordered French Chicken.

As the hostess was about to seat him, he saw Lt. Colonel Richard Decker. Thanking the hostess, he made his way over to Decker and sat down at his invitation. They exchanged an enthusiastic handshake. The men had been friends for many years, and it was an added bonus of the trip to find him here.

"Why you old coot, I haven't seen you in five years – and look here, full bird Colonel hardware!" he said tapping Eppinger's shoulder."

After pleasantries, Eppinger leaned forward. "I got the worst assignment. I'm transferred to Asheville and the hillbillies."

"Now, Hans, don't go calling them hillbillies or they'll show you a thing or two you won't like. I had some property up there years ago, and they are pretty smart folks."

"Hey, ever tried the French Chicken they serve here?"

Decker shook his head, "Can't say that I have – good?"

"The best, and I'm going to order it. I encourage you to try it."

"Sold."

After getting some water for the added guest, the waitress took their orders.

"So, you're headed to Asheville. Word is that is the garbage pit of assignments – a lot of insurrection. Were you aware the last Commander, Lt. Col. Syme, committed suicide?"

Eppinger nodded, "Yes, he really screwed his division up. I heard that many of his men deserted him – all at once. I hear they were a large number of Christians in his Command and they got away. Can you imagine that, right under his nose, a bunch of Jesus Freaks?"

"That's not all I heard," said Decker, "I heard his men ran from those Jesus Freaks, when they tried to capture them. Can you believe it, our soldiers running from a bunch of Freaks?"

Eppinger raised a finger while looking around. "Not so loud, I would rather that be put in the past and forgotten. Anyway, he's gone, and that's the end of that," said Eppinger raising a knowing eyebrow. "So, what have you been up to lately?"

"Nothing out of the ordinary – trying to stay outta trouble," Decker smiled. "I heard some news about the war though. I think there's gonna be a peace treaty."

"Really? I didn't think Israel was gonna sign a treaty with

69

anyone – the other side wanted too much and wouldn't guarantee any lasting peace."

"The Visitors found a way around that. They are gonna guarantee Israel peace – in fact, I understand the missing pyramid is gonna come down somewhere near Israel, in the Mediterranean Sea."

"You're kidding – I thought they said it was going to complete that structure they got going here.

Decker shrugged, "This is just what I heard, but I think it's on pretty good authority. I also heard that it is huge – I mean bigger than huge. They say that the pyramid is a hundred miles square at the bottom. Can you believe that?"

"It seems unbelievable – how can you bring something that big down from space. I guess there was a scientist in California who said he thought that if it wasn't done just right, it could hit the Earth with such force that the Earth might crack."

"Well now, that sounds like crap to me. Scientists – what a bunch of losers. What we need are more men who can defend their country," said Decker, then smiled, "Against who, I haven't got a clue," he smiled. "Anyway, if it's true, it's about time there was peace treaty in the Middle East. It'll be good to pull all the troops outta there."

Eppinger nodded. "At the rate things are being settled, we won't have any wars around anymore."

Decker smiled, "Yeah, outta business."

Decker filled him in briefly about his assignment, adding he was up for his own Colonel's bird hardware in two months. "I'm being transferred to the Orange Brigade in the Mid-West as Deputy Commander."

The two old buddies finished dinner, then had a drink before going their separate ways. Eppinger was happy to see his old friend. It had been too long since they had talked and he resolved to correct that in the future. Arriving back at his room, he discovered he was actually tired. Evidently, the plane trip, the drinks, and the dinner were having their effect. He decided not to fight it, and retired early, anxious for the morning to come.

* * * * *

Eppinger was up early the next morning. He showered, shaved and dressed before heading to the mess hall on the 26th floor. He loved the morning breakfast of cooked ground beef & gravy on toast – affectionately known in the service as SOS. He'd been eating it for twenty years and liked it as much as he did when he first joined. He took his time eating, and then strolled up to the Personnel floor in time for his appointment. Things were running a bit late though, and he had to sit for twenty minutes before he was escorted in to see General Powell.

As he entered, a portly man wearing four stars rose from his chair and came around to shake his hand. Quickly Eppinger saluted before reaching for the outstretched hand.

"It's great to see you, General," Eppinger said. "I think the last time I saw you – about a year and half ago if I recall – you were in New Orleans."

General Powell nodded, smiling as he sat down, "Yes, at the awards ceremony." The General pulled his chair up to the desk and opened a folder he had in front of him. "Well, Hans, you know why you're here. I know you must be a bit disappointed with your transfer to the Red Brigade. If I were you, I'd be expecting a commendation for the work done in California – not an assignment to the worst Brigade."

"Well, sir, I was a little surprised, but I'm happy to go wherever you think I can serve best," he lied.

"Cut the bull, Hans. I have been in this army too long to swallow that stuff anymore. You should be mad – I don't

71

blame you. However, this may work out for you. I personally selected you for this job precisely because of your success in California. We need that same success here – and I promise you this, Hans: do a good job, and I will personally pin that first star on your shoulder."

Eppinger was stunned. He had not expected that. "Well, sir, I – yes, I'll do the best I can. You can count on me, sir."

"I am, son, I am. I got General York breathing down my neck. He wants my job – did I tell you that he and I were classmates at West Point?"

"No sir, I don't believe you did."

"Yeah, we were. He was a jerk then and he still is. He never has forgiven me for graduating higher on the class list than he did," smiled Powell. "Yeah, he thinks I cheated on my Tactical Theories final exam and that's why I keep one star ahead of him now." This time Powell chuckled as he remembered.

"Well, he's just bitter. I think it's about time he stopped thinking such a thing about you," said Eppinger.

"Well, he can't. See, he was right!" This time the General laughed aloud, getting several looks from adjoining tables. "Yeah, I cheated – but who cares now with space pee-on's running everything?"

"Did I hear that General York is here at the pyramid?"

"Yes, he's here. He is running the Southeast Asia show. He would love to run mine, and will if I screw up. That is why I need you to do a good job, Hans. I can watch your back, but I need you to take care of mine."

"I'll do my best, sir."

Powell nodded, and then paused for a moment. "Hans, about this Worker Program you were doing in California. They aren't happy about it. They don't like the Jesus Freaks going about their business with the good people. Bunch of crap, if you ask me," volunteered Powell. "Now, you didn't hear me say that, right? Now, tell me a little about the program."

"Well, sir I'm very surprised to hear that. I thought the Worker Program was a good idea. Rather than killing these religious fanatics, I put them to work. I took a city in California, near Gorman, and we evacuated all the residents and gave the city over to anyone without the Mark. I put a fence around it and made sure I knew who was going in and out. I emptied out the prisons and directed the Goonies not to kill any Christians with families – I even offered a bonus for any they brought in to us. There were some rules – first, only married couples and families could live in the city. Second, only one member of the family could go outside the city at a time – later I amended that allowing two parents to go out as long as their children remained inside."

"I see. I can understand why it worked," smiled Powell. "If you don't come home that night, the children are killed."

"Exactly – same with the couples – one stayed and worked inside the city while the other was out."

"Do many run?"

"A few, but we make sure the punishment is done swiftly. There are no exceptions. Come 9 PM, you have to be back in the city – unless you have a night job. If you are not back by nine, the sentence is carried out immediately. Don't run out of gas. Don't lose your way. Don't fall down and break a leg. At 9:01, the family's dead."

Eppinger nodded. "And it's working pretty well, I understand."

"Yes sir. Actually, the Christians like it. You see, I don't allow any Goonies or other outsiders inside the city. The Christians are not hassled and they enforce their own laws. It is just like a town of twenty years ago. They feel very secure in it. They know their families are safe. They love it," he smiled.

"And, I understand that the necessary tasks are being done on the outside."

"Yes sir, some are garbage haulers, gas station workers, waitresses, cooks, hotel clerks – just about every job you can think of is being done by them. It is not as it was before, there just aren't enough Freaks to do all of the work. Over the past couple of years, we have killed so many of them, they're starting to get scarce. But, the essential jobs are being done. Planes fly between the large California airports, buses run, plus, a lot of the surrounding stores are open for business."

Powell smiled. "Well, I don't know how long they'll let you keep this program, but until I hear otherwise, I'll look the other way, how's that?" he smiled.

"I appreciate that, General. It makes life a lot more enjoyable for everyone concerned."

Powell nodded, and was silent for a moment. Finally, leaning forward, he gave a quick look around as if to see if anyone was within earshot. "Hans, you and I have been friends for a long time. I look at you like a step-son; so, let me ask you a question," he said, looking around again. "Do you think all the stuff about going to the stars is true?"

Hans pursed his lips while staring at the table. He gave a quick glance at Powell's face, judging the old man. He felt a need to be cautious. These days who knew who was listening to what? "Does it matter?" he answered, "I've been taking and giving orders so long, I just follow them."

"Well, son, I tell you what I think – it's a bunch of crap," said the General. "They always have some reason why they can't take all the folks just yet – kill a few more Christians, Jews, and Muslims, that'll do it. But it never does."

Eppinger nodded, preferring not to make any verbal sounds that could be recorded.

"I can tell you this," continued Powell. "I'll never go there. I am too old, too many aches and pains – and they want me to live forever like that? No thanks, just shoot me before you go, that's what I say."

"Now, General, you don't mean that," smiled Eppinger.

Powell grew quiet. "Yes, I think I do. Oh, there is one more matter I want to talk with you about. In your new assignment, I understand there is a group of Jesus Freaks up in the hills; perhaps you are aware of them already? I understand they've grown to quite a few in number: Some say 5,000, some say 10,000 – but whatever the number, you are going to have to do something about them."

"Yes sir, I know. I understand they are led by a man they call the Prophet."

"Yes, we had him locked up once. Your esteemed predecessor, a civilian, Regional Prefect Bernard Krantz, had him locked up – next thing we know – not only does the Prophet escape, but Krantz joined him! Can you believe it? So, they send in Lt. Col Syme. He decides to make a name for himself and charges up the hill to where these Jesus Freaks are living. It was a disaster. I guess, from the reports I have heard, they got half way up the hill, and then turned and ran! Can you imagine that Hans – they ran?" Powell looked around to see if anyone was listening.

Eppinger nodded. He had heard this story before.

"So this Syme jerk shoots some officers and wants to pretend like nothing happened – blames it on those men, labeling them cowards." He shook his head slowly. "I'll tell you what... those men weren't cowards. I had someone check their service records. They were fine officers. We were fortunate to have them. I think they did see something – something that scared them and their men to death. Be careful Hans. That Prophet fellow, there's something about him that could ruin your day."

Eppinger nodded. "Yes, I had come to the same conclusion. No, we aren't going to fool with him right away – oh, we'll get him in good time – you can bet on that. I don't know if you know it or not, but I understand we have an informant in the camp."

"Really?"

"Yes, its Top Secret – I'm not surprised you didn't know. They only told me two days ago. I don't know what his status is right now, or what kind of information he is feeding us. However, rest assured, I won't make any moves 'til I'm sure they are the right ones."

But Jesus said, Suffer little children, and forbid them not, to come unto me: for of such is the kingdom of heaven.

– Matthew 19:14

Chapter 7

Mickey discovered the problem with being a spy was finding someone to spy on, yet not make them mad about it. He definitely needed someone to practice on – to learn how to watch without being seen; to walk without making noise; and to listen without being heard. There were so many other things he thought he should learn, like how to pick up trash to get information, or maybe make drawings of their footprints so he could search around and see where they had been. He knew he should keep notes – really good spies kept notes. He resolved that he would always carry a notebook and pen with him. He was sure he could learn all of these things, though it might take a little time.

He just needed to practice on someone. Not Tim, he would get mad, that was for sure. He didn't know how that girl Mary Kegler would like it, and he certainly couldn't follow Mrs. Moore around – she might tell the Prophet – and who knows what he would do. Maybe prophets, if they got mad enough, could turn people into something else, like a dog or cat. Who really knew? No, the only person he knew, who shouldn't get too mad was the Major. After all, it was he who made him a spy, so how could he get mad? It was settled. The Major would be the person he would spy on.

However, his spying job would have to wait because it was raining. Instead, Mickey sat on the front porch impatiently waiting to go to school. The rain was falling at a steady rate, and didn't look as though it had any thought of stopping soon. "So, you just gonna hang around here after school?" Tim asked, as he came out on the porch, struggling with the zipper on his rain jacket.

"No, but I don't know what I'm gonna do. I might see if Mr. Kegler needs help. He asked me yesterday to help him fix the sink at the Great House, but I couldn't 'cause I had to get here. Maybe he's got some job today for me.

"Mickey, about this spy business, I don't want you being a nuisance to Major Frost. You know, if someone were following me around like that, I'd get pretty mad."

Mickey nodded, "I know – at first, I was gonna follow you, but I knew that it would make you mad, so I'm not."

Tim put the jacket's hood over his head. "Mickey, don't let your imagination get you in trouble. I am telling you to take a break from your spy game. Besides, I think you need to concentrate on your school work more – I haven't seen you do any homework all week."

Mickey rolled his eyes and let out an exasperated sigh. He turned his head away from Tim and laid it on the railing. Tim was getting on Mickey's nerves – do this, don't do that, blah, blah, blah.

"You hear me?" asked Tim, an edge creeping into his voice.

Mickey nodded, without turning around until he heard Tim's footsteps retreat down the street. Then, turning his head until he could see Tim walking, Mickey stuck his tongue out. Then, giving his 'before school' sigh, ran down the street until it joined up with Circle drive, and from there to the small schoolhouse.

At school, Miss Yeager said it was raining too hard to go outside for recess; she was sure they would all get too muddy. Didn't she understand that was the whole point? Grown-ups! The older they got, the weirder they got... though, Mickey had to admit, Miss Yeager was a nice lady.

Finally, the school day was over and life could begin

again. Mickey made his way to the garage, careful not to miss any puddles. He entered the horse stables which had been converted into the motor pool. Several vehicles were parked in the barn, and Mickey saw the figure of a man bent over one of the cars.

"Hi, Mr. Kegler," said Mickey.

The man straightened up, bumping his head on the open hood. It wasn't Mr. Kegler, it was Reverend McDonald – but everyone called him Reverend McDee for some reason. Mickey didn't know him really, though he had seen him around. One Sunday he saw him preach at church – all the ministers took turns.

"Well, hello there young man; now, who might you be?"

"My name is Mickey Streeter. You're Reverend McDee aren't you?"

The Reverend wiped his hands off, before extending one for a handshake. "Yes, that's who I am, and I'm pleased to know you," he smiled.

Mickey knew who Reverend McDee was. Everybody seemed to know him. He had a ready smile on a round face that seemed to light up when he looked at you. His jovial face sat upon an ample body, which the Reverend had no thought of changing, for better or worse. Mickey knew he would like the Reverend.

"Can I tell you a secret, Reverend McDee?" asked Mickey.

"Son, you can tell me anything you want," replied Reverend McDee, as he stuck his head back under the hood.

"I'm a spy."

"Really?" said McDee, his voice a little muffled by the hood. "Are you spying on me?"

"Oh no, not you – on Major Frost," replied Mickey.

McDee took his head out from under the hood. "Major Frost… do you think that's a good idea? The Major has many important things to do, you know. Maybe your spying on him will get in his way, and that wouldn't be good, would it?"

"Oh, I'm real careful. I make sure he never sees me. I'm gonna keep notes so that I can show him how good I was, and then maybe he'll give me a real job to do."

"Here, give me that wrench by your left hand there," said McDee, pointing to one of three socket wrenches on the bench. "So, why are you spying on Major Frost?"

"I'm just practicing."

"I see."

"Why do you think the Major needs to go up on Bolder Mountain so much?" asked Mickey.

"I dunno. Maybe he needs a place to look around."

"Is the car broke?" asked Mickey.

"Oh, no, I'm just making sure everything is in tip top shape. When I was young, my daddy got me interested in cars. Even when I became a minister, I still liked to fool around with cars." answered McDee. "Now, I'm gonna tell you a secret – can you keep a secret?"

"Yep. That's what spies do – they keep secrets. I've kept it secret about me being a spy already."

"Well, this here car is what they call a 1995 Mustang – a real fast car. When Detroit built it, they wanted to give it some real muscle, so they put in a 5.0 liter V-8 with 4.00 inch bore and 3.00 inch stroke. It had 215 horsepower and could go about 140 miles per hour. Pretty fast, eh, Mickey! I could make it go even faster by adding some racing pistons and camshaft! I'm just giving it a good cleaning and oil change. This is the fastest car in camp!"

"I don't know what any of that stuff you said means," grumbled Mickey.

"Well, I'm teaching you. You see, that's how young men learn things. Old guys like me teach them," McDee said, burying his head again under the hood.

"Are you gonna marry Timmy and Mary?"

"Am I what?" asked McDee bumping his head on the hood again.

"Marry Timmy and that girl Mary, the one who used to be blind," repeated Mickey.

"Now, where did you get an idea like that?"

"Just watching them," he smiled. "I told Timmy he should marry her."

"You did?"

Mickey nodded, "I think she would be fun to have around. I like her. The twins think they will get married too, but they think if Timmy gets married, he won't want us around anymore."

The Reverend, putting his hand on the car's fender for help, knelt down until he was able to look Mickey in the eye. "Now, you tell the twins that is never going to happen. I know Tim, and he loves you kids more than life itself."

Mickey smiled. "That's what I told them."

"Well, good," said Reverend McDee. "Now, why don't you give me a hand here to get up, Mickey," said the Reverend, as he tried to get up. "Seems somebody put some lead weights in my pants," he smiled.

Mickey took the Reverend's left arm and helped him up. "Why'd they do that?" he asked.

"Don't know, son, don't know."

"Are my parents in heaven?" asked Mickey suddenly.

"Oh, I'm sure they are. Did they love Jesus?"

"Yes, sir," answered Mickey matter-of-factly.

"I'm sure they are in heaven as we speak, waiting for the rest of us to join them," replied Reverend McDee.

"That's what I think, too. I didn't cry too much when my parents died, 'cause I knew they were in heaven looking down on me. That's right, isn't it?" asked Mickey.

"You bet, son. You bet," said the Reverend, wiping his hands.

81

"Does God look down on us all the time?"

"Of course He does," smiled McDee.

"Even when I'm in the bathroom?"

"In the... Uh, well..."

"How about when I'm eating, or watching TV?"

"Well, now..."

"What if I killed somebody, would He see me do that? And, I was thinking about when I sleep – does God sleep too, or does He just sorta hang around 'til I wake up? What's He doing while I'm sleeping?"

"For a young man, you certainly have a lot of questions," said McDee.

"I would ask Tim, but he's mad at God right now, and he doesn't wanna talk about it, ever. I ask him stuff, but he tells me I shouldn't bother him."

McDee threw the soiled towel in the metal can by the door, then turned and faced Mickey. "Here's my answer to all your questions. See Mickey, when we believe in God, we believe 'cause we feel it's right. We have faith. Do you know what faith is?"

"Sure, it's like when I think something – no, maybe it's – no, I guess I don't know."

"It is knowing something is so, but you can't prove it. When Jesus tells us about Heaven, and we believe Him, it is because we have faith He is telling the truth. We have faith in Him."

"I believe."

"Yes, and so do I."

"So, I have faith?"

"You do, and isn't that wonderful? I tell you what – why don't you go around for the next couple of days and see how many things you have faith in? Then, we'll talk about it. Now, I gotta get back to work here."

"Okay. I gotta go – don't tell anyone I'm a spy, 'cause it's suppose to be a secret."

Reverend McDee, using his fingers, gave the okay sign before ducking under the hood again.

Leaving the Reverend, Mickey headed toward the Great House. The rain had almost ceased and was promising to quit altogether. Mickey kicked a rock that was in his way. He was bored. Life seemed to get that way sometimes. He thought about spying on someone else, because he was tired of climbing up that stupid mountain. And, since he decided to take notes, nothing had happened to make many notes about, except climbing up that stupid mountain.

Arriving at the Great House, he saw Tim, but decided to leave him alone. He was with that girl, Mary. They were doing the 'lovey-dovey' junk. Instead, he went into the kitchen where he saw Sergeant Evans eating a sandwich.

"Hello, Sergeant Evans," smiled Mickey.

"Hello there ,Mickey, what's up?"

"Oh, nothing," said Mickey as he slumped against the counter. "What kinda sandwich is that?"

"This here is an egg sandwich."

"Do you like it?"

"It's delicious."

"Do you like it 'cause you have faith in it?"

"No, 'cause it tastes good."

"Can you keep a secret, Sergeant Evans?"

"Well, I can sure try."

"I'm a spy."

"Really, wow."

"Yes, it's official."

"I see, and who are you spying on?"

"Well, right now, I'm just practicing, but as soon as I get pretty good, I'll spy on someone for real."

Mickey left Sergeant Evans and wandered around the kitchen, before going back out to the dining area. He sat down at one of the vacant tables and then rested his arms on the table. He put his head in his hands, and sighed, "What to do, what to do." It was just a crummy day.

Chapter 8

The next day the ever-present clouds tapered off. They usually did after a rain cooled the ground. Although it wouldn't last long, it was nice to have the sun shining and even casting sharp shadows here and there. Mickey felt good, now that school was over for the day. School was just boring.

He ran to the cabin to check if there were any notes from Tim. Not finding one, he changed into his fatigue pants. He resolved this was definitely a Spy Day. He had seen the Major heading for the motor pool, and thought, if he hurried, he could catch him there.

Tim grabbed a sandwich, before running up Grand Circle Drive to the motor pool. Bordering Grand Circle Drive were many mature trees and Tim picked one near the motor pool. Kneeling down behind the tree, he began waiting for the Major. Time seemed to drag. This wasn't as much fun as he thought. Even practicing, was boring. Mickey shifted his position from resting on his knees to sitting, but it didn't help much.

Suddenly, he saw the Major exit and begin walking westward on Grand Circle Drive. Reaching Knob Hill Trail, he turned left. Knob Hill Trail led out of the camp toward the surrounding hills. At the point where Knob Hill Trail ended, the Major began climbing up the steep embankment toward Bolder Ridge. Bolder Ridge was part of the mountainous ridge that surrounded the camp.

Mickey had seen him do this before, and wondered if he wanted to follow him up the sometimes steep mountain trail again. Maybe he could just wait here for the Major to return. Then sighing, he began following him up the mountainous ridge. This spy business was not easy.

Mickey hung back. He knew it was the practice of the Major, for some reason, to keep looking around as he ascended

85

the hill. Bolder Ridge was only one hundred feet to the top, but just beyond was Bolder Peak. Now, that was a climb. He heard it was over thirteen hundred feet. Posted every twenty feet were signs forbidding people from climbing, but sure enough, the Major headed past them. Mickey considered giving up the game for the day – that was just too far to climb, but again persuaded himself that it was the price of his training.

It took the better part of the hour to reach the peak, the highest point of land on the east side of camp. On the West side, was Black Mountain, almost as high, at twelve hundred feet. Mickey sat down behind a rock outcropping trying to recover his breath after the long climb. He took out his note pad and scribbled his notes. Peaking around the rock, he saw, some fifty yards ahead, that the Major seemed to be standing and resting too. Then, with another look around, the Major went north and disappeared. Mickey was astounded. He had not seen that before. Last time the Major just looked around and then made his way down again.

The only place where the Major could go was a narrow ridge leading around the backside of the mountain. It didn't seem possible he went on that narrow path around Bolder Peak. One false step and he would plunge down a thousand feet to Bolder Chasm.

He was sure the Major didn't go that way; nobody would. He waited to see if the Major would reappear, but he did not. Carefully, Mickey traced the Major's steps, and discovered a large section of granite, some fifteen feet high, by thirty feet wide, just in front of the ridge guarding the back of Bolder Peak. There, an opening, not immediately visible, and measuring some three feet wide, allowed access to the other side of Bolder's Peak.

Venturing through the three-foot opening, he carefully peered through the gap to see where the Major had gone, but could not see him. Yet, he was sure this was the path the Major took. Mickey was tempted to follow the Major through the opening, but decided there was too much danger of being caught. Better to wait until sometime when the Major wasn't here to explore and take more notes.

He grinned, anticipating Major Frost's surprise, when he would tell him of following him here. With all Mickey's past exploration of the area around camp, he was surprised he hadn't discovered the opening before. He was sure not many others had either. Mickey began to go over the words for his report that he would hand the Major – 'followed', 'stalked', 'spied', and 'dangerous' all came to mind. This spy school was turning out better than he thought.

An unexpected yawn escaped his mouth. Spy stuff would have to wait. He was tired. He had to be home by five o'clock and the sun was beginning to sink. If he started back now, he could make it easily, maybe even have time to stop off for something to eat, before he went to the cabin. The climb down wasn't nearly as hard as the climb up. Now it was his turn to look back to see if there was any signs of the Major. There were none. Whatever the Major was doing, it was taking him some time. This was good news for Mickey.

Finally reaching the Great House, and checking the clock inside, Mickey found he had ten minutes before he had to be home. Besides, Tim never complained if he was a few minutes late – a few, anyway. Mickey made his way past the counter where they were beginning to lay out the dinner for the evening. Instead, making his way into the kitchen, he found several people, including Mr. Kegler who was lying on the floor, half in and half out of one of the dishwashers.

"Hi, Mr. Kegler, what you doing?"

Kegler looked down toward his feet and saw the smiling face of Mickey. "Oh, still working on the dishwasher son, just working. Why don't you help me out and hand me that screwdriver next to you?"

Mickey grabbed the screwdriver and handed it to Kegler. Then, scooting closer to the opening, and sticking his head inside he whispered, "Mr. Kegler, can I tell you a secret?"

"Well, first, this space isn't big enough for both of us, and second, if you told me, it wouldn't be a secret anymore, would it?"

"But you won't tell anyone, right?"

"I'll try not to, but I'm getting old and sometimes I forget what I should and shouldn't say."

"I'm a spy," whispered Mickey.

"Really? For who?"

"Major Frost. He made me an official spy, and today I wanted to train, so I spied on Major Frost."

"How does he feel about that?"

"Oh, I didn't tell him. I followed him up Bolder Mountain, to the very top."

"That's not a good idea Mickey. You could hurt yourself up there. Didn't you see all the signs saying not to go there?"

"I was real careful."

"Mickey, it's too dangerous. The drop on the other side is sheer down. No one is allowed on that ledge – and that, mister, includes you," he concluded with some sternness.

"I was wondering why Major Frost would want to go up there."

"I'm sure he has his reasons," groaned Kegler as he squeezed out of the opening. "Now, there – that should do it. You gonna help me put this thing back together?"

"No sir, I gotta get home – it's almost five o'clock. Remember, Mr. Kegler, it's a secret."

Kegler nodded and smiled as he watched Mickey leave. Oh, to be young again with mysteries to keep and share.

* * * * *

88

The next day some sunshine was still poking through the clouds above the camp. The rare rays continued giving a lift in attitude around the camp. Everyone, including Mickey, was feeling and acting more jovial.

Mickey planned to scale Bolder Peak in the morning, but was asked to help clean the Great House after breakfast. It didn't take long for the cleanup crew to turn the appearance from a cafeteria to a lounging area. Mickey got permission to leave and immediately made his way for Bolder Peak. For some reason, the climb this day didn't seem as hard as the previous day. Reaching the top of the peak, Mickey took a careful look around making sure that no one else was there. Assured that was the case, he ran behind the boulder and through the opening he had found the previous day.

Here he paused, listening for any sounds that might reveal someone else, but there were none. Assured he was alone, he walked further out onto the wide ledge. The ledge was a space with an area with fifteen to twenty feet to the edge where it dropped off suddenly. Mickey had no desire or intention of looking over. Staying to the back of the cliff, he made his way around to the other side, but was distracted by the sight of a narrow opening five feet above him. It was a small cave, one he was sure could not be seen from below, as the cliff's ledge would block the viewer's angle.

Getting up to the cave was simple, a small series of level areas acted as good as steps to reach the cave. Mickey climbed it with ease. Once there, the light streaming in revealed an area about twenty feet wide, ten feet tall and running back about thirty feet. Mickey was about to walk to the rear when something on the floor of the cave caught his eye – a wire. Mickey was astonished. Slowly he bent down and picked it up. One end of the wire went to the mouth of the cave while the other went back into the cave, eventually disappearing around a corner at the rear.

He had not expected to find anything like this. It was getting scary. For a moment, he debated whether he should investigate or leave. However, he decided danger was just part of the spy job. Slowly he traced the wire back into the darkened cave, becoming aware that fear was growing within him with each cautious step. Toward the rear of the cave, the light faded, and Mickey slowed until he was slowly putting one foot in front of the next. Arriving at the dimly lit back wall, he found the wire made a sharp left turn, leading through a passageway into a second, smaller area. Here, the light was almost gone. It took several minutes of contemplation before he decided to venture into the darkness. Finally, one slow step after another, he crept into this smaller, darker area. As his eyes became accustomed to the dark, he found himself looking at a table. Discovering the table brought a sudden shiver of fear within him. His first instinct was to run, but knew that would not be right; yet, clearly, something was wrong. On the table were some electronic-like boxes, and the wire he had been tracing, was connected to one of the boxes. Mickey was sure it was a radio. Beneath the radio was a contraption that looked like the pedals of a bike. A cord ran from the pedals to the back of the radio. The whole thing brought an increased level of fear. On the old table were a couple of books, microphone, and kerosene lamp. Mickey felt his heart beating harder in his body with each new discovery.

Suddenly, he heard a noise from the outer cave, instantly he was filled with an almost paralyzing fear. Looking around, he ducked behind a ridge in the wall where he waited as silently as he could. Even his breathing, escaping in low stuttering gasps, seemed too loud to him. Within a few minutes, a presence filled the opening, reducing even the small light that had drifted between the two rooms of the cave. Around the corner came the figure of a man, almost six feet tall with weight equal to the height. The figure turned to look back toward the cave's entrance, and the movement allowed the weak light to reveal his face.

"Major Frost!" exclaimed Mickey with joy. "Boy, am I glad to see you! Look what we found!" he exclaimed, his fear of a moment ago, vanished.

The Major jumped at the unexpected greeting, and then stood still as Mickey rushed to the table.

"Look here, Major," he excitedly said, "A wire! It goes to this thing that's probably some kind of radio! And I found it! I was being a spy, just like you said, and I found it!" shouted Mickey.

He smiled up at the Major, "Pretty good spying, right?"

* * * * *

Tim was growing angrier by the minute. The rule was, everybody had to be here, in this cabin, no later than five o'clock. They could go out after that but then they had to be back when the lights went on in the Great House. Tim went out to the porch again, looking first one way, then the other. He stared toward the Great House, clearly visible were its lights, shining through almost every window.

That was it. Mickey was a good kid, but even good kids needed some discipline now and then – just to show them they couldn't push people around. Tim would confine him to the cabin for a week – maybe two, if he didn't show up soon. Turning, he went inside to see if the girls were doing their assigned homework. The girls, on the other hand, were no trouble. They went to school, came home, did their chores, played outside and were always back when the lights went on. Mickey could take a lesson from them. Yes, he could. He checked the clock again – six o'clock.

When he checked the clock again, it was eight o'clock. Anger had been replaced with fear.

* * * * *

Every now and then, Andy thought a particular day was a very, very good day. Today was one of them. He stretched out on the couch. He even felt so good that he had encouraged Stephanie to pick out a movie at the Great House for them to watch tonight. He was sure she would pick out some girly flick that had as its theme, how the world would be a better place, if men didn't make women cry. That was okay, he didn't care. He even took out one of the two small bags of popcorn they had been allotted. He was surprised, and impressed, when Stephanie showed up with one of his favorites – a Bugs Bunny movie. Seemed few people in camp even knew who Bugs Bunny was – how could that be.

Andy shook his head. Of course, they didn't know who Bugs Bunny was. Many in camp weren't even born when Elmer was chasing Bugs. He glanced at their clock and saw it was eight o'clock – the agreed time to start the show. Andy called to Stephanie, and received a 'hold your pants' reply.

A frantic pounding at the door brought Andy quickly to his feet. Alarmed, he reached the door quickly with Stephanie not far behind. It was young Tim Barter.

"Mr. Prophet, something's wrong!" he nearly shouted, his voice betraying his anxiety. "Mickey isn't home. He always comes home before the lights go on. I looked everywhere, but I can't find him, please, will you help me find him?" he pleaded, his tone revealing his fears.

"Okay. Let's slow down."

"I've looked everywhere, I…"

"Hold on. Did you have a fight with him, or is there some reason you know of that would make him not want to come home?"

"No. Not at all. He was all excited about being a spy. He

92

was the happiest he has been since we arrived.

"A spy?"

"Can you help me find him?" pleaded Tim.

"Of course we can," Andy replied, then turning to Stephanie, "Put a call through for the Emergency Response Team to assemble. Also, tell them to put out a general alarm. I want everyone else up and out searching as well."

Stephanie didn't reply, but ran to get her walkie-talkie.

Turning back to Tim, "We'll go to the Great House and be there when the team arrives. Now, tell me, what has Mickey been doing lately? Is he a member of any of the clubs? Does he have a girlfriend? Tell me anything that might influence his voluntary absence. I wanna hear more about this spy business. Let's eliminate those possibilities before we look at anything else."

On their way to the Great House, Tim briefed Andy. No, he wasn't a member of anything. No, no girlfriends – no, he hadn't been in any fights that Tim knew of – the only new thing in his life was this spy thing.

"Tell me about that."

"Well," said Tim, shaking his head, "Not much to tell really. He told me he was a spy now. That Major Frost made him a spy. I guess Mickey wanted to join the soldiers – at least that's what he had said to me, but I told him he was too young. Next thing I know, he's a spy."

"Well, we'll talk to Major Frost. He should be coming to the House as soon as he hears of the ERT alarm."

Andy found Major Frost was already waiting for them at the entrance to the Great House, still buttoning up his shirt from getting out of bed.

"What's up?" he asked.

"We've a missing child – do you know the young boy that lives with Tim called Mickey Streeter?"

"Yes, a little; I talked to him for a minute, day or so ago."

"He said you made him a spy?" asked Tim

The major nodded. "Yes, said he wanted to join the army, tried to tell me he was sixteen, but finally admitted he was only twelve. I told him he could be my personal spy in camp and that seemed to please him."

"So, did you send him on a special mission or anything?" asked Andy.

"No. Of course not. It just seemed his heart was set on defending the camp, so I thought he would like to be a spy. Why? Do you think it had something to do with his being missing?"

Others were now arriving, and Andy motioned them into the House while he pondered Major Frost's question. "No, I don't think so," he said finally. "Did you happen to see him after that?"

Major Frost shook his head. "No."

Once inside, Andy, then Tim, briefed the assembled group on the missing child. Major Frost finished the briefing by assigning teams to search around the camp. He promised more would join them as help arrived.

The clouds overhead were not thick that night, allowing more illumination than usual which made searching easier, though no more fruitful. For the first hour, the teams searched likely areas that might seclude a child. Finding nothing, the Colonel broke up the entire search area into smaller grids, and they began a slower, more methodical search.

As morning broke, they still had no success, nor did they until one o'clock that afternoon when they found his body at the bottom of Bolder Chasm.

Hearing the news, Tim began running for Bolder Mountain. By the time he reached the Chasm, his lungs were in pain and he was struggling for oxygen. "Where...is...he?" he gasped.

The Major motioned to the edge of Bolder Chasm.

Looking over the edge, Tim could see several lines running a hundred feet down the sides of the deep crevasse. At the bottom, four men were bending over Mickey's body.

"They'll bring him up in a minute," said Major Frost. "I'm deeply sorry for your loss, son," he added quietly, while tenderly patting Tim on his shoulder.

Slowly, the stretcher began rising. The team had tied ropes around both the body and stretcher to give it some security. As careful as they were, the stretcher bumped against the uneven walls of the chasm in its slow journey upward. Tim watched it rise with his tears flowing so fast, it was difficult for him to see. Occasionally, anguished sobs escaped him without his noticing. The sounds of tortured sorrow touched the hearts of those standing silently with him.

At last, the stretcher reached the top and Tim rushed over to help settle it on the rock. Mickey's face was ashen. There were deep bruise marks on his cheek, forehead and bare arms, while his right arm was at an unnatural angle. Tim lightly touched Mickey's hair, remembering how it flopped in the wind when they were camping. Reaching down, he picked up Mickey's hand gently with both of his own, and held it to his cheek as he looked down at his lost friend. Tim half expected him to open his eyes and speak.

Tim thought about how Mickey trusted and counted on him for everything. He had failed Mickey. He should have been able to keep him safe. Mickey could not be dead. He still had three Baby Ruth candy bars saved for him. Then, laying his head on Mickey's body, Tim began sobbing, "I'm sorry Mickey, I'm sorry!"

Blessed is the man that walketh not in the counsel of the ungodly, nor standeth in the way of sinners, nor sitteth in the seat of the scornful.

– Psalms 1:1

Chapter 9

Finished with packing for his return trip to North Carolina, Eppinger wandered over to the large picture window that overlooked the busy harbor below. The busy scene impressed him: ships as far as the eye could see, waiting their turn at the docks; planes overhead cueing up to land at the Pyramid Airport. All this was set in the vast Antarctic Ocean, which lay strangely quiet for miles in all directions. Given the fact they were in the southern Atlantic, long famous for its wild seas, he was amazed how it never stormed here.

A knock at his door broke into his thoughts. He was about to open it, but thinking better of it, peeked through the security hole. What he saw brought chills, as always. Outside stood two Ancestral Brothers in white and black robes, with a third Brother robed in all back, behind them. It was Abdon. Eppinger opened the door, and all three of the tall and silent creatures walked past him. Their black hoods were drawn up over their heads, but drooped slightly at the edges, partially hiding their faces. He could feel a breeze as they passed, and detected a slight acrid odor. Silently, they went to the end of the hallway and into the living room before stopping and waiting there for Eppinger.

"This is an unexpected pleasure," half-smiled Eppinger, hoping his voice did not betray his nerves.

"You know who I am?" asked Abdon, his deep voice resonating in the room, even though he spoke in an almost subdued tone.

A red rim surrounded his eyes, a characteristic common to the Visitors. The eyes and height made them stand out along with the chiseled features of their face and body. They appeared more like mythical Greek athletes than alien beings. Some said the red around their eyes allowed them to see inside a person's soul. Eppinger considered that ridiculous, although there was no denying they seemed to know a lot more about individuals than could be explained. Nobody was comfortable under their unwavering gazes, regardless of the reason.

"Yes, sir," replied Eppinger. "You're Abdon, leader of the Ancestral Brothers. It's an honor to meet you, sir," Eppinger hoped his nerves did not show in his voice. The fact Abdon was here in person was impressive and scary.

"I am the leader here, but there is one greater than I. Now, the area you are being given has been known for its difficulty. Are you aware of this Colonel?"

Eppinger nodded, adding, "Yes, General Powell and I had such a conversation. He wanted me to know he had high expectations for the pacification of the area."

"As do we, Colonel, as do we. This area has been a particularly embarrassing problem for the General. I wanted to pay you a visit to emphasis how much we are counting upon you to solve it."

"Yes, sir – and solve it we will." He smiled, but did not get one in return.

Abdon walked to the window and stared out for a moment or two. "What is your opinion of General Powell?" he asked finally.

"Well, he seems very capable. I've known the General for much of my military career and I've always been impressed by his abilities."

Abdon turned slowly giving Eppinger a searching stare. "I know his capabilities!" he snapped. "I'm asking about his commitment to our cause," he said curtly.

Eppinger was taken aback by the tone. "I don't understand," said Eppinger, feeling his face beginning to warm. "As far as I know, he is committed to it, as am I."

Abdon nodded slowly, but without expression. "I know you are loyal to General Powell, but I want to advise you to make sure your loyalty does not interfere with your dedication to the mission. We of the Brotherhood expect to be your first loyalty, do you understand?"

"Yes, yes sir, of course," stammered Eppinger. "I didn't mean to imply that I placed my loyalty to General Powell on a higher..."

"I understand," interrupted Abdon. "Those who demonstrate great loyalty will be rewarded when we take everyone to their new home. You understand that, of course."

"Yes sir, completely."

"So then, I don't have to worry that your new area will continue to be a problem?"

"No sir. I will bring this district under complete control. The Red Brigade will do you proud, sir." Eppinger paused before asking, "Is there something I should know about General Powell, sir?"

Abdon was quiet for a moment before answering. "I think you know all you need to know, Colonel." Abdon attempted to smile. "I think you need to forget about General Powell, and concentrate on things closer to your home. Your wife, Colonel, she is fully committed to our cause?"

The question took Eppinger by surprise, and a look of confusion traced across his face, "My wife sir? Well, yes my wife is fully committed to the cause." As he answered, questions raced through his mind searching for the reason why Abdon would ask such a thing. Lorraine had given him no cause to doubt her commitment, not only to himself, but also to his mission.

Abdon turned to Eppinger, staring so intently into his eyes

that Eppinger was forced to look away.

"I think you would be wise to have a talk with her soon," advised Abdon.

"I – I will, sir. But I assure you she is every bit as committed to this great project as am I."

Abdon turned to leave.

Eppinger gathered his courage and spoke, "Sir, about the length of time it is taking to rid our societies of these Christians. Some of the Elect are growing impatient. I hear murmurings asking when the migration to the stars will begin. It has been quite awhile, sir, and I hear..."

Abdon whipped back around focusing upon the Colonel. "Are you questioning me?" he snapped.

"No, sir. I would never question you. I understand completely this takes time. I was just wondering if you could give me an estimate when this Christian business will come to an end? I simply ask so I may make preparations for the final elimination."

For a moment, silence hung heavy in the room. Finally, Abdon's mouth moved, trying to smile, but was only partially successful. "All in the proper time, Colonel, all in the proper time. You bring up an interesting topic – the Christians." Abdon put his hands behind his back, and seemed to rock on his heals while thinking. "I understand you were using these Christians in menial tasks in California, is that true?"

"Yes sir, using them in this way has enabled the communities to continue to function. However, I assure you, I'm ready to eliminate them at the proper time."

Abdon looked down at the floor for a moment, before looking at Eppinger. "I'm not sure I approve of this, but for the time being I will allow it to continue; however, be prepared to eliminate them."

"Yes sir, of course."

Abdon nodded then, without a word, turned and walked to

the door, with the two Brothers following.

Eppinger did not move as he watched the three exit the room. He breathed a sigh of relief as the door closed behind them. His former Sergeant would have said, "Those are some scary dudes."

* * * * *

Captain Beiner was about to close his office when the telephone rang. His first instinct was to let it ring; however, it might be the General trying to reach him.

"General Powell's office, Captain Beiner speaking," he said in his practiced tone.

"Captain, this is Lieutenant Colonel Eppinger, is the General still there?"

"No sir, he left about fifteen minutes ago. Is there something I can help you with?"

There was a pause before Eppinger said, "No, Captain. Can you get a message to the General for me?"

"I'll try Colonel, but I can't guarantee it," replied Beiner. It was his standard answer, regardless of the caller's rank. General Powell's privacy was part of his concern, and he wasn't going to let every Tom, Dick and Harry constantly interrupt him, regardless of how much hardware they wore.

"I'd appreciate it if you could, Captain," replied Eppinger. He knew the game. "Tell the General it's important that I see him. Tell him I just had a visit from Abdon, and he mentioned the General's name."

Beiner felt a pang of fear at the mention of Abdon's name. "Yes sir, I'll try to reach him. Will you be in your room?"

"Yes," replied Eppinger hanging up the phone. It was important to inform the General that the Aliens were asking about him. That was not a good sign, at all; but what about those questions concerning his wife, Lorraine?

100

Perhaps Powell knew something about Lorraine he was not sharing. Maybe, he could trade information with the General; however, offering a trade was risky. Right now, he had the General's favor, but if the General suspected he was being blackmailed, things could get ugly very quickly.

Almost an hour later, a knock came at Eppinger's door. Quickly Eppinger went to the door and saw General Powell's face through the peephole. Powell was not in uniform. Instead, he had on civilian clothes that appeared to be a size too big. On his head, pulled down over his ears, was a Tigers baseball cap – a decidedly non-General appearance, which apparently was the goal.

Opening the door, Powell quickly entered.

"So, now, what's this about Abdon?" he said curtly as he ripped off the hat and threw it on a chair.

Eppinger put his finger to his mouth and motioned Powell to follow him. He led the General out the dining room door onto the balcony and chilly night air. He wasn't sure if the rooms were bugged, but one had to be careful. His Mother had taught him it was better to be safe than sorry. He waited until the General had closed the door.

"Abdon was here," hissed Eppinger. "I don't like that jerk," he added, shaking his head. "He asked me about you, and what I thought about you."

Powell was silent for a moment. Then swearing, hit the railing with a closed fist.

"He asked me about your commitment to the cause," said Eppinger.

"My commitment?" shouted Powell. "My commitment? How dare he question my integrity?" Powell slammed the railing again. "What else did he say?"

"A couple of things – but the one that alarmed me was when he mentioned my wife."

"Your wife?"

"Yes, do you know anything about that?"

"Me? What would I know? Besides, even if I did, I couldn't tell you. You know that. So, what else did he say about me?"

"Well, sir, I think Abdon told me these things in private, I really shouldn't tell you."

Powell looked at Eppinger, and for a moment, his eyes burned with anger, then he smiled. "Now, Colonel, you wouldn't be trying to pressure me, would you?" he asked.

Eppinger returned the smile, "Absolutely not, sir."

"That's good," replied Powell. "It does seem to me that your wife's name was mentioned. I wish I could tell you exactly what was up, but I don't know. However, the interested people were with Intelligence."

"Intelligence?"

Powell nodded. "It didn't make any sense to me either. She isn't a spy, that's crazy – besides, most of the intelligence people are out of the business now, anyway. The only thing they do now is dig Christians out of the woodwork. And we know she isn't a Christian, for heaven's sake, so go figure."

"Could it be a mistake – could they be confusing her with someone else?"

"Son, I'd like to say that was the case, but it isn't. They know you, and they know she is your wife. If I were you, I'd go home and have a real heart-to-heart talk with her."

Eppinger felt his heart skip a beat. What in the world could Lorraine have done that would attract the attention of Intelligence, or 'Jesus Sniffers', as some called them." He felt a pang of fear as he suddenly thought he might know why – that housekeeper. She was a Jesus Freak and she was real buddies with his wife – in fact, he had thought they were getting to be too good of friends.

"Now, what else did they say about me?" asked Powell.

"You?" asked Eppinger "Nothing, really. Just said they

102

were worried about your commitment to the cause. That is all. I tried to get more information, but they wouldn't tell me anything – just said I needed to worry about my wife, and not you."

"How dare they question me!" exploded Powell. "They give orders as if they own me, and still, I've carried out every last one! I have over twenty years in this man's army. I have not complained once – not once. They have turned me into a sniveling 'yes boy', but do I complain? No sir!"

"If I hear anything else, I'll let you know, General."

Powell nodded, too angry to trust himself to speak.

"I'd appreciate it, General, if you would do likewise," said Eppinger.

Powell took a deep breath and tried to relax, "Of course, son, of course."

The two old friends said goodbye, each wondering if they would ever see the other again.

Chapter 10

Seven slow, agonizing days had passed since they buried Mickey in the small cemetery at the edge of camp. Tim had not been able to grieve the loss of Mickey. Each time he felt his grief approaching, he shoved it aside. He was not ready. Instead, he concentrated on helping the twins get through their own ordeal. There was no time for his tears. However, even if there were time, he was not ready.

In the ensuing days, while it seemed the girls were dealing with Mickey's death, they appeared more withdrawn. It was as if Mickey's death awakened within them the awareness that life was a serious business. Perhaps it was the sobering realization that not everyone grew old.

"Do you ever think about Mommy?" asked Katie as the two sat on the cabin porch.

Alison nodded, "A lot."

"Timmy said Mommy's dead, but I think he's wrong," said Katie. "Sometimes I wonder if Mommy is looking for us."

"Sometimes I dream about her," ventured Alison. "I see her waiting for us by a highway. Like maybe we are coming on a bus or something, but we never get there."

As the days past, in the wake of Mickey's death, both twins had became melancholy, as did most of the camp. The happy boy, running around wanting to help everyone, singing songs with the wrong words, enthusiastic about everything, could not be heard anymore, and the camp seem to feel it.

Reaching their cabin one day after school, the twins found Tim at the kitchen table. There was a cardboard box in front of him. It was obvious that he was waiting for them.

Tim smiled as the twins entered the cabin. "So, how was your first day back at school?" he asked, smiling.

Alison shrugged her shoulders, "Okay," she answered with

no enthusiasm.

Katie came over to the table. "What's in the box?"

"Well, I thought maybe it was time we faced facts. This is Mickey's box. I thought maybe we could go through it together."

Alison shook her head slowly. "Not me, I'm not touching that stuff."

"Me either," echoed Katie.

"I thought maybe you'd feel that way, but listen – we have got to face the fact that Mickey is no longer with us. I think if we go through his things, it will bring back some nice memories. I think Mickey would like us to take care of his things. In fact, I am sure he would like each of you girls to have something of his, so you could keep him close. What do you think?"

The girls shrugged unenthusiastically.

Tim pawed through the few remaining effects recovered from Mickey. There was a pen, a quarter, and the key Tim had given him long ago. The 'mystery key' they called it because neither knew what it unlocked. There was a rubber band and then there was a small notebook.

Opening the notebook, he saw a tic-tac-toe game with marks looking like the twins made them. The next page appeared to be Mickey's handwriting. There were notes about some conversation with Reverend McDee. The word 'faith' was circled, and something about God being in the bathroom. It was the third page that interested Tim the most. It contained his spy notes. Tim knew they were the Spy Notes, because in large letters across the top of the page, was scribbled *SPY NOTES*. However, there were not many notes. He had written something about Bolder's Peak and Major Frost. There was something about a 'secret passage', and that was all.

"Here, Alison, why don't you take Mickey's Lucky Quarter?"

Alison opened her hand and Tim dropped the quarter in it. "How do you know it's lucky?" asked Alison as she turned the quarter over examining it.

"Oh, it is. See, the year it was made is the same year Mickey was born. And here, Katie you can have his Lucky Key."

"That stupid old key," said Katie. "It never unlocked anything."

"Oh, but it did. Mickey told me it unlocked happy days for him. I think he had that key for a long time. He said his father gave it to him. He was the one that told him it was a lucky key."

Katie put the key in her pocket. "I guess our family is getting broken up," said Katie with some emotion creeping into her voice. "Mickey is no longer here, and you are getting married."

"Who said I was getting married?" asked Tim, shocked.

"Mickey said you were."

"Oh, well, Mickey was just guessing. I'm not getting married."

"I think that Mary girl wants to get married."

"Now, don't go putting words in other people's mouths." Tim sighed, putting the notebook in his pocket.

"Tim, Timmy, you here?" It was Mary's voice from the front door.

Tim waved her in.

Mary smiled as she entered, "I hope you don't mind my coming by. I thought maybe you needed someone to talk to, or just have someone make you hot chocolate."

"I'd like some hot chocolate!" said Alison with Katie in unison.

Tim smiled. "That hot chocolate idea sounds good."

Tim showed her the canister where he kept the hot chocolate for the twins.

"You girls let us know when that water is boiling. Mary and I are going out on the front porch," said Tim.

On the porch were a couple of chairs and a handcrafted bench with a back. Showing Mary the bench, he sat down beside her.

"So, how are you doing?" asked Mary.

Tim shrugged. "Okay. I sorta think I'm recovering, and then I see, or hear something that sends me right down to the bottom again."

Mary nodded. "That's how grief works, I think. First, there is the shock of it and then, when that goes away, grief sorta bubbles up again and just when you think it's over – up it comes again."

"Sounds like you've had some experience with it."

"No. Not really. My life has been pretty much grief-free. Some might say that sounds funny coming after my being blind and all, but I never really grieved about being blind. That's just the way life was for me, and I accepted it."

"I was sitting here talking with the girls about Mickey. They are having a tough time, I think. I was also thinking about the way he died. They say he was walking on the path that goes around Bolder Peak, but I don't think that could be true. From what I hear, that path is pretty narrow and high up. Mickey was deathly afraid of heights. I am surprised he even went up on the mountain."

"You don't think he fell off that path?"

"Oh no, I'm not saying that. I just want to know what happened, for sure. Sorta keeps poking at me that I don't know exactly how it happened. Maybe I'm just working out my grief... think that could be it?"

"I don't know – doesn't really matter. We do what we think we have to do, and that's the end of it."

Tim folded his arms and sat back, smiling at Mary. "How come you haven't been scooped up by some guy?"

Mary smiled, "Well maybe, cause there haven't been any boys around. My mother and father lived out here for a long time, and the only time there were boys was when the church groups came. Then, in two weeks, they were all gone, and we were alone again 'til the next group."

"Sounds like a pretty lonely life to me," said Tim.

"Oh, I really didn't mind. I had lots of things here to keep me busy, and really, I had already marked having a boyfriend off the list of possibilities. So, I concentrated on doing other things."

The two sat there in silence for a few minutes – comfortable with each other.

"C630887777086," said Mary,

"Excuse me?"

"Your driver's license number."

Tim smiled, "That's impossible."

"The pots boiling!" yelled Alison from inside.

Mary and Tim got up and went into the kitchen where Mary retrieved three cups from the cabinet.

"Aren't you going to have a cup, too?" asked Tim.

"Can't," replied Mary. "I've got to get home, but if you come by later, maybe we could have a cup together at the Great House."

Tim smiled. "That's a deal."

Mary poured the hot water over the cocoa in each cup and then brought them to the girls and Tim. "You all just enjoy your cocoa and I'll see you later," she said, touching Tim's shoulder lightly.

Tim watched her leave, then got up and looked out the window. He followed her with his eyes as she walked down the street, still feeling her tender touch. As he watched her, he knew, he just knew. He picked up his cocoa and poured it out in the kitchen sink. He did not like cocoa.

Not expecting to see Mary until later that afternoon, Tim

decided to fill the time by having a talk with Mickey. Had someone else said that to him, he would have thought it was sick. However, he had some things he needed to say – things he had not got around to saying while Mickey was alive. He put the last two Baby Ruth candy bars into his left pocket and his gun in his right and set out for Bolder Mountain.

Though Bolder Mountain was not where Mickey was buried, it was where Tim thought he would feel closest to him. After all, it was there that Mickey took his last breath, and Tim had the strange notion that somehow his spirit might still be there.

The journey up the mountain was slow, mostly because Tim did not feel like hurrying. He used this time for reflection. He thought about the church killings, and helping Mickey out of the hiding place after the Goonies had murdered their parents; how Mickey loved those Baby Ruth bars; about their nights hiding in the hills; or times Mickey was a lookout. It occurred to Tim that if they had never left that hill, Mickey probably would still be alive. Tim felt in his pocket for the candy. He had been saving these Baby Ruth bars for some special occasion, such as passing a test at the camp school, or doing something around the cabin, or for the camp. He had waited too long. Buttoning his jacket against the growing chill, he made the last steep accent to Bolder's Ridge. Reaching the summit, he looked out over the camp. He resolved to come to this place more often; the camp appeared so beautiful from here. Perhaps, he thought, that's why Mickey had been there.

Finally, approaching the shear drop where Mickey had fallen, he looked down. Tim tried to recreate a sense of what Mickey might have felt. Perhaps he felt a slipping, the stones beneath his feet moving, sliding, followed by nothing – nothing at all as he plummeted. Perhaps there was not enough time to fear, regret, or wish – indeed, nothing at all and then, the sudden impact – followed again by nothing, nothing at all. If there were a God, He would not have permitted this to happen. If there were a God, He would know the world needed more Mickeys. Shaking those thoughts out of his mind, Tim reached into his pocket and retrieved the Baby Ruth bars. He held them for a moment, thinking he should say something, but could not think what. He did not speak; he simply let them drop, one by one, to the bottom.

Taking a deep breath, Tim looked around at the peak of the mountain, examining the ridge that ran around the peak to the other side. It was narrower than he remembered, and he was convinced Mickey would never have attempted to walk on it.

If that wasn't how he died, then what was the answer? What happened? He moved to the face of Bolder's peak, and slowly began searching for the opening Mickey made mention of in the notebook. Tim looked toward the large boulder forming the actual peak of the mountain. It was as large as a three-story building – and as big around as a small city block. He traced the edge of the boulder. A dark space in the rock unexpectedly appeared. It looked like a crack in the huge rock, yet, as he drew closer it proved to be deeper than he first thought.

In fact, he saw it was not simply an indentation in the rock at all, but actually a passageway. Tim felt his heart jump. Surely, it was the opening Mickey noted as the 'secret passage'. Although some three feet wide, it was so well hidden, it would be invisible to all but the most discerning eye. Carefully venturing into the passage, Tim saw it made a sharp right turn, narrowed a bit then opened on the other side. Tim was astonished. Why hadn't he been told about this? Who knew, or should know about this? Certainly, Roy Kegler should know, and the Major – in fact, Mickey had mentioned the Major coming up here, not just once, but several times.

Tim walked out on the wide ledge that ran around the

outer side. To his left was the granite peak, and to his right, a flat ledge area extending fifteen to twenty feet out, before dropping off. Tim slowly walked as far as he could around the peak. On the other side, he found the narrow path from which they said Mickey fell. Looking at it, Tim was even more convinced Mickey would never have ventured on it.

Slowly walking back toward the entrance, he inspected the rock above him that formed the peak of Bolder Mountain. He was half way around when he spotted an opening of a cave about fifty feet above. At first, it looked almost impossible to reach. As he neared the far side, he could see a succession of natural flat rocks acting almost like steps. Slowly, Tim climbed them toward the cave.

Reaching the cave entrance, he peered in. However, the daylight only penetrated part-way into the cave. Cautiously, he entered and found it was deeper than expected. There was no sign of habitation by either man or beast. Turning back around, he looked out over the valley. Perhaps, at this height, something unusual would be revealed. Why would the Major come here so often? Why didn't he just station some men here to guard this corner of the mountain? Turning, Tim went further into the cave. He paused, allowing his eyes to adjust to the growing darkness. His eyes adjusted, he could see the end of the cave; however, there was no sign of anything unusual.

Finally, he sighed, and gave up. He admonished himself for always being so suspicious of everything and everybody. As he neared the entrance, his eye caught something, nearly hidden on the floor of the cave, just at the point where the floor and wall met. Bending down, he saw it was wire. It had been laid so close to the side of the cave that in some places it disappeared beneath the jutting out of the rock. Tim felt his heart jump a few beats. He quickly looked around, half-expecting someone to be watching. Drawing out his revolver, he began tracing the wire toward the back of the cave. Had

Mickey done this? He was sure he must have.

Grasping the pistol tighter, Tim walked as quietly as he could, squinting to see the back of the cave. He tried to remember how many bullets he had. It was eight, he thought. Reaching the back, Tim was surprised to see the wire did not end there, but made a sharp left turn around a protruding rock. In addition, now he began hearing some kind of small motor running.

Tim froze. The noise was seeping out from behind the protruding rock. In addition to the motor, he could hear something else. He couldn't identify it – it was too short. An animal scratching or a clicking sound – he couldn't be sure. Quietly, and slowly, placing one foot in front of the other, he rounded the rock.

His breathing seemed loud to him, and he tried to take slow, even breaths. A light began to show. He stopped and listened again. This time he definitely heard the sound of a man's voice, speaking low. A few more steps and the wall rounded again, to his right. Carefully, Tim peaked around the corner and saw a man wearing headphones and speaking into a microphone while sitting at a table with radio gear on it. It was Major Frost. Alerted by something, Frost's head turned and he looked directly at Tim. Frost jumped to his feet, reaching for the forty-five strapped to the side of his hip.

"Stop!" shouted Tim, pointing his gun at Frost with both hands and extended arms. For a moment, neither said anything, and then Tim nodded, "It's you," he said quietly. "I don't know how I knew, but I did. You killed him."

"Now, Tim," said Frost, managing a smile, "Don't go assuming things." Frost slowly removed his headphones. Carefully, and slowly, he laid them on the table, while keeping an unwavering focus on Tim, all the while maintaining his smile. "I know what it looks like, son, but you're wrong."

Frost took a slow step forward.

"Stop right there Major," snapped Tim, his voice showing resolve. "Why did you have to kill him? He was a good kid! He admired you! Did you know that?"

Frost, very slowly, slid his foot forward, just above the surface. "Of course, he was a good kid – I liked him quite a bit. Certainly, I would never hurt him," said Frost in a low soothing tone while maintaining an unwaveringly focus on Tim.

"You take one more step, and I fire," Tim said, in a measured tone.

Frost stopped.

"Now, Tim you wouldn't do that. Besides, that little pea shooter couldn't do much damage anyway. Why, I'd be on you before you could get another shot off," said Frost, widening his smile, as his right hand slowly reached his holster.

"I'm warning you, Major."

Suddenly Frost grabbed his gun.

BAM! BAM!

Both shots found their home in Frost's chest. For a moment, the Major stopped, a look of surprise on his face, followed by a smile. Slowly, he began raising his gun again.

BAM! BAM! BAM!

The impact of the bullets staggered the Major, who steadied himself, only to suddenly collapse without uttering a sound.

Tim went to the fallen body and stood over the Major whose eyes, remained wide open, though not focused. He pointed his gun at the Major's chest and pulled the trigger.

BAM!

The body jolted as the round impacted. Tim stared down at the body. Feelings of hate, disgust, and rage, mixed with grief, flooded him as he continued to point the gun at Frost.

He thought of sweet Mickey, who trusted this man, and Tim pulled the trigger again.

BAM!

Mickey's smile came to him. The boy found joy in everything – especially Baby Ruth candy bars.

BAM!

All that Mickey wanted was to help.

Click.

Running here, then there; he always had a project, always busy.

Click.

How Mickey counted on him, always willing, always smiling.

Click.

Click.

Click.

[Less ye corrupt yourselves,] And lest thou lift up thine eyes unto heaven, and when thou seest the sun, and the moon, and the stars, even all the host of heaven, shouldest be driven to worship them, and serve them...

– Deuteronomy 4:19

Chapter 11

Andy hoped the G-bus had enough electric juice left to get him back to the cabin. He had forgotten to charge it last night, and the labored whine of the motor told him he might be in trouble. He was returning after accompanying Roy Kegler on their monthly inspection of the generators at the falls. While the generators seemed to be working fine, the water flow was down again, significantly. If it continued to drop, it would mean cutting back on power within the camp. Both he and Roy were justifiably concerned.

Nearing Grand Circle, he saw old Elmer Dorby waving him down. Andy slowed the cart, and stopped next to the old man. As usual, Elmer was dressed in a clean shirt with a tie that sometimes didn't match. His shoes, while not spit polished, obviously had received some attention, as did his slacks, which sported a crisply ironed hem. Elmer believed an old man should have dignity.

"What's up Elmer?" asked Andy.

Elmer looked down at the ground for a second, then back at Andy. "Well Prophet Andy, I need your help."

"Sure, just name it."

"I think what folks have been saying about me is finally true, maybe I really am crazy, you know, just losing my mind in my old age," replied Elmer.

"Now, what would make you say a thing like that?" asked Andy.

115

"I've been having strange thoughts, things that don't make any sense."

"So, that makes you think you're crazy?" smiled Andy. "Hey, some think I'm crazy."

Elmer didn't smile. "Do you remember what I said in the Great House about dinosaurs?"

"Sure."

"Do you think I was crazy when I said that?"

"Look Elmer, you said what was on your heart. You said what you thought was right. Don't apologize for that. Trust that the truth is in the Lord. Let's see what happens."

"Well, it's worse now," whined Elmer. "I'm starting to dream about them. Last night I dreamed I was at one of those big pyramids down south. I was going into the pyramid and when I opened the door, it was filled with dinosaurs! That's crazy isn't it, Andy?"

Andy smiled and leaned over. "You just keep on preaching what you think Jesus wants you to say."

"And you don't think that's crazy?"

"No, I don't. I have been having some wild dreams myself lately. I am pretty sure when God reveals to us all His truths, a lot of folks are gonna say, 'See?' Maybe you will be one. I think there are gonna be quite a few surprises in store for us. Well, gotta go before the juice in this baby runs out," smiled Andy

Elmer returned the smile, and gave a goodbye wave.

Fortunately, the road from there into camp was downhill, and the G-bus hummed right along. Andy turned the corner toward his cabin, and spotted Tim Barter. As he neared, Tim put out his hand to stop Andy.

"Hello there young man," greeted the Prophet with a smile. "I was headed home, but why don't you and I go and have some watermelon? I can plug this baby in at the Great House."

116

Tim shook his head slowly.

His somber expression caught Andy's eye. "Now, what seems to be the problem, son?" he said, concern slipping into his voice.

"I was headed to your house to tell you something. I just killed Major Frost," he said.

"You what? You killed the Major?"

Quickly Tim explained what he found, and what had happened. For a moment, Andy was without words. Finally, he ran his fingers through his thinning hair and motioned Tim to get in the cart.

"Come on, we'll go to the Great House, then up to that cave and see what we have. I don't know if I have enough power here to get us there, but we'll give 'er a try. Tell you what, when we get to the House, call that Alevertz, or Alvarz, or whatever his name is—"

"I believe he pronounces it, Alverez, Armando Alverez," said Tim.

"Yes – the one that's handy with computers. Maybe he can look at some of that equipment you told me about, and tell us what we have."

The short trip to the Great House was quiet except for the labored whine of the G-bus. Both men had to deal with their private thoughts. As Andy pulled up to the Great House, he turned to Tim. "Now, young man, don't go blaming yourself for something that couldn't be helped. If everything is as you say, then I think you did this camp a great service. We knew there was something strange going on. The Visitors seemed to know what we were doing almost before we did." Andy shook his head. "I just never figured it was Frost."

Tim smiled, "Thanks, I hoped you would say that."

Tim put in a page for Alverez while Andy, spotting Roy Kegler, quickly explained what happened.

Kegler shook his head slowly, "You just never know, do

you?"

Soon, Captain Essex joined the group bringing with him two enlisted men. Quickly, Andy explained to all of them about Frost, adding, "I want all of us to go up to that cave where he was operating, and see what was going on. I have asked Lieutenant Alverez to come with us. I think he can give us an idea how active Frost was with his information."

Andy left his cart at the Great House and, climbing into one of the two other G-buses, headed for Bolder Mountain with a few others. It wasn't long before the group reached the point where they had to climb toward the summit, called Bolder's Peak. While Tim, Alverez, Essex and two security men arrived at the top in short order, both Kegler and Andy struggled with the climb. Reaching half way, Andy paused, "Hold on Roy, let's take a little break," he smiled. I'm not as young as I used to be."

Roy smiled, "Know what you mean, Andy."

"Well, I think it proves one thing though, I'm not fat. If I were fat, I couldn't have made it this far, right? I just need to get in shape," he added.

"Sure," smiled Roy, "You ready now?"

Andy took a deep breath and nodded, "Just had to catch my breath was all."

Arriving at the top, they found the others already making their way around the crevice to the other side.

"Did you know about this passage to the other side, Roy?"

"Yes, I found it a long time ago, but we put it out of bounds for the campers. All those signs you saw declaring the place off limits, well, I put those up about seven years ago. Tell you the truth, I just forgot it was here. It's been years since I thought about it."

Finally, Andy and Roy arrived at the mouth of the cave and could hear the others talking within. Following their voices, they arrived at the rear of the cave. The four men were waiting for them, not wanting to disturb anything until Andy arrived. Using their flashlights, they slowly ventured further into the cave. Tim stopped abruptly as his beam fell upon the inert body of Major Frost.

The Major was lying on his back staring, with unseeing eyes, at the ceiling. Captain Essex approached the body and knelt down while motioning one of the enlisted men to work the electricity generator pedals. Quickly, the lights came on. Then, while Essex searched Frost's clothing for any information, Alverez sat in the chair and surveyed the equipment.

Alverez looked over the equipment, front and back.

"Well, what do you make of it?" asked Andy.

"Prophet Andy, I thought the reason you wanted me to come up here was that there was a lot of computer stuff – that's really my playground. This is all radio stuff. I am a little familiar with it though, I did some work a few years ago that required some interface with this kind of equipment; plus, my roommate in college was a ham radio freak."

Alverez resumed poking around, looking at the various dials, gauges and screens.

"He really had a nice operation here. The manufacturers mark shows it's a RB-4800. That's got a 32-bit floating DSP. Probably something like a 40 dBm intercept in HF bands, plus..."

"Oh, I don't wanna hear about all that stuff – where was he transmitting?" asked Andy.

"Sir, with this equipment, he could reach just about anywhere in the U.S. that he wanted. Now, ham radios use frequencies from 535 to 1605, but this is set a little lower than that – the 453 range. That sorta sounds like police channels to me."

"Police?" asked Andy.

"Well, if you think about it that makes some sense. There

119

really aren't any police anymore, at least like we knew them. All law enforcement that is around is military now, and they have their own channels. I will bet no one else ever gets on this channel, and that's why they picked it. The range is not that far, another reason why they chose it – so they could keep the broadcast local. They probably have the receiving station fairly close – or maybe a tall antenna in Asheville could pick it up."

"Could we move it and still listen?" asked Essex.

"I don't think so. Our camp being down in a bowl, the radio waves couldn't reach us. Even if they did, I don't think our reception would be very good. That's probably why he located here."

Andy nodded. "Okay, let's set up a monitoring station right here then. Essex," said Andy, looking at the captain, "Essex, can you assign people to man this place twenty-four hours a day?"

"Yes sir."

Andy nodded again and turned to leave. "I want to be informed of any activity on the radio immediately. In fact, Alverez, do you think we have any equipment in camp that could pick up these same frequencies? I'd like to bring it up here and monitor the other police channels to see if anything is going on with them that we should know about."

"Yes sir," responded Alverez.

"Oh, and by the way Essex, I am promoting you immediately to the rank of Major. Now that Frost is gone, we will need someone in charge of security. You will be in charge of the garrison, reporting to Stephanie, who reports to me, is that agreeable with you?"

Immediately Essex went to attention and saluted Andy, who acknowledged the gesture with a nod. "Have your men assembled at the Great House today at 2100 hours and I'll address them there."

"Yes sir."

"As for you, Tim," said Andy, "This camp owes you a debt of gratitude. Who knows what things this man had planned? If you want to serve in our military force, I will be happy to appoint you as a Corporal in the army."

"Yes, sir, I would like that."

"Done. Colonel Essex will see to it that you are properly instructed as to your duties. Now, it is time I went home and finished something I was working on there."

Andy and Roy left the men to take care of the Major's body and to arrange for a twenty-four hour staffing of the radio. The climb down the mountain was much easier for the two older men and they arrived back at their cart only slightly out of breath.

As Roy climbed in the cart, he turned to Andy. "My wife and I were talking, Andy, things are not going well for the camp."

Andy nodded. "I agree."

Roy grunted. "The water is going down. Did you know the lake water temperature is climbing? We got a bunch of dead fish out of it yesterday morning, and there were more today."

"Yes, I know. I think we all are uneasy about it. I noticed the crops are not doing as well as they had been, and the cloud cover is thinning."

Roy nodded. "So, I was talking with my wife, and we're thinking maybe the time is near, like real near."

Andy smiled, "I think you're right, and I think a lot of others feel the same way. It is one of those things we all sense, but nobody talks about. It's as though, if we don't mention it, then we avoid it."

Roy smiled, "Seems strange don't it? I mean this is what we have all been hoping for, but as it draws near, we want to delay it."

Andy nodded. "Just being human, I guess. It is easier dealing with what you know than what you don't. Even though, for centuries, Christians have been singing about these days, and praising God – even praying that the time would hasten – still, when it's almost here, we find some fear in it."

"So, you agree, it won't be long now."

"It won't be long."

* * * * *

Mary Kegler knocked softly at the door of Mickey's house.

Alison opened the door, and tears welled up in her eyes as she saw it was Mary. Mary opened her arms and Alison rushed in them and began to weep quietly. Soon, Katie joined her sister and the three girls wept softly together, remembering Mickey. Finally, Mary straightened up and stroked the hair of each twin. "Still having trouble? Me, too, but come on, I'll fix you girls something to eat. You'll feel better if you have something to eat, at least that's what my mother always said. Have you had anything to eat today?"

"I had a piece of bread," answered Katie. "Timmy's been up on the mountain most of the day. He just got back."

"Well, we'll look and see if we can do better than a piece of bread. Where is Tim?"

Alison pointed toward the back of the hallway. Mary nodded, and then began fixing some wheat cereal for the girls. The kitchen was quiet as she worked. Words didn't seem to fit the occasion. When the cereal was ready, each of the twins began eating quietly as Mary walked down the hallway toward Tim's room. She waited outside the closed door pondering whether she should knock. Finally, she knocked softly. Hearing something that might be a response, she opened the door slowly and went in the room.

Tim was sitting on the floor with his knees tucked up to his chin, his back resting against the wall.

122

"I heard about Major Frost," she said quietly.

At first, Mary didn't think he was going to answer, but without looking at her, he finally said, "I went up there to talk to him about you."

"Talk to Major Frost?"

"No," said Tim with some aggravation. "I went up to talk to Mickey. I went where he died, like maybe I was closer to him there than at his grave."

Mary sat down next to him, also wrapping her arms around her legs. "And did you?"

Tim looked at her, "No, I didn't get a chance. I got sidetracked, then I found the cave, and the Major – so, I just never got a chance. " Tim shook his head. "Nothing about this makes sense – none of it... my parents dead, the girls' parents dead, Mickey's parents dead – and now Mickey. Isn't there ever an answer? Can't somebody just make me believe that it all matters?" Finally, Tim turned his head to look at Mary. "That old midget up on the hill – does he make sense to you?"

"Who?"

"The old guy, 'bout three feet high."

"Oh, the Hermit – I've never seen him, few do. My father said he saw him once when he came back to fix up the camp. Said he talked to him about how important it was to get the camp ready. I think the Prophet has seen him. I think he told my dad he had seen him, but nobody else has, that I know of. You've actually seen him and talked to him?"

Tim nodded, "Strange old 'coot." He was silent for a moment before speaking again, "Something about him though. I wonder what he'd say about this."

"Well..." began Mary.

"He'd probably go off spouting something about God, about how everything does make sense, we just don't know how yet. Somebody asked me once, 'Why do bad things happen to good people?' I didn't know the answer then, and I sure don't now. And, I'm sure not going to let some half-pint tell me he does."

"You shouldn't talk about the Hermit like that. Maybe, the answer is that we just have to have faith."

"I need something more. Faith is fine, if it makes you feel better about some stuff. However, when it comes to life and death, I need something more that shows me our lives matter. That somehow all of this matters. That God gives a hoot."

Mary carefully reached over and grasped Tim's hand. "I care Tim."

Tim squeezed her hand and looked at Mary. Her light brown eyes seemed to see inside him, while her face, framed by her rich hair, seemed to swallow him. Tim reached out, softly touching her face with his fingertips, while slowly drawing her toward him. He kissed her softly with an emotion that took them both by surprise.

Tim closed his eyes for a second before speaking. "Mary, I know this sounds crazy, and I'm not even sure I should be saying this, but I have to." Reaching down he put both hands over Mary's hand. "I love you."

Mary tried to say something, but Tim raised his finger to silence her.

"Let me say all of this. I have thought about it day and night. I know we haven't known each other for a long time. I also know we don't have the years our parents had to grow old together. I don't want everything to end before I have a chance to tell you that I love you."

Mary put her hands over her mouth while staring at Tim. Then, leaning forward, wrapped her arms around Tim saying, "I love you too."

Tim kissed her, and was surprised how wonderful it felt.

Finally, Mary pulled back, then gasped, "You want to marry me?" she asked.

"Marry?"

"Yes, that's what people do when they fall in love."

"Well, yes, but–"

"Then you have to ask me," said Mary. "Not me ask you."

Tim looked into Mary's beautiful eyes, and the thought of marrying her brought joy to his heart. He smiled, "Mary, will you be my wife?"

"Ohhh," squealed Mary, then kissed him intensely.

Tim thought he might suffocate, but Mary released him and ran out of the room squealing, "I've got to go!"

Tim heard her burst through the front door.

"What's wrong with Mary?" asked Alison when Tim slowly arrived at the kitchen.

"She's a woman," answered Tim.

Alison turned to her sister, "What's that mean?"

* * * * *

Mary ran from Tim's cabin all the way home. Reaching her family's cabin, she burst through the door, stopping for a moment to catch her breath.

Mrs. Kegler hurried over to her. "What's the matter, honey? Is something wrong?" Her concern showed in her tone.

"Mama, he asked me to marry him."

"Marry? Who? That young man? Don't be silly, you don't know him. Now, don't go talking foolishness."

"What's this about marrying?" Roy Kegler asked as he entered the living room from the kitchen.

"Daddy, he asked me to marry him!"

"Married? Who? When?"

"When?" asked Mary. She thought a moment, then turning on her heels, ran out the door.

"Mary!" shouted her mother. "You come back here!" However, it was no use. She was already half-way up Circle drive.

Betty Jo turning to her husband shook her head. "Can you beat that? I was afraid of this from the first time that boy came calling. Well, she's too young – plus, we hardly know the boy. Absolutely not, Roy – I want you to talk to them, and tell them that! Get some common sense in them. That's what they need."

Roy went over to the kitchen table, motioning for his wife to take a seat. When she had done so, he smiled and said, "She's of age, Betty. These times are different from when you and I started dating. Times are a lot different. I gotta say I'm not surprised that she wants to get married. I remember her talking to both of us once – thinking no one would ever want her because she was blind – well, now someone does. Times being what they are, who knows what's gonna happen tomorrow. I think she deserves to be happy – that's what I think."

"But she's just a child – and what do we really know about this Tim fellow?" asked Betty.

"Not a lot, but I've spent some time with him. Betty, he is a good kid. He works hard and is respectful."

"But I hear he doesn't even believe in God."

Roy nodded, "Yep, that's what Mary has told me. I figure it is between Tim and the Lord. I think he lives like a Christian, because maybe he believes more than he knows. Look how he loves those kids – I'm surprised he's able to survive after losing Mickey, knowing how he felt about him."

Betty got up from her chair and went over to her husband, and sat on his lap while wrapping her arms around his neck. "But she's our baby, Roy. She's all we got."

"I know honey, I know."

Again, Mary was out of breath when she reached Tim's cabin. Bursting through the door, she found him in the kitchen getting snacks for the girls. "When...Tim?" she gasped.

"When?"

"When do we get married?" she managed to blurt.

Tim smiled and went over to Mary. "As soon as possible, I say, just as soon as possible."

Mary smiled. "Did I tell you that I love you?"

"Tell me again."

"I love you," she gasped. "Did I say 'yes'?"

"I didn't hear it."

"Yes!" she gasped. "I do want to marry you!"

"I can't tell you how happy you have made me, Mary!" exclaimed Tim as he grabbed her and twirled her around. "I'm also happy because I know Mickey would be pleased."

"I think he's watching over us now," said Mary.

Tim was quiet for a moment before saying, "I hope you're right."

"You're getting married?" asked Katie.

Turning, Tim smiled his answer.

"Woo Hoo!" shouted both twins.

"I wanna be Bride's Helper!" announced Katie.

"Me too!" echoed Alison

"I said it first, didn't I Tim? I said it first!"

"You both can be my bridesmaids," smiled Mary.

That night, before he fell asleep, Tim did something he thought would never do again. He talked to God. It was the first time he had talked to God in a long time. It felt good. Tim wasn't sure God was listening, or even there, but, even though it felt strange, it felt right. He asked the Lord to watch over Mickey, wherever he might be now, and to watch over the twins, and Mary. And then, he added his thanks for Mary.

Chapter 12

Reverend McDonald's name was on the sign outside Bachelor Cabin One. Along with several other single men, the Reverend had one of the two-rooms, single bedroom apartments. Tim hoped the Reverend was home – he never knew, though. The Reverend was always going out of camp to meet someone or to help bring new people into the camp's safety. He would never tell who it was or when he was going.

Entering the building, he went down the narrow hallway, passing doors marked with the names of other men who lived there, until he saw a nameplate with Reverend McDee's name on the door. He knocked on the door and the smiling face of the Reverend greeted him. "Well, hello there Tim, this is an unexpected pleasure, come on in," he said.

"Did you just get back?" asked Tim.

"I did. I did," smiled the Reverend. "I tell you Tim, life outside the camp is changing all the time. They got a new deal going with Christians now. They are turning them into workers. They get up in the morning and go to a job, just like before. They keep everything running and then, at night, they go back to their compound. A new Commander for this area started the program. You remember the old one, I think his name was Syme, well he up and committed suicide. The rumor is that it was because he messed up the invasion of this camp."

"Really!" said Tim

"Yep, they were going to replace him 'cause he messed up so bad. So, now there is a new Commander; his name is Eppinger. Don't know much about him, but he's doing something really different. Instead of killing all the Christians, he's only killing some, and turning the rest into workers."

"Sorta like prison labor?"

"Yes, I think so. But enough about that; why don't you tell

me what's on your mind?"

"Well," said Tim suddenly worried the Reverend might object, "I see you have a wedding ring on your finger."

Reverend McDee smiled, and touched the ring, fingering it gently. "Yes, I was married to the love of my life, Tilly."

"Tilly?"

"Yes, short for Matilda. We got married a month after I got out of seminary school. We were married for over twenty years, and then she was in a car accident and died." Reverend McDee touched the ring again, "I guess I just can't bring myself to take it off after all these years."

"Well, sir, I guess being married is a wonderful thing, wouldn't you say?"

McDee smiled, "Yes, and I think I'm being led down a path here."

"Well, sir, I'm getting married."

"Why, that's wonderful!" exclaimed Reverend McDee "And I'll bet it's to that pretty Kegler girl, Mary."

Tim smiled, "Yes, sir – how'd you know?"

"Why young man, I think half the camp knew you were sweet on her," laughed McDee. "Well, wonderful – when were you thinking of getting hitched?"

"As soon as possible," smiled Tim.

"Oh, my," laughed the Reverend. "Well, we'll have to start our pre-marital counseling right away then."

"What's that?"

"Well, getting married isn't just a simple thing. It involves a lifetime commitment. Couples are all heated up about getting married and are sure they will live happily-ever-after. However, that is not the case. Life is a day-to-day thing, with problems, disappointments, and trials as well has hugs and kisses. I like to have a few sessions to talk to people about those challenges so they are better prepared."

"Well, thanks Reverend McDee, but we won't be needing

that. You see, we are really in love."

"I'm sure you are but…"

"The thing is, times are different. Every day may be our last day – don't you agree? Who knows when this is all going to end? I don't want to waste any days I could spend with Mary as my wife."

Reverend McDee shook his head, "Nobody wants counseling anymore. I used to have my calendar filled with couples coming and going. Now-a-days everybody is in such a rush." The Reverend sat back and sighed. "I suppose we can do that. I can sorta understand why people don't want to waste any time these days."

Tim jumped up. "That's wonderful! I'll run and tell Mary and let you know what day we want to be married. I think it'll be within a day or two – can you do that?"

"Oh, I guess so, son. I'm not that busy anymore," smiled the Reverend.

Mrs. Kegler's response, when Roy informed her, was not as obliging, "No! Absolutely not!" she said, raising her voice for emphasis.

"Now, Betty, we talked about this already. It's time," said Roy quietly.

It took Betty Kegler two more days of both her husband's and daughter's cajoling before she agreed; however, once she committed herself to the marriage, her enthusiasm grew by leaps and bounds.

Soon the news was all around. The camp began treating the event as an excuse for a camp-wide celebration. Tim had wanted a small affair with Reverend McDee possibly letting them say, 'I do' in his living room. However, Mary's mother would not hear of it – nor would Mary.

"This is the day I dreamed about as a child. I used to practice walking down the aisle and saying, 'I do'. I want this to be special," she said. With a few complaints, Tim relented, while voicing his leftover complaints to the sympathetic ears of Roy Kegler and the Prophet.

"I remember they threw rice at my wedding and I got a piece in my eye!" complained Roy.

"I remember at my wedding I had to wear a suit that was so small, I felt like sardine!" countered the Prophet.

"Hey, that was my suit – and it was beautiful. I remember at my wedding I drank so much I passed out, and didn't wake up 'til the next morning!"

"I remember at my wedding, I got married and then they threw me in jail!"

"Oh, yeah, that's right," said Roy. "Well, you win, your wedding sucked more than mine."

"I think most guys would like to say 'I do', get some kissing, and just get leave for the honeymoon," smiled Andy.

"Amen," said Tim.

"So," asked Roy. "You gonna stay at the Honeymoon Hideaway?" he asked, referring to a cave that had been made into a getaway place for weddings years ago. "Back when the church owned the property, they had me completely frame out that cave, and they turned it into a honeymoon space," smiled Roy. "That Honeymoon Hideaway has all the comforts of a nice hotel room, including a wonderful view of the other side of Black Mountain."

Tim smiled, "Yes, Mary has already mentioned it. I think she said some of the women would go there and spruce it up for us. I don't wanna stay there too long though – the twins need me to be at home. I thank your wife for letting the twins stay over at your house while we are up at the Hideaway."

"Yep," said Kegler. "Now, don't go rushing to get back, if you know what I mean, young man," he winked.

Over the next two days, Mary, her mother, and many of the women in the camp, were busy fixing up the Hall and the Honeymoon Hideaway. The wedding would occur at the chapel and then the wedding party would walk to the Hall for a planned big dinner. From there, he and Mary would be driven in one of the carts to the path that would lead them to the Hideaway. The whole thing was way beyond what Tim wanted, or was comfortable with, but then, it was Mary's Day.

For himself, he spent most of the next two days away from the hubbub, preferring instead to spend the time at the Prophet's garden. He liked the peace and quiet. Small work parties who came to harvest or care for the camp's garden were his only interruption. Everyone complained the crops weren't doing as well lately. Tim had seen that the Prophet's vegetables were sparse. Some, in fact, had never germinated. At first, he worried it might be his fault, and dreaded telling the Prophet. Hearing others were having the same problem, brought a sense of relief, but at the same time, concern. These crops were one of the major sources of food for the camp. If they could not correct the problem, there would be grave consequences for those in the village below.

Yet, while this concerned him – on this day – he shoved the concerns back. Soon he would become the head of his own household, and the husband of Mary. He liked that, 'the husband of Mary.' He only wished it would hurry up and happen. There was just too much activity in the village. Women constantly stopping him – kissing him, giving him hugs – and the men were no better. They would slap his back and shake his hand, and raise their eyebrows and say stuff like, 'Atta boy' or, 'save up your strength, you'll need it'.

Tim was content to stay in the garden away from the hubbub, spending much of the time sitting on an old tree stump and looking out over the camp below. He found one moment he was deliriously happy about getting married, and the next, deep in depression over losing Mickey. However, the time he spent alone helped him reconcile Mickey's death, and he came to think of it as a 'healing time'. He talked a lot to Mickey. It made him feel better, thinking maybe Mickey's spirit was there; and that his young friend approved of the coming marriage. He even found himself saying a prayer now and again. The prayers made him feel better, whether God was there to hear, or care, he did not know – but they made him feel better.

It seemed his wedding day would never come, but it did. Suddenly, he thought everything was happening too fast. Major Essex gave him some polished shoes to wear, and they even fit. Mary's father drove the cart over. It was decorated with all sorts of flowers and ferns. Predictably, someone had tied a whole slew of cans to the back, and the banging could be heard from some distance as the cart approached. Ken Johnstone came with Roy in the cart and brought Tim the wedding suit he had hanging at the store. Andy Moore was there when Ken Johnstone brought the suit in. He carried the pants and jacket over his prosthetic arms with a white shirt folded up and held with his metal claw. Ken handed it to Tim then quickly left. He wanted to check on the last minute preparations at the great House.

Andy stepped up, and examined the suit, "Now, Tim, be sure this suit fits right. My suit was too small for me and the results were not pretty."

Roy Kegler laughed, "That's for sure."

As the time for the ceremony approached, Tim took his shower. The men discussed whether they should cut his hair, and finally decided they should. Over some protestations from Tim, Roy Kegler brought out the scissors, and a few minutes later, they congratulated each other on how much better the young groom looked. A similar discussion occurred regarding the beard that Tim was taking some pride in growing. Soon a razor was produced, and again over some objections, he was soon clean-shaven. They helped him dress, and brushed him off – along with a quick check of the time. The men agreed that

133

getting the groom to the wedding on time must happen and they congratulated themselves again.

Finally, Roy brought the cart around.

"Are all of you getting in?" asked Tim

"No." smiled Andy, "this is just for you. Here, get in the back seat and we will all meet you at the church in a few minutes."

Tim climbed into the back seat, smiling sheepishly. Roy put the cart in motion so quickly, Tim had to grab the front seat to prevent his falling out the back. This brought laughter from his well-wishers who had begun to follow.

At the church, Reverend McDee was thoroughly enjoying the event. He walked around shaking any willing hand he could find, and patting as many backs as possible. Officiating at a wedding was his favorite duty – that and baptisms. He only wished he had had time to provide a proper pre-marital counseling to these youngsters. Marriage was always a difficult adventure, even in the best of times, and now, even harder.

Finally, the time arrived. Tim arrived in the official Marriage Cart amidst the clanking cans. He was quickly ushered into a waiting area to the left of the altar. He waited with Johnstone. He was much more nervous than he ever suspected he would be. In fact, the nerves were affecting his stomach. He had obviously sampled too many sweets.

Someone was playing soft music at the piano, and the assembled people were quiet. He glanced quickly at the group and saw the church was packed – there were even some people standing at the back. He walked slowly to the altar where Reverend McDee stood waiting and exchanged smiles with him. Tim turned and focused his attention on the outside doors. He knew Mary would enter there.

The piano, after pausing for a moment, came to life again with Bach's, *Jesu Joy of Man's Desiring*; its music filling the church. The double doors opened and the smiling twins, dressed in identical gowns, walked down the aisle. At each step, they would reach into their baskets and spread flower pedals. Although twins, one seemed to favor the underhand toss while the other an overhand fastball. Arriving at the altar, they smiled at Tim and Katie gave a wave.

There was a pause in the music, before the piano began banging out Felix Mendelssohn's Wedding March. The entire room stood as Mary came through the doors on the arm of her father. She was dressed in a borrowed white wedding gown trimmed with delicate white lace, with a hint of pink thread running through it. The gown came to the floor with its white train trailing three feet behind. She wore a white hat with a wide brim and beautifully embroidered lace that ran down her back to her knees. A finely stitched veil covered Mary's face, but Tim could see she was smiling. Their eyes met, and Tim broke into his own smile, despite his queasy stomach.

The ceremony went just as planned, except Tim thought the Reverend talked too much. Finally, he found himself putting the loaned ring on Mary's trembling finger, with his equally trembling hand. The combination of the two made the task take longer than it should. At last, it was on, and they turned to face Reverend McDee. "I pronounce you man and wife," he smiled.

Then quietly, Tim threw up on Reverend McDee.

But Jesus said, Suffer little children, and forbid them not, to come unto me: for of such is the kingdom of heaven.

– Matthew 19:14

Chapter 13

Katie Myers rolled over on her back and stared up at the ceiling. "How do you know they're gonna have children."

Alison, in the bed next to her, gave an exasperated sigh, "Cause that's what people do when they get married – they have babies."

The girls lay staring at the ceiling, each remembering yesterday's wedding: the piano playing; walking down the aisle with flower pedals as the official bridesmaids; Tim being so scared that he threw up; then, later, there was all the delicious food.

"Children?" said Katie, in an exasperated tone. "Why does Timmy want children? He's got us!"

"Of course he wants children. That's why they get married! They have children just like Mama did, and they are a family. That's what it's all about. I don't think we belong here anymore. We'll just be in the way."

"Mary seems nice. I like her a lot. I think she would like living with us," ventured Katie.

Alison shook her head. "Nope. They wanna have their own kids. People get married, they have kids and they are a new family. We are the old family." Alison was quiet for a moment. "You ever think about Mommy?" she asked.

Katie nodded quietly.

"I had a dream about her two nights ago." Alison said softly. "I dreamed she was smiling at me."

"Really? I had a dream about her too. She was washing out my ears. I hate that," said Katie.

Katie was quiet for a few minutes, before turning to her sister, "Do you think she is alive – I mean, really alive?"

Alison thought for a moment then nodded, "I do."

"So do I," said Katie. "Timmy said he would help us find her, but if he gets a new family, I don't think he will. I think we should go find her ourselves. She's probably back home wondering where we are."

Alison wiped a silent tear from her eye. "I miss her, Katie."

Katie came over to Alison, and the two sisters embraced, as each let their quiet tears to roll down their faces. At last, Alison straightened up, "Let's do it – let's go find Mommy!"

"Where? We don't know how to get home from here – and it's a long, long way, I think."

"I know, let's ask Mr. Prophet. Maybe he'll tell us. Mr. Prophet knows everything. He talks with God all the time, you know," smiled Alison. "Why, he might even know where Mommy is himself!"

Quickly, the two girls jumped out of bed and, a few minutes later, found themselves headed to the Prophet's cabin. However, they were disappointed when they arrived.

"No, sweetheart," said Stephanie with a smile. "I think he went up to the garden that's on the hill."

It was a long hike up the dirt road. Reaching the hill, they found the climb up to the garden was made harder by the crude steps set further apart than was comfortable for their short legs. Finally arriving at the top, they stood for a couple of minutes to catch their breath.

The level area where the Gardens were located was beautiful. Everywhere there were vegetables, with rows and rows of different colors from a wide variety of plants. Although some of them looked a bit limp.

"Wow," said Katie, "This is pretty."

Alison nodded. "Why didn't we come here before?"

They began walking between the rows, discovering at the far end, another garden. This one had a homemade sign that said "The Prophet's Garden." It wasn't as pretty as the large garden because there were more weeds.

"Mr. Prophet!" yelled Alison. Hearing no response, she shouted again, "Mr. Prophet!" Again, there was no response. However, to their left, they heard a rustling. Emerging from the garden's rows was a little, bent-over man, with a white beard, and long white hair. He was walking with the help of a cane, but bent over so far that he nearly had to look through his bushy eyebrows to see them.

"Hello there," he said, smiling.

"What's your name?" asked Katie.

"Most people around here call me Hermit. I guess we haven't met before. I take care of the gardens. Well, I don't take care of it all alone – I have lots of help from the people in camp," he said continuing to smile.

"I heard of you," answered Alison. "I hear people talk about you all the time. Some say you plant new veggies, and some others say you're crazy. I heard the Prophet tell someone that you were a Holy man," Alison paused for a moment. "What does that mean, 'a Holy man'?"

"Well, first, I'm not a Holy man, only Jesus is that. Second, it means sometimes He speaks to me and tells me secrets. And, sometimes he has me meet little girls and talk to them about Jesus. Do you believe in Jesus?"

"I do," said Katie. "We sing songs in Sunday School about Jesus."

"Yes," added Alison, "once, before we came here, we were in a class to learn about Jesus, and at the end they gave us our very own Bible. But, then..." Her voice trailed off, and an awkward moment of silence ensued.

"I know, Alison. I know," said the Hermit.

"Do you know where the Prophet is? We have a very

important question to ask him."

"Well, he's not here right now. Why don't you ask me the question? You know, I'll bet I could answer it for you. I'm a pretty smart fellow."

Alison looked briefly at Katie, then back at the Hermit. "Okay. Well, we were thinking that we should find our mother. Timmy was supposed to help us find her, but he's gotten married, so we thought we should find our mother on our own. Do you think we should?"

The Hermit stared at them for a minute and then, motioned the girls to follow him to a tree stump. He sat down and motioned the girls to another one nearby. "You miss your mother a lot, don't you?"

"Yes," said Alison softly.

"I'd let her clean my ears all day, if she wanted," echoed Katie.

The Hermit smiled. "Well, I think you will find her – how about that?"

"Really? We can see her again?"

The Hermit nodded. "Now, do you trust Jesus enough to do some scary things?"

"I do!" blurted out Alison. "Momma said we should always trust Jesus."

"Me too!" echoed Katie, then in a more subdued voice, "I trust the baby Jesus."

"Well, you know, I think you do too, and so do I. So, here's what I think you should do..."

* * * * *

It didn't take long for Colonel Hans Eppinger's presence to be felt at the headquarters of the Red Brigade. First, he moved his headquarters from its former location to the old Biltmore Train Station in Asheville. He didn't want any association with Lt. Colonel Donald Syme's past regime at all. The new location gave him just as much area, plus it was lighter, and brighter. He had offices designed and built and left room for a very large lobby area. This was located in what used to be the main terminal ticket area. He installed a coffee shop and a few other support businesses. His aim was to give his men a brand new feel about their job and to forget past failures and disappointments. This was a new day and he wanted them to have a new attitude. The days that followed showed he was successful in this.

Hans wasted no time in having his wife Lorraine join him. He located a wonderful four-bedroom colonial home on Town Mountain Road. It had a wonderful view of the Blue Ridge Mountains. Both he and Lorraine were thrilled with the location. When he had told Lorraine it was four bedrooms, she smiled knowingly at him. They both wanted a family. This was a house was perfect for a growing family. They had tried in the past, but no children had come. Maybe here with a new beginning, things would be different

Lorraine snuggled up to her husband as they shared a cup of coffee in their comfortable bed. The bed faced a beautiful, stone fireplace. "This is wonderful, Hans. I always wanted a home like this – away from all the hubbub of the city."

"Really? You never told me that."

"I know. I didn't think there was any point to it. We go where the Army wants, right? Why make you miserable trying to give me something you could not. But here we are!" She snuggled closer and then took a sip of coffee.

"Lorraine," said Eppinger. "I want to talk to you about something."

"Oh good, 'cause there's something I want to talk to you about, too."

"When I was at the Pyramids, some Brothers visited me. They mentioned you."

"Me? What on Earth for?"

"That's what I'm concerned about. Has anything happened in your life that would be any cause for concern?"

Lorraine was stunned. Why on Earth would they be talking to her husband about her? She was doing nothing other than being a supportive wife. Unless...

"What?" said Eppinger alerted by the slight change in her expression. "I know your looks very well, honey. What did you just think of?"

Lorraine shook her head, "Nothing, absolutely nothing." That wasn't a lie – really. "Well, I just thought – when you said they were concerned about something – the only thing I could think of was Rachelle," said Lorraine, referring to Rachelle Myers, their housekeeper. Lorraine had begged Hans to let her come with them from Ohio to California and now to North Carolina.

"That's exactly who I thought of too," nodded Hans. "She is getting too close to you – I mean these Jesus Freaks are supposed to be employees, not friends."

"I know, dear. It's just that Rachelle is a very nice person. She is always willing to do whatever I want, so I like her; what's wrong with that? I don't think you should worry about my liking her."

Eppinger thought for a moment. He wanted to be reassured by his wife, yet having Abdon speak about her was unsettling. He feared there was more than what his wife was telling about this Rachelle person. Perhaps it was time for him to step in and have her replaced.

Rachelle had described to the Eppingers how Goonies had come into her church while the congregation was singing. She heard screams while she was in the kitchen getting snacks ready for after church. Immediately, she ran to the door, where she saw three Goonies headed toward the kitchen. She barely had time to squeeze under the sink, behind small double doors before she heard them enter. She mentally traced their footsteps around the kitchen as they opened and shut doors, searching. However, they did not open the double doors under the sink, where she was hiding. Finally, they left, and soon after, the screaming stopped. She continued to tremble and thought her whole body would become one big cramp, yet she was too frightened to move.

Waiting until there were no sounds, she cautiously opened the sink doors, crawled out, then tip-toed to the door leading into the hall. Hearing nothing still, she ventured out and down the hall into the sacristy. There she saw bodies draped over pews, or lying in the aisles. Some were lying on top of another – all with their right hands missing. Finding her husband was the worst part. He lay there unseeing and unhearing. She bent down and attempted to embrace him until thoughts about the twins intruded. Immediately, with a panicked cry, she ran downstairs to the Sunday school area, but there was no sign of either twin. Describing that day to Lorraine Eppinger brought tears to her eyes from the depths of her soul. She told Lorraine she prayed every day that her daughters were in Christ's care and were safe.

She was captured shortly after that, but rather than be killed, she was brought to a detention center that had been set up by Eppinger to distribute Jesus Freaks to jobs. It was there Lorraine Eppinger had first seen Rachelle.

Lorraine remembered she was curled up in the corner of a filthy barrack at Fort Knox. After being captured in Ohio, she, along with many other Jesus Freaks, were transferred to Ft. Knox for distribution. Lorraine remembered having to hold her nose when she entered. Her husband had agreed she could pick someone out of the camp to help care for household.

That was in Ft. Knox, Kentucky where Hans was briefly stationed. It was the first camp where her husband had set up the controversial worker's camp for Jesus Freaks. Many said it should not be done, yet it was now being copied in other areas around the U.S., including his last station in California.

Then he was transferred to Asheville. He wasn't happy about the transfer initially, but a soldier does what he is told – and he did it with a will.

"Hans? Are you listening?" His wife's voice broke in upon his thoughts, bringing him back to their conversation.

"Yes, certainly – tell me more about Rachelle." asked Hans.

"Just that she is a Christian, but we knew that. That is no secret. You can't find good help these days unless it comes from the Jesus Camps. I was just wondering if it wasn't her that they were concerned about."

"Well, has she tried to preach to you, or tried to make you join some group?"

"No, of course not," now, this certainly was a lie. She didn't like to lie, especially to her husband, but what was the alternative?

Hans sat up, facing his wife, "You'll tell me if there's anything I should be concerned about?"

Lorraine smiled, touching her husband's cheek gently, "Of course."

"So, now what did you want to talk to me about?"

For a second Lorraine had to gather her thoughts, "Hans, I love it here in Asheville – and we talked about having a family some day."

"Uh, oh," said Eppinger with a smile.

Lorraine snuggled closer to her husband. "I was thinking since we can't have children of our own, perhaps we could be part of the adoption program. You know, find a child that we could raise as our own."

Eppinger kissed his wife on the forehead. "For once in my life, I'm ahead of you," he grinned. "I was saving it as a surprise, but since you brought it up, today I arranged for the first television broadcast showing the children available for adoption and I brought home one of the first display books printed about the program for you to see.

Lorraine squealed with excitement, "Gimme, gimme, gimme," she said, holding out her hands and wiggling her fingers.

Eppinger went to the briefcase and brought out the inch-thick, eight-by-ten book. He smiled as he handed it to his eager wife. "I guess we know what you'll be doing the rest of today, and probably the rest of the week," he smiled.

Lorraine opened the book enthusiastically and immediately began reading the copy and looking at the accompanying the pictures of the children. Hans left his wife – it was time for him to get ready for the day. In fact, she did not hear him say goodbye, but as the front door closed, she looked up. Suddenly, some of what her husband said came back to her in a rush.

She jumped out of bed and ran to the window. Lorraine watched him drive out of the driveway and down the street toward town. Satisfied he was gone, Lorraine ran into the basement to Rachelle's apartment. Lorraine banged on the door twice, but didn't wait for an answer, instead she opened the door and went in, "Rachelle!" she shouted.

Rachelle came out of the small bedroom, looking startled. She was a smaller woman barely reaching five foot two inches, and just over a hundred pounds. She was wearing the bathrobe Lorraine had given her last year. "What's the matter, ma'am?" she asked, with a look of concern.

"I'm in trouble. Those Elect people were asking about me. I think they know. How could they know? Did you tell anyone? Anyone at all?"

"No, Mrs. Eppinger, no one. I would not have to tell anyone. We are not dealing with earthly abilities here, but with spiritual dangers."

"I think I better quit being a Christian – that would be best," said Lorraine, as she began to pace up and down the small hallway. "What if they find out? They would destroy my husband, and you, and me. Oh my, God! Lorraine put her hands on her face and starred at Rachelle.

"Perhaps we better pray, Mrs. Eppinger. We are not alone you know. Satan may have his angels, but so does Jesus. He can protect us."

"I should never have started. Why did I let you talk me into this?" said Rachelle as she began pacing back and forth again. Suddenly, she stopped. "Well, that's it. I quit. I am no longer a Christian – don't talk about Him to me anymore!" She turned and reaching the door, turned around, "And if you mention Jesus to me again, I will turn you in and deny ever knowing God." Exiting the room, she slammed the door behind her, but then quickly opened it again. "So, where is that Bible? Where have you hidden it? No, no, don't tell me I don't want to know. Just make sure it is hidden, do you hear me?"

"Yes," said Rachelle meekly.

Again, Lorraine slammed shut the door. Rachelle did not move, shocked by Lorraine's announcement. She stood there for a minute or so, and was about to turn, when the door opened again.

Lorraine stood in the doorway, with tears running down her face. "What am I going to do Rachelle? I am a Christian. And, I'm going to have a baby," she said meekly.

Rachelle went to her and put her arms around her, as Lorraine began crying. "What's going to happen to my husband? And what about the child?"

Rachelle patted her back saying softly, "You're going to have a baby?"

"Yes, any day now!" sobbed Lorraine.

Quickly she explained about the adoption program, and how Hans had agreed to their taking in a child, and how it would be their own.

"Adoption? That's wonderful!" exclaimed Rachelle.

"Yes. It is actually going to happen. And," she said, "Hans knows that I want a girl, even though I know he would like a boy. Am I being selfish? I have always wanted a girl. This morning," continued Lorraine, "Hans gave me a brochure and told me about a television program coming on today with pictures of the available children. He wants me to choose one. And now that they know I'm a Christian – they will never let me have a little girl."

Rachelle shook her head slowly, "No, I don't think you are being selfish." She sat down next to Lorraine. "I will pray for you. I will pray He will keep you safe, and that you will have a child come here."

Lorraine turned toward Rachelle, "Oh," she said, putting her hands over her mouth, "I'm sorry, Rachelle. It must be awful to hear me talk like this after losing your own children. I'm so sorry, will you forgive me?"

Rachelle smiled, "Yes, of course. I can imagine how excited I would be in your place."

"Yes, I know. I'm so sorry." Lorraine was silent for a moment. "Please tell me if I'm being too personal Rachelle, but I can't imagine how terrible it was to lose your twin girls. How did you survive?"

"Sometimes I wish I hadn't," answered Rachelle, pain in her voice, "and, at the time, I didn't want to – I used to beg God to take me so that I could be with my babies but He didn't. I thought many times of ending it all myself, and I would have, if I weren't a Christian. In one afternoon, I lost my wonderful husband and my two babies. I haven't stopped crying yet."

Lorraine leaned over and put her arm around Rachelle's shoulder. "If there's anything I can do honey, you just tell me."

Rachelle took a deep breath and let it escape slowly. "There's nothing anyone can do. It is the times we live in now.

I pray every night that God will end it all soon so that I may be with my family again." Rachelle smiled sweetly, "But, don't let my troubles dampen your joy. I would be as happy as you, were I able to have my children back."

"Why don't we pray about it? Let's say a prayer that God will direct you to the baby He wants just for you." said Rachelle, smiling. "And let's pray that these Visitors will leave you alone and not discover you are a Christian."

The two women joined hands and asked Jesus to guide Lorraine to the baby He wanted her to have, and to give her the strength and wisdom to raise the child as a Christian. They prayed God would confuse those who would reveal she was a sister of Christ.

* * * * *

Watching the Lions beat up the Bears was almost as good as the real thing. The game took place six years ago, yet watching it on tape was almost as good. Andy didn't really care whether the Lions or Bears won. It was the noise, the chatter, and the roar of the crowd – all perfect for a peaceful evening nap. Tucking a pillow under his head, he stretched out and clicked the remote to start the tape.

The tape had just started when there was a frantic pounding at the front door.

"Good heavens, who is that?" exclaimed Stephanie from the kitchen. Quickly she went to the door as Andy rose from the couch.

Standing at the door, in obvious distress, was Tim Barter.

"What is it, Tim?" asked Stephanie

"The twins, I can't find them anywhere – and look, I found this note."

Tim handed Andy the note with a trembling hand.

147

Deer Timmy
me and katie have gone to find mommy. Mr. Hermit
said it was good
Idea. thanx for all you done for us. have a happy
time with mary."
"Love, Alison Myers xxxxx
Katie Myers xoxoxoxooo

"When did you find this!" asked Andy.

"Only a few minutes ago. It was on my bed, but I don't know how long it was there – Mary and I just returned from the Honeymoon Hideaway. I went into the bedroom and found it. Please, help me find them, I can't lose them too."

Andy turned to Stephanie, "Call Roy and have him get three vehicles ready, and alert the Guard. I need four men in each of those trucks." Then, turning to Tim, "Go home and get what you need for the road, and meet me at the stables." Tim turned immediately, and began running toward his cabin, while Andy ran toward the stables. At the same time, Stephanie ran to the phone.

Andy beat the others to the stables. As he looked over the available vehicles, he remembered Reverend McDee telling him he had just finished working on the black Mustang. Quickly he began packing the Mustang with two rifles, and was about to follow-up with some ammunition, when, out of the corner of his eye, he saw a figure standing inside the open garage door. It was the Hermit, watching him.

"Where did you come from?" exclaimed Andy. "I haven't got time to talk now, the twin girls that were living here have run away, and we have to get going."

"I know," said the Hermit. "That's why I'm here." He walked over and put his hand on Andy's arm to stop him. "Don't do this," he said slowly.

"Do what?"

"Leave the girls alone. Send only Tim and his wife Mary to search for them."

"I can't do that. I should be sending more people, and will, once we get these trucks on the road–"

"Andy, I told the girls to go and search."

"You? You told them to go?" exclaimed Andy. "How could you? These are two little girls!"

"Andy, these are two little girls that Jesus loves. The Lord has heard their prayers, and now He is going to answer them. Tonight should not be a cause for concern, but celebration. We should celebrate, in faith, for joys not yet seen."

"Am I supposed to tell Tim not to go – why, he wouldn't pay any attention to me if I did."

"Tim and Mary should go. This journey is for them as well." The Hermit paused, and stepped back. "Do you believe me?"

Andy was silent a second, finally saying, "I do. I know you have been sent here by God to guide us. I trust you, and I will do as you ask."

The Hermit smiled and turned to leave, but Andy said, "Wait. There's something I have been wanting to ask you," he said, then suddenly feeling self-conscious, looked down as he asked, "Are you," he began, then looking up, saw he was alone in the stable. "...an angel?"

Chapter 14

General Brian Powell grumbled to himself as he pulled on the last boot. He hadn't accumulated four stars in order to be summoned like some errant schoolboy. Being stationed in this pyramid had its disadvantages. Always being at the beck-and-call of The Brothers, or Visitors, or – whatever they were calling themselves, was one of them. He felt like he was their houseguest. Much better if he was back in the States on good ol' USA soil. Then he would show these space-jerks a thing or two. Who did these creeps think they were? Powell stomped to the bedroom door and shouted out, "Beiner!"

Within moments, Captain Beiner came to the bedroom.

"Yes, sir," he said. Beiner was a career soldier. There was no doubt in anyone's mind about that. He was fiercely loyal to the General, dedicated to the Chain of Command, and was career motivated. He was the perfect aide to the General. In addition, he had the look of the perfect soldier – six feet tall, close-cropped hair set on a square face with sharp brown eyes. The only imperfection on his face was a number of pockmarks – the result of childhood pimples his mother tried to stop him picking.

"Help me get my coat on here," snapped the General. "Didn't used to be like this, you know," said Powell, as if Beiner was interested. "There was a day when four stars meant you could be god if you wanted. Now, these jerks will probably be giving me a mop and pail soon. Mark my words!"

"There," said Beiner, brushing off the General's shoulders, "You look great."

Powell went to the full-length mirror to inspect his appearance: A grunt signified his approval. Turning towards Beiner, he motioned for the Captain to close the bedroom door. Waiting patiently until he had done so, Powell went to his

150

bed's lamp stand and pulled open the drawer.

Powell sat down on his bed, motioning Beiner to come closer. "Larry," said Powell, realizing it probably was the first time he had ever called his long-term aide by his first name. "I need your help."

"Yes, sir," responded Beiner who, for a second, allowed some emotion to play across his face. Powell had never called him by his first name, nor had he ever asked him for his personal help. He felt some kind of emotion, but he wasn't sure of its nature. "Anything you need, just tell me."

Powell nodded, remaining quiet while he thought, then he nodded again. "Suppose I have something for you to do that was absolutely confidential – I mean no one, not even the Visitors should know this. What would you think about that?"

The nature of the question told Beiner this was serious, and probably out of bounds. He relaxed, allowing his hands to rest upon his waist and a small smile to infect his lips. "Well sir, I'd say you were going to ask the right person. The Visitors aren't my boss, you are."

"I could not have asked for anymore loyal aide than you – and now I am hoping you will do one more thing for me. I have a bad feeling about this meeting, a very bad feeling. Therefore, I have done a little 'in-case-of' preparation here. First, this envelope contains my orders promoting you to Major."

"Well, really sir–"

"Shut up. It is long overdue, and we both know it. If you had a Command in the field, you'd already be wearing those gold leafs. Now, the second envelope is a letter to Colonel Hans Eppinger. You're familiar with Colonel Eppinger?"

"Yes, I am, sir."

"Larry, I need you to deliver this letter to him, personally. If I am not back by tomorrow morning take the first available flight outta here. You will see, along with the letter, I also put in orders transferring you to his Command. And, this here pouch," said Powell, retrieving a bag with drawstrings from the drawer, "contains some good old American cash. I know they say not to use it now, but you may have to anyway. Now, son, do not wait for me to come back – if I'm not back by morning, don't even pack – get on that plane. Do I make myself clear?"

"Yes sir."

"Good, now when we get to the Brother's – or whatever these idiots are calling themselves now – I want you to leave me. Do not come back here, or go to your apartment. Find somewhere to hang out 'til morning. Do you understand me?"

"Yes, sir... but why–"

"All I want you to say is, 'yes sir', and then shut up."

"Yes sir," responded Beiner.

"Okay. Now, let's get this show on the road."

Walking out of the bedroom to the front of his apartment, they were joined by two other aides. Outside the apartment, a cart and driver were waiting in the hall. While all Senior Officers could call for transportation, Generals had transportation standing by at all times. Here in the Pyramid, an electric cart was essential to get around, especially if time were a factor. General Powell's cart had three rows of seats.

Climbing in the back seat of the cart with Capt Beiner, he waited until the others climbed in the middle row before motioning for the driver to start. Quickly, the whine of the cart grew to a high pitch as the driver kept to the center of the extremely wide hallway. Not many people were on this floor since it was reserved for Senior Officers only. The officer's elevator would take him to the floor where Powell knew the jerks would be waiting for him. Aliens. Screw 'em. They never smiled and they looked at you as if you were dirt. Always watching, listening. Plus, they wanted humans to live with them forever. Nuts, just nuts.

The cart unwound as they neared the doors to the Visitor's wing.

"This is the Visitors Wing, Sir," announced the driver.

"Visitors. Humph," growled Powell to himself. Every year it was a new name – had to be politically correct and use the new name. He couldn't keep up with them. They were creeps and would always be that, no matter what anybody called them.

Powell got out of the cart with Captain Beiner behind him. He straightened his coat and, from thirty years habit, wiped the toe of each shoe against his opposite trouser cuff. Finally, Beiner opened one of the double doors for him and Powell went inside. He looked back at Powell and gave him a smile. Beiner hesitated before turning and leaving for the cart.

On either side of the inner door were two very tall alien Visitors. Powell ignored them, as usual, but he could feel them looking him over. Neither said a word to him and he continued down the wide and long hallway. At the opposite end, the hallway widened into a reception area. Here couches and chairs were set about in an orderly fashion, looking much like an expensive doctor's office. He approached the cubical where two Sergeants were sitting, with a third on the phone. Behind them, he could see a Lt. Colonel reading a paper.

General Powell received immediate attention from the Sergeant who called the Lt. Colonel's attention to the General. Immediately the Lt. Colonel escorted Powell into a sitting room where he was the only occupant. The minutes dragged on as he waited, and with each passing minute, he became more agitated. They were keeping him waiting on purpose. He was sure of it. Those alien jerks did this each time he was summoned to them. Jerks. He was about to leave when a side door opened and two black robed Visitors motioned Powell to follow them.

"Jerks," repeated Powell to himself. "Don't even have the courtesy to smile, or say hello, just point as if he were some servant summoned to the master's quarters."

The two robed creatures led Powell down the hall, and

then made a right turn into a much narrower hall, not wide enough for two people to walk comfortably side by side. They stopped near the end of the hall, and to Powell's surprise, a section of the wall slid open revealing what would pass for an elevator. However, it was large, almost like a freight elevator, with a ceiling Powell estimated at around twenty feet.

One of his robed escorts pushed a very large button, certainly larger than Powell's entire hand, and the elevator began to descend so fast that he felt his stomach jump into his throat. The descent ended with a deceleration that matched the beginning. Powell had to steady himself on the wall to keep from falling on his face.

The door slid open and Powell found himself looking into a large room with a ceiling even taller than the elevator's ceiling. His two escorts led the way out of the elevator and into the room. It felt exceedingly warm and humid to Powell. The two creatures approached a very large man who was waiting for them in the center of the room. Each of the creatures went to either side of Powell's new host.

This man was taller and more massive than even Abdon. He had a robe that was red and had double rows of piping red, black, and gray on the hems. His collar was white, trimmed with gold piping. The hood of the robe was pulled over the top of his head to a point where the face was hidden by the dark shadows of the hood. The shape of the hood over the head did not seem right – it was not round, but triangular.

"Do you know who I am, General?" he asked.

"No, sir, I don't."

"I have many names. Once I was called Heylel, which means, 'The Morning Star' – some say, 'The Day Star'. I always liked, 'Morning Star'. Once I truly was, and shall be again. Some have called me Beelzebub, but that is not correct, for Beelzebub serves me as does Apollyon, Diabolus, and Abdon. There are so many that serve me – Lords Belial,

Cerberus, Legion and Python," He stopped and smiled at Powell. "General, tell me, do any of these names sound familiar?"

"Yes sir," answered Powell, who was beginning to experience some discomfort in his stomach. "I am familiar with Abdon. He is the leader of the Visitors."

"Wrong. He is not the leader, I am. Abdon means, The Server. He serves me. I am Abaddon, the Morning Star, he who is of Praises, of Glory, the Renowned. I am he who shall be as the Almighty One! I am the light bringer to heavenly domains." Abaddon paused, and remained silent for a moment, as if reveling in his self-descriptions. At last, he focused upon the General, as if suddenly recalling what he had asked him.

"You may call me Heylel, but I prefer Abaddon," he said slowly. He put his hands together, "General, why hasn't your man, Colonel Eppinger, moved against the Christians?"

Powell was about to answer, when Abaddon held up his finger for silence. "And what is this about turning Christians into workers? My instructions were for the elimination of all Christians and Jews – were they not?"

"Yes, sir," answered Powell, clearing his throat for a second of reprieve while gathering his thoughts. "Colonel Eppinger is very concerned about the welfare of the Elect. There have been many Christians killed and many of the Elect no longer work. He keeps essential services going by using the prisoners as a work force. So many of the Elect simply wait for that glorious day when they will be taken home that he..."

"That he allows the Christians to live, is that it? We cannot take the Elect to their home in the heavens until all Christians have been eliminated, yet you continue to let them live?" Heylel approached Powell. "Tell me, General, does this make sense to you?"

Powell straightened up, "No, of course not, sir."

Heylel grunted, "Humph. I want to know what you have

done about it."

"I plan on putting an immediate stop to the program. I will order the execution of the prisoners, forthwith, sir," said Powell. Fear had begun to grow within him, as he sensed this would not end well. Whatever he needed to say in order to get out of this place, he was going to say.

Heylel nodded while his unwavering gaze was making Powell feel uncomfortable. Finally, Heylel put his palms together, while shaking his head. "You plan, you plan, and you plan, but you don't accomplish! All excuses. That's what you do!"

Powell started to speak, but Heylel cut him off. "There is another matter. It concerns the Christians that are encamped in the hills outside of Asheville. You are aware of this encampment?"

"Yes sir and I have discussed this matter with Colonel Eppinger. He has assured me that he will be taking action against them soon."

"Soon?" said Heylel drawing the word out.

"Yes sir, I believe he needs time to reorganize his command. Lt. Colonel Syme left the command in very poor shape. But Eppinger has assured me he will take all necessary action against those Christian encampments at the earliest opportunity."

Heylel remained quiet, leveling an unflinching look at General Powell, which began to bring perspiration to Powell's forehead.

"Tell me General," Heylel said, finally, "Do you think this Colonel is the right man for this job? I understand he turned Christians into workers in California also. I have already given the order for their extinction. It is being carried out as we speak. Yet, this Colonel Eppinger asks for time – delay, delay and more delay."

Powell cleared his throat, "I will speak to the Colonel

immediately when I leave here."

"There's more," said Heylel. "Were you aware the Colonel has a Christian woman working in his house – in fact, has made her almost one of the family?"

"No sir," said Powell.

"Yes, and she is much more than that. In fact, my sources tell me that Colonel Eppinger's wife may, herself, have become a filthy Jesus Freak."

Powell felt his face flush, "Sir, I can't imagine that! I am sure your sources must be mistaken. I've known the Colonel and his wife for many years, and I assure you they cannot be Jesus Freaks."

"How come all of this is news to you? You do not seem to know much about the men under you at all. Do you know my name? No. You don't even know my name, do you?"

"Heylel?"

"No fool – that is how I am described. My name is Abaddon. Sounds like Abdon, doesn't it? He is but a servant of mine. Does the name Abaddon mean anything to you?"

"No sir."

Abaddon shook his head. "Such ignorance." he said. "Do you know some say they named your planet Venus after me, General?"

"What? Uh, no, no sir. You must be quite flattered."

"General, please – why would I be flattered that one of your filthy planets is named after me?" Abaddon smiled. Tell me General, you do not believe I even exist, do you? In fact, most of you filthy humans do not believe I exist. I'm some fairy tale made up to scare little children, isn't that right? 'Better watch out or the Devil is gonna get 'ya'- isn't that what they say?"

"Are you saying, sir, that you are the... the devil?" Never had Powell experienced the degree of fear that now possessed his body.

Lucifer smiled. "Soon, the final section of the pyramids will come down, and the final chapter will unfold." Lucifer walked a few paces, before stopping. "But you know – or perhaps you don't, you are quite ignorant – that I must set up my throne somewhere other than at the Pyramids? Now, tell me General, where do you think that would be appropriate?"

General Powell felt the moisture on his forehead beginning to run down to his cheeks, "Eh, where? Well, I suppose at the UN, maybe – is that right? At the UN, in New York?"

Lucifer shook his head, "So ignorant. No, General, why would I honor my little play-things with my throne? There is only one place where I must locate my glory, and that is Jerusalem. If you had any clue what was going on, you would know that, General."

"Yes, sir" stammered Powell.

"Do you think they will love me, General? Some would say, I'm not pretty. Would you say I'm pretty, General?"

"Yes, of course. You are very handsome."

"How would you know, you don't even know what I look like, but soon you will. In fact, soon everyone will know. I am preparing many to love me for who I really am. Can you guess how I am doing that, General? No, of course not, you have such a small brain. The children – General – the children – that is how. Now the children are beginning to love me, you know. They are beginning to grow fond of my appearance. They do not think I am ugly. They play with me, and sleep with me cuddled next to their chest. They have television shows, which show me as being loveable. Children all over the world wear T-Shirts with my image. You see, General, they do not think I am ugly. They think I am pretty and cute. Soon, they will regard me as majestic. Power brings majesty. Did you know that? Of course you did, all Generals understand that power brings majesty. Men stammer when they speak to you. Women flirt with you. These things occur because a General's stars carry a little majesty, is not this true? They shall with me too. Only mine will be of such great power and glory that all of creation shall bow to my name!"

Fear engulfed Powell's body. He wanted to leave he wanted this to end. "Sir, I'm sorry if I offended you. Please, tell me what I can do to apologize. Do you want me to kill all the Christians today? I will order it done. Just tell me what I can do," whined Powell.

"You're pitiful, General." Lucifer turned his back on Powell again and stepped away a few feet before he turned back. "How He could think that insignificant creatures such as you could be in charge of the Word. I am the rightful prince of heaven and Earth; I, who know the Word so well, I can fetch every syllable of it, I can shape it to my will, craft it to my purpose, my glory, as no other creature in heaven and Earth could ever do. I, to whom even He will soon pay homage. He has named you pitiful creatures His heirs. How could He do that?" The last words were delivered with such anguish and volume that Powell thought tears would follow.

For a moment, there was silence. Finally, Lucifer wrapped his arms around his robe and spoke. "I knew we would meet, you and I," he said, in a deep, grave voice. "I did not think it would be so soon. Now, do you know who I am?" he asked. "Tell me, do you know what battle we fight?"

"Yes sir. I do." answered Powell, his voice reflecting a breathless fear.

The hood appeared to nod a little. "You humans, use your puny logic to search for me, and for Him. Did you really think I could be revealed so easily?" How could creatures so ignorant think they could rule over me?" he asked, but did not wait for Powell to answer. "General, you were given a lot of responsibility. We trusted that you would serve us well in preparing the Earth for her final days."

"Yes sir, and I appreciate that. I've done my best."

"Have you now, General. That is not what I see. I do not think you have tried your best, at all; no, not at all. Your description of my servants was, I believe, 'Jerks'. Isn't that so?"

"Well, ah, sir..."

"I think there is another word you used. I believe it was, 'idiots'. Right?"

"Sir, I was just joking – we do that a lot here, you know, make fun of..."

"Silence!" snapped Lucifer with a volume that reverberated off the walls and even the tall ceiling.

Instinctively, Powell took a step back.

"You have no idea who we are. You have no concept of the battle that is taking place – of the stakes or consequences. That's because, General, it is not we who are the idiots, it's you!"

For several seconds there was no sound in the room as the creature's eyes bore into Powell. Finally, Lucifer turned and walked back to the two standing Ancestral Brothers.

"Now, General, I'm going to show you who we are. I am going to show you true beauty. I am going to enjoy watching you see who we are," his voice showed he might even be smiling.

The two Brothers stepped forward. They slipped off their robes and stood fifteen feet in front of Powell. As their robes hit the floor, Powell could see something happen to each of them. They changed. Their bodies mutated while they rapidly grew in height. Their smooth skin turned into coarse, rust-red scales that appeared over their entire body.

Powell began backing away, not believing what he was witnessing.

In a matter of moments both creatures had transformed from beautiful men into huge, ugly beings resembling creatures from some prehistoric age. They towered over Powell, large oblong heads showed teeth that protruded from a mouth too small to contain them. He felt the stench of their hot breath flowing over him as they bent down within a foot of him. Their feet where huge, resembling bird claws, yet encased in a reptilian skin. There were two appendages which could pass for arms; yet, their smallness seemed to mock the size of their body.

For several moments, they did nothing but stare at him with their protruding teeth, and blood-red eyes.

Powell was nauseated from fear and the smell from their foul breath, which wafted over him.

"Tell me, General, aren't these creatures truly beautiful? I find it is you, not we, who are ugly. That smooth skin, I don't even want to touch it – and you constantly shed it everywhere you go. You have hair all over your body. It even sticks out at the top, and you walk like a monkey. You are disgusting, and all the time you think you are the chosen creatures of creation. You're not!" he shouted. "I am! I am the chosen one! I was the Prince. I was the Chosen One. He loved me above all others! He loved me first!"

The volume made Powell instinctively cover his ears again.

"Once I was like you, created in His image, the most beautiful of His creations – but now His creatures are repelled by me. He has changed me into something even His angels find disgusting!"

Powell had slowly sunk to his knees and, for the first time in his life, wanted to curl up like a child.

"These are my creatures," said Lucifer. "I created them in my image! They are not ugly. They are beautiful!"

He took a couple of steps toward Powell. "And here is something that will thrill you, General. I know you are not a Jesus Freak. Never cared for all that religion business, did you? No, not a Jesus Freak; therefore, General, you are mine. You crouch here, fear dripping through your skin, you want to get away, don't you? You cannot. Soon you will think death better than life. Now, here is the wonderful part – death will not save you from me. You are mine – forever. Forever, General – mine forever!"

Suddenly, he barked to the others with sounds like no others Powell had ever heard. Slowly, the two creatures reached down to Powell. He began to back away until he hit the wall. Turning, he began scratching at the wall. He searched for the door, while growing sounds of fear escaped his lips.

"The time has come, General, but I don't know if I should say 'goodbye' or 'hello'."

Chapter 15

Alison peaked out from behind the tree and looked east, then west, down the highway. Finally, she motioned for Katie to join her.

"Which way do we go now?" asked Katie

"I'm dunno," answered Alison. She thought for a moment, looking right then left. "I think we should pray," she said finally.

"I brought my mini-Bible," volunteered Katie

"Okay, let's hold it. Do you know the Lord's prayer?"

"No, do you?"

"Some of it. I'll start it and you repeat what I say, okay?"

"Okay."

Alison paused a moment, collected her thoughts and began, "Our Father, who ark in heaven hollow be my name" Alison stopped.

"Well?" asked Katie.

"That's all I know." Alison thought for moment and then said, "Close your eyes."

"Why?"

"Because I'm not done praying," Alison cleared her throat, before beginning. "Dear Mr. God," she said, "help us find Mommy."

"You gotta say 'amen'," said Katie.

"Amen," said Alison, with attitude. She didn't like Katie telling her what to do.

"I say we go this way," volunteered Katie, pointing east.

"No, wait. That way or, maybe..."

"It's this way," announced Alison finally, starting toward the east. Katie followed.

Both girls found walking in the dark on the deserted highway, unnerving and soon held hands. The night was cool and got cooler as it aged. Alison buttoned her sweater and encouraged Katie to do the same. They realized they should have worn a jacket. It was colder here, away from the camp. After walking close to an hour, Katie whined, "The Bible is heavy."

"Here, give it to me. I have a pocket I can put it in," said Alison reaching for the small Bible.

Suddenly, the flash of headlights came across them.

Instinctively, Katie started to run, but Alison grabbed her, "Wait, let's do what Timmy did," she said, and stuck out her thumb. "Don't forget to smile," she reminded Katie.

A van slowed, finally stopped next to them. Alison tried to see into the cab through the passenger's window, but it was too high. "Can we have a ride?" she asked.

"Yes," said a masculine voice. "Get in the back."

It took the combined efforts of the girls to get the door to slide open, but it finally did and they climbed in the back. There were two rows of seats plus space behind the second seat for luggage. Separating their seats from the driver was a mesh screen. Through the wire mesh, they could clearly see ahead.

"Don't forget to buckle in," cautioned the driver looking in the rearview mirror. The brief dome light did not reveal too much about the driver. He was a man, and he looked like he might be tall – but other than that, they couldn't see. "So where are you going?" he asked.

"Ohio," answered Alison.

"We're gonna see Momma," added Kate.

The driver nodded as he put the van into drive and pressed the accelerator. "Well, I'll help you out as best I can," he said. His voice sounded as if he were smiling.

Alison and Katie sat back in their seats and relaxed. It was good finally to be on their way. If they could get a few more rides, they would be with their Mother in no time. The driver was silent and soon the motion of the van, and the late hour, made their eyelids heavy, and both girls fell sound asleep.

A speed bump jolted them awake.

Alison yawned. There was a little tint of dawn in the sky, as the van stopped at the guard shack. In a practiced motion, the driver showed his pass and the guard waved him in.

"Where are we?" asked Alison, a note of concern in her voice.

"Oh, I just have to make a stop here," the driver announced. They could see him clearly now in the day's first light. He was indeed a tall man, even though he was sitting. As the van stopped, the driver turned around and smiled. He was very good-looking and had deep blue eyes that almost looked black in the half-light, and he was wearing an Army uniform. Leaving the van, he went into one of the several buildings located near them.

Looking out, the twins saw they were in, what appeared to be, a good-sized town. There were vehicles parked all around, and most of them were Army.

"I don't like this," ventured Alison.

"Look," said Katie, "there are a lot of soldiers," she said pointing to several walking in the early morning. "Are we at an Army place?"

"Come on, let's get outta here," said Alison, unbuckling her seat belt while looking for the door handle; but there was none. "Try your side," she said with a note of anxiety.

Katie, unbuckled her belt and rattled the door to no avail, "Alison, what are we gonna do!" she whined, a note of panic rising in her voice.

"Don't worry Katie," said Alison, with uncertainty in her voice.

They saw their army driver emerge from the building. Reaching the van, he unlocked his door, and without a word, started the vehicle and began slowly driving further into the base.

"Where are we going, Mister?" asked Katie, her voice trembled.

"Don't worry girls, everything is fine," he replied.

The girls scooted together and began holding one another. It had been like that since they were babies. At the first sign of danger, they sought comfort from one another.

Finally, the van stopped outside a multistoried brown building. Again, the driver went into the building. A short time later, he emerged with two other soldiers, one of whom was a woman. She approached the van, opened the side door, and smiled at the two girls sitting with their arms around each other.

She had a nametag reading, Sgt. G. Armest. Reaching in, she took hold of Alison's wrist. "Come here, little girl," she said in a stern voice. "There's nothing to be scared about."

Both girls tightened their hold on each other. There was something in the woman's voice that told them they should, indeed, be afraid.

The guards led the girls through an office with a high counter, into a smaller room, where a bad height chart was painted on a dirty white wall. The first number on the chart was over the twins heads. Sgt. Armest motioned for the girls to stand against the wall while another soldier flashed two pictures. Armest then motioned toward a second door leading further into the building. "Follow me, ladies," she said.

Alison and Katie followed her with two guards behind them as they all walked between two rows of large prison cells. Some had bars running vertically, a few had mesh screens and then there were a couple which were all metal with only small-hinged portals. Silently, both girls held hands as they walked, too scared to talk, and only able to steal glances of one another. Occasionally, there were voices on either side of them whispering and sometimes shouting. Some yelled epitaphs at the guards, while others said, "Don't worry children, it will be alright," or, "God be with you."

Finally, Sgt. Armest stopped and pointed to the cell door she wanted the guard to unlock. That done, the Sergeant motioned toward the girls, "You two, inside," she said curtly.

Still holding each other, the two girls entered the cell.

Surrounded by many children, a group of women prisoners stood at the back of the cell. Some of the women came forward a step or two, as they saw the twins enter. They were silent as they watched the guards leave. Satisfied the soldiers were out of earshot, one motioned for the twins to come to them.

At first, the twins did nothing. Fear had frozen them to each other and to the floor.

One of the women came to the twins and, after shooting a glance down the hall, smiled and reached out. "My name is Margaret, girls. Do not worry. All the ladies here will make sure you are taken care of now," she said softly while smiling. "This is where they keep the children who are up for adoption. Soon you'll have a new Mommy and Daddy."

Both girls could see as many as fifty children, some of whom were even playing with toys strewn about the floor. A group of women watched the children and some held the children on their laps.

Over the next hour, both Alison and Katie relaxed as the friendly nature of the women flooded over them. Everyone was excited to have new young children. Most of these women had lost their own children in the past – either dead or missing. "So, ladies," asked Margaret, "What are your names?"

"I'm Alison and this is my twin sister, Katie."

"Well now, aren't they just the prettiest names. So, you are twins. Do you like having a twin sister?"

"Yes, ma'am, my sister's my best friend, most of the time," smiled Alison

"And is your sister your best friend?" asked Margaret of Katie.

Katie nodded. She was still too shy to talk to the women directly, even though she felt they meant no harm.

"Now, we know your first names, what's your last name?"

"Myers."

"Myers? Miss Myers, where did you live?"

"In a camp," answered Alison.

"I mean, where did you live before – before all this trouble began?"

"Oh, we lived in Perkins, Ohio. So did Mickey and Tim," added Alison.

"My, that's such a long ways. Did all of you walk this far?"

"No, we got a ride, and now we live on top of Cloud Mountain."

There was a murmur among the gathered women.

"We've heard about Cloud Mountain. That's where there are a lot of Christians living, right?"

"Uh-huh," ventured Katie, "and you can fish all the time!"

"I'll bet you know a lot of people on Cloud Mountain, right?"

"Well," began Alison, "not everyone, there are a lota, lota people, but we know some – like Mr. and Mrs. Kegler, and the Prophet..."

"You know the Prophet?" gasped Margaret.

"Yes, ma'am. He's a very nice man."

The woman named Margaret knelt down and looked closely at both girls, and then examined their clothes. "Say now," she said, "what do we have here?" Reaching inside Alison's pocket, she withdrew the small Bible.

A couple of the women groaned.

"What's the matter?" asked Katie.

"The only children they allow here are those who aren't Jesus Freaks." said Margaret sadly.

"I'm not a freak."

"What they mean, honey, is that you can't be a Christian. They think that all children under seven years old are not contaminated yet with Jesus, so they let them live. If they knew you had this Bible, they would have put you in the Termination Cell. Your being here puts all the other children at risk," she sighed closing her eyes.

"We won't hurt the others," pleaded Alison.

"Of course you wouldn't, but those Goonies think you would. They let these children live because there are a lot of families out there who want kids. So, they think they can raise these children to be good grown-ups who don't like Jesus."

"Do you want that?" asked Katie.

"Of course not, I just want these children to live."

Margaret walked a couple paces away from the girls while motioning the other women to follow her. They talked, sometimes loudly, for the next fifteen minutes. Finally, the group turned back toward the girls and Margaret went to the cell bars, and began knocking on them while calling for the guard. It took twenty minutes before a clearly annoyed guard came to the cell. "What's the matter!" he challenged.

"Those two girls you brought down can't stay in this cell. Look," Margaret said, holding up the small Bible, "this was in one of their pockets. These kids are Jesus Freaks, and they will infect the other children if you let them stay. Somebody messed up and put them in this cell."

The guard examined the small Bible Margaret held in her hand, then grunted. "Okay, bring them here."

The women brought the two girls to the cell door. The expressions on Alison's and Katie's faces showed they clearly did not understand what was happening.

The guard opened the cell door and reached in for Alison's hand, but the frightened girls began to back away until he grabbed their arms and pulled them out the door.

"Where are we going?' asked Alison with fear in her

voice. She was clearly choking back tears, as she looked at the women. The expression on her face pleaded for help.

Margaret pressed her face against the bars to catch a last glimpse of the girls being half-dragged down the hall. Now, the girls' fear was punctuated with tiny sobs. Finally, Margaret turned back. The women were silent for a few minutes before Margaret addressed them. "I know. It's terrible – but it had to be done."

The others slowly nodded. They all knew, for the safety of the other children, it had to be.

"Then shall they deliver you up to be afflicted, and shall kill you: and ye shall be hated of all nations for my name's sake."
– Matthew 24:9

Chapter 16

Tim drove out the back way, alongside the river, up the embankment, past Ken Johnstone's country store and past the gas pumps to the edge of NC Highway 280. He stopped the black Mustang and tried to decide which way the girls would take.

Mary looked at the map the Prophet had given her before they left camp. "280 seems to run into 26 which runs south of Asheville, and then hooks up with US 40, headed east." Tim nodded as Mary pointed it out. He then eased out onto the road and headed toward US 40. Was this the way the girls had taken? Did the girls even know how to get to Ohio from here?

Mary could see emotions playing across Tim's face. Leaning over, she rubbed his back without saying a word. It had the desired effect, and Tim looked at her briefly and smiled. After a few minutes, she broke the silence, "God will guide us," she said with confidence.

They drove in silence for thirty minutes both lost in their thoughts. They arrived at a road with an arrow pointing to their left indicating US 26 was ahead.

"Did you notice we haven't seen any cars at all?" asked Mary.

"Yes, creepy."

"A few years ago 280 was pretty busy – not bumper-to-bumper, but busy," said Mary.

"Times have changed, honey, they have changed indeed."

Turning left, they began to head toward US 26. They were coming up to speed when, in the distance, both could see two pickup trucks coming their way."

"Well, just as we were talking about no traffic, here come two pickups," smiled Mary.

"Um Hum," said Tim. "Let's keep our eye on them, they make me nervous," he said.

Tim checked his speedometer to insure he was not speeding. The two pickups flashed by, but not before Tim could see three men in the back of the first truck with some sort of gun mounted in the pickup's bed. The second pickup had two men in back, with boxes in the bed of the truck. Tim watched the view mirror as the trucks flashed by. Suddenly, he saw the brake lights of both trucks come on.

"Trouble," said Tim.

Mary watched as both trucks made a u-turn on the highway and began coming toward them. "Honey, they are coming after us!" she squealed.

Immediately, Tim punched the accelerator. The Mustang jumped so quickly the tail wanted to fish around. Tim caught the road just in time, and the car straightened out. "I've got it almost to the floor! Fasten your seatbelt tight!" shouted Tim as he tried to will the Mustang to move faster.

Quickly the needle began climbing: 65, 75, 85. "What's happening?" he asked Mary.

"They are gaining on us! They're gonna catch us, honey!"

Tim pressed the accelerator as tight as he could to the floor. The needle continued to climb reaching 90, then 95 finally it touched 100. "What about now?" he asked showing some real fear in his voice.

For a moment Mary did not answer, trying to make sure her perception was correct. "I don't think they are gaining anymore.

Tim continued to press the accelerator, unsure how much the car could take before it threw a rod. The Mustang seemed to be in its element as the needle continued to rise, 110, 115, and then 120."

"Tim, we're losing them!" shouted Mary with a smile, then seeing the speedometer, "We can't go this fast!"

The road ahead seemed to be long and straight. That allowed Tim to keep his foot to the floor. The little car seemed willing and able to give more. Not until the speedometer pinned itself did Tim ease up a bit, though not enough to slow the car by much. The speedometer dropped to just below 120, but the car's bucking and drifting did not ease up.

"Any sign now?" asked Tim

"None," said Mary. "Tim can we slow down a little?" she asked nervously.

Tim relaxed his foot again, allowing the car to drop to below one hundred until it was down to seventy-five.

"Okay?" he asked.

Mary smiled her answer, and then turned her attention again to the rear window for any sign of their pursuers. "Do you think they gave up?"

Tim shook his head slowly. "Nope, we probably just made them angry. They will keep coming. Look on the map and see what might be ahead."

"We are about to cross Brevard Road, then if we keep going, we'll turn into US 40, or we can bear right and get on 240 which runs around Asheville."

"We need people and traffic. We are sitting ducks out here all alone on the road. We'll take 240 and get into Asheville. Maybe we can find a place to lie low for awhile and then start out again."

"Okay, honey," said Mary, turning around in her seat after taking a last look behind.

Highway 240 brought them closer to Asheville, and then merged into a bi-pass circling the city. At the Patton Ave exit, Tim turned right and headed for downtown. Finally, they ran into some traffic, but certainly less than one would expect.

Once in the heart of downtown, Tim made another right onto Church and then into an alley. The alley serviced several of the stores and a few cars, probably merchants, had parked behind the stores. Tim parked the Mustang in one of the available spaces.

"Now what?" asked Mary.

"We gotta ditch the car for awhile – they'll be looking for it," he said. "I hate to do it after the Reverend put so much work into it, but we'll come back to it when we think it's safe."

The two got out of the car, and after looking around, started toward the street.

"Here," Tim said to Mary, "carry this under you right arm, like this." He said handing her a package; then curled her hand under the package so that it rested more in the crook of her arm. "This way, they can't see the back of your hand, and it looks pretty natural."

Tim grabbed a bag containing some extra underwear and did the same. By carrying the parcels in their right hands, they concealed the fact they didn't have any marks.

"Mary," whispered Tim as they walked. "Look how a lot of the people are dressed."

"Yes, I noticed that too," she answered noting a number were dressed in identical blue smocks. However, she also noticed that their movements were not confident, nor carefree. Many hugged the walls of the buildings while passing people, while others stepped off the sidewalk and walked in the street."

"Did you see their hands?" asked Mary.

"Yes, they're all Christians."

"I think this is what I heard about in camp. This is part of this new Worker Program."

Tim nodded, as he saw someone push one of the blue-smocked individuals off the sidewalk into the street.

As they came out on Patton, Mary saw a cafeteria across the street. There appeared to be a number of people eating there. "Let's go over there, Tim," she suggested.

Due to the traffic, they had to wait for a bit before crossing Patton Avenue. It was a good sign that did not escape Tim's notice.

The cafeteria was larger than either had first estimated. Easily seventy-five to a hundred people were inside eating or picking out their food. There were still many vacant tables available. People in blue smocks were cleaning tables, and serving food at the cafeteria line. Tim picked a table by the wall, which still had dirty plates and silverware. From this vantage point, he could see both main entry doors leading in from Patton Avenue.

Sitting down at the table, he arranged the plates and silverware to appear they were still actively eating. Tim looked around and saw a number of television screens attached to the walls. Once upon a time, he imagined, this was probably a sports bar. Now, there were only two television stations left – both run by the Visitors. The sound was turned off on the sets, but it was obvious what was being broadcast. Half of the screens showed a cooking show while the other half was showing some kind of program showing children's pictures that looked like Wanted Posters.

Tim slowly took stock of the rest of the room, but there didn't seem any cause for concern. Everyone was talking and eating. No one seemed interested in either Mary or himself being there. He could see Patton Avenue clearly from here. Suddenly, something on the street caught his eye. The two pickups that had been pursuing them were driving slowly down the street. The men behind the trucks were checking out the parked cars. The second truck stopped. Two men from the truck jumped out and headed for the cafeteria.

Tim looked around quickly to see if there was another exit. To their right were two swinging double doors, obviously leading to the cafeteria's kitchen. He looked at Mary who seemed engrossed in the television.

"Keep quiet, honey," he cautioned. "We have visitors."

Mary nodded, as she watched TV.

Tim watched the two men enter the cafeteria. However, he saw that, rather than search for someone, they immediately went to the cafeteria's line and took two plates.

"Oh, my God!" screamed Mary.

"Quiet!" admonished Tim.

"It's the twins!" shouted Mary, pointing to the screen.

Looking up, he saw both Alison and Katie. They were holding each other while looking with fear-filled eyes at the camera.

Tim gasped, and quickly looked back toward the two men. Their eyes met for a second, and then both Goonies dropped their plates as they yelled.

Grabbing Mary, Tim bolted for the double doors behind them.

"Hey, you!" he heard as he and Mary burst through the kitchen door. Several of the cooks looked up, surprised by the sudden and noisy entrance.

Tim ran past them, holding Mary's hand, before they could be stopped. A couple of the cooks shouted something as they passed. Ahead, he saw a door he hoped led outside. Grabbing the handle, he yanked the door open and found it led to an alleyway. He pulled Mary through the door.

"Run!" he yelled at Mary as he slammed the door shut behind her. Looking quickly around, he spotted an old three-foot long, piece of wood. Grabbing it, he wedged it against the door then ran off the porch and down the alley after Mary. She was trying the rear doors of the stores as she ran, but found them locked from the inside. Tim caught up to her and yanked on the handle of a car parked next to one of the doors. The door opened and he yelled to Mary. Quickly, they both ducked inside the car and lay on the rear floor. Tim pulled out his gun, ready for anyone that might open the car door.

In the distance, he heard some noise and surmised it was the lumber giving way. This was followed by shouts and the sounds of running feet. Tim could tell some were running away, while, at least one, was coming toward them. He listened as the feet slowed as they approached the car. He could hear someone checking the doors to the buildings and finding them locked.

He heard him shout to his companions, "Check the cars!" followed by the sound of approaching footsteps. Tim slowly raised his gun then, gripping it with both hands, pointed it at the car's window and waited. He was ready.

"Hey!" he heard a distant voice shout. "They found their car!"

Immediately the steps stopped, then started running away from them, toward the restaurant.

Tim felt himself breathe a deep sigh of relief. For several minutes, both he and Mary maintained their silence. Finally, Tim lifted his head to look around. He didn't see anything, yet felt they should remain in the car for a little while longer. "Let's make sure they're gone," he whispered to Mary, who nodded in return.

Several quiet minutes went by until Tim felt it was safe to leave. He began to get up, but quickly ducked back, hearing approaching footsteps. He put his finger to his mouth warning Mary. The steps stopped and the driver's door opened. Tim gave a quick glance toward Mary and tightened his grip on his gun.

The driver tossed a package on the passenger's seat and got in. There was a brief rattle of keys, before the car started up.

Suddenly, Tim rose up, holding his gun at the drivers head. It was a woman, and she gave a short scream.

"Quiet!" commanded Tim. "Do as you're told and you'll

be alright. We don't want to hurt you," he said. He and Mary rose to a sitting position on the back seat.

The woman remained frozen in place, her hands on the wheel of the car. Through the rear view mirror, Tim could see she was studying them. She appeared to be in her late thirties, with curly hair kept trimmed just above her shoulders. She was wearing a blue smock, which came to just below her waist.

"Let me see your right hand," commanded Tim

She held up her hand revealing smooth clear skin.

"You're a Christian?" asked Tim.

She nodded.

Tim stuck his right hand forward so she could examine it. "So, are we," he said.

The woman sank back into the seat, dropping her hands from the wheel, "Thank God," she said, relief evident in her voice. She began turning around.

"Don't turn around," snapped Tim. "I don't want anyone to see you talking with us. Where are you going?"

"I was headed back to the Worker Camp. They let me off work a little early today, and I was going to spend it at home," she said.

"Where are they keeping the children?"

"The children?"

"Yes, the ones that were on TV."

"Oh, the Adoptee Children – I don't know too much about it really. It is a new program they just started. All the children under a certain age, and judged not to be contaminated by Jesus, are put up for adoption. I think they are keeping them downtown in the building that used to be the Headquarters building."

"Please, take us there," pleaded Mary.

"Yes, please," echoed Tim. "I've been taking care of those twin girls since their parents were killed."

The woman looked down at her watch, and thought for a

moment. "I have a little time, but not much. I'll drive you there," she said. Then, reaching over to her bag on the passenger's seat, she pulled out two wrinkled blue smocks. "Here, put these on. Sorry about the mess they are in. I was taking them back to camp to clean. They will give you some cover if you have to walk around."

Tim and Mary quickly donned the smocks. "My name is Tim and this is my wife, Mary," he said.

"My name is Barbara Bourne," said the driver as she started the car. "How did you come to be here?"

"It's a long story," answered Mary.

"How are you going to get around, do you have a car?"

"We did," answered Tim. "We had to ditch it – some Goonies chased us. I think they already have found it. So, it would be too dangerous to go back to get it."

The drive to where the children were held didn't take long. They were in the heart of Asheville, yet the traffic was, at best, moderate.

Bourne pointed ahead to a building some three blocks away. "That's where they keep the children," she said as she pulled into a parking space.

"Why are you stopping?" asked Tim with some edge.

"This is where I work. It will look natural that I came back here. I can even work some overtime. I will tell them I have to finish something. They won't know the difference. We don't get paid by the hour, you know." She said this with a wry smile. "I figure I can keep myself occupied for a couple of hours. That will give you time to take the car, do what you have to do, and get out of town – but make sure you ditch the car within two hours. That's when I'll report to the authorities that the car is missing."

"Thank you Barbara. God bless you for helping us," said Mary.

"Yes," echoed Tim, "it's wonderful; but, we need you to

do something first. We need to know where the children are right now. How about you go down to the building, check to see if they are there, then come back here and tell us what's happening?"

Barbara nodded. "What's the children's names – oh wait, they don't go by names. They list them by number."

"Yes, that's right," said Mary. "Let me think a minute, I'm pretty good at remembering numbers," she said closing her eyes. There were two numbers beneath their faces on TV. Underneath Alison was the number KB2475-14 and under Katie was the same number, except it ended in 15."

"I'm impressed," said Barbara as she wrote the numbers down.

"Don't let her see your driver's license," smiled Tim.

"I'll be right back. You two wait here," smiled Barbara as Tim and Mary exited the car.

Nearby was a bench, one of several bordering the sidewalk. Picking one, Tim and Mary sat down. Mary reached over and took hold of Tim's hand without a word. Tim squeezed hers for reassurance.

Arriving at the city building, Barbara entered through one of the revolving doors. Inside, there was a large lobby with elevators lining both sides of a long hallway. Barbara looked around and spotted a sign that read, *Adoptions Room 125*. An arrow pointed toward the hallway.

A short walk down the hallway, Barbara spotted and opened the door to Room 125. There was a short high counter and behind this, a single desk. A woman about Barbara's age of thirty-seven, also dressed in a blue smock, was reading a book.

She smiled at seeing Barbara. "May I help you?"

"Yes," said Barbara, returning the pleasant voice and smile. "I'm interested in locating two of the children which were televised today."

The woman rose from her desk and made her way to the far end of the counter where a single computer station was located. She moved the mouse to bring the screen to life. "What were their numbers?" she asked.

Checking her paper, Barbara read off the numbers.

"Oh, yes. Here they are." she said, turning the monitor so Barbara could see. Looking at Barbara through the screen were two girls, holding each other, their eyes pleading with the camera for help.

"They are twins!" said the clerk with a note of surprise. "Wow! That's neat."

"They really are darling," said Barbara as she continued to look at the girls.

"Oh, no," said the clerk as she read down, "that's too bad. I see here that they were taken off the adoption list. They shouldn't have been on that TV program. That's too bad, they're so cute."

"Really? Why have they been taken off?"

She was silent as she read further, "Seems a Bible was found on one of them, which disqualifies them from adoption. They are now considered Jesus Freaks." She paused before looking up at Barbara. "They've been scheduled for execution."

Chapter 17

Lorraine gave up watching the televised pictures of children. Though this was the third time she had viewed available children, she still didn't see the one child for which she was searching. It seemed ridiculous, after the many prayers she had said for a child. Now, here was the chance to have one, and she could not find the one she felt God wanted for her.

Lorraine heard Rachelle come into the living room with the vacuum cleaner.

"Why Rachelle? Why isn't God showing me the child He has chosen? Do you think God knows I would be a good mother?"

Rachelle put the vacuum cleaner upright and turned it off. She came to the couch, putting her hand on Lorraine's shoulder. "God has a plan. I know it doesn't seem like it, but He does."

Lorraine looked at her Christian friend, "I know how hard it must be for you to say that, having lost your own children."

Rachelle didn't reply at first, but smiled. "Sometimes it's very hard, but that's what faith is all about – getting us through those times. Do I believe God has a plan for me? Yes, I just haven't got a clue what it could be at this point."

Rachelle sat down on the couch and looked at the sweet faces of the children on TV. They all seemed so cute, yet so lost. She could see fear residing in their beautiful eyes as they looked at the camera.

Next to her, Lorraine felt bad for Rachelle. She couldn't imagine how it would feel to lose twin girls.

Suddenly, Rachelle screamed, and rushed to the television set, putting her hands on the screen. She screamed again.

"What's wrong?" shouted Lorraine.

For a moment Rachelle couldn't speak, but finally

managed, "My babies, my babies."

* * * * *

The Asheville airport hadn't changed much from the last time he had flown here, almost seven years ago now. Leaving the plane, the bright Carolina sun made his brand new Major leaves sparkle. Beiner had thought about rubbing them with some grit to tone down their newness, but in the end, decided he liked the way they sparkled.

The plane's departing passengers were military, as always, these days. Few people had the money or prestige to get an available seat. His ride was waiting for him at the terminal, and in short order he arrived at Colonel Eppinger's office. He was impressed with the efficiency of his staff and the overall appearance of the Headquarters. Beiner was a career soldier and he believed in things being done by the book, and that included ship shape living and working areas.

He was ushered into see the Colonel immediately, and Eppinger greeted him warmly. The Colonel's appearance impressed Beiner as one worthy of command. Eppinger stood only five foot eleven, and at almost two hundred pounds was considered overweight by some; however, that was not Beiner's impression. What extra weight the Colonel carried was the result of muscle development. Eppinger extended his hand with a warm smile. His brown, almost black hair was trimmed to regulation length, and his brown eyes looked intelligent, yet friendly. Beiner was certain Eppinger was performing as many evaluations of him, as he was of Eppinger.

"Have a seat, Major," said Eppinger finally, pointing to one of two overstuffed chairs situated on the side of the room. Beiner liked that he didn't want him to sit at his desk, but accorded him a more personal sitting, perhaps a hint of the prestige his new Major leafs brought. "I was surprised to learn that you were coming," began Eppinger. "General Powell made no mention of it to me."

"Yes, sir," answered Beiner. He gave a quick look at the office door to assure that it was closed. He reached in his vest and withdrew the letter Powell had given him to deliver to Eppinger. "The General wanted me to deliver this letter to you personally and immediately," said Eppinger. Then he withdrew another paper and handed both to Eppinger. "This second one is my transfer to your Command."

"Really?" stated Eppinger, as he opened the envelope and slowly read the letter.

Beiner could see emotions tracing across the Colonel's face as he read, then re-read the letter.

"Are you familiar with the contents of this letter?" asked Eppinger in a flat voice.

"Not exactly, sir," said Beiner, choosing his words carefully. "But I think I know the gist of it."

"Which is?"

"From what I gather, both you and the General are in big trouble. I'm not exactly sure why, but I think it involves your wife, as well as yourself."

Eppinger jumped up from his chair and began pacing. "This is beyond ridiculous!" he shouted. "General Powell says those space jerks think I am a Christian sympathizer and that my wife is a Jesus Freak. He says they are coming to arrest me. Are you aware of that!" shouted Eppinger.

"Not exactly, sir."

"He says they intend to arrest my wife as well!" Eppinger ran his hand through his hair as he continued to pace.

Beiner waited silently, unsure of what the proper protocol was, exactly.

Finally, Eppinger stopped, and looked at Beiner. "Let me ask you Major, what is your role in all of this?"

Beiner thought for a second, and then stood up. "General

Powell is more than my Commander. I have been with the General for many years. I look up to him as a father – the one I never had. If he had allowed me, I would have stayed with him and would have defended him with whatever means I had. He thought it would be best if I came here and warned you. I now am under your Command. If the General held you in such high regard, then I must too. Colonel, I'm yours to command, whatever that may be."

"Thank you Beiner, I appreciate that."

"However, I must tell you, Colonel, I don't think you have many options left here. If you think you will convince anyone in authority to stay, delay or dismiss any charges against you, I believe you are sadly mistaken. I worked at the Pyramid long enough to know how they work. Once the decision is given, there is no recourse. Either individuals in the Chain of Command execute their orders, or they, themselves, are eliminated. General Powell has put his life in danger by the fact that he sent me here. I hate to say it, but I would be surprised if General Powell is still in charge of anything, including his own life. These are mean folks."

"Yes, you're probably right, and you also put your life in danger – and I am grateful, believe me. Tell me, from your experience, how long do you think we have?"

"I would guess, at the most, one week. They've got to get someone to replace the General, and then he has to send someone here to replace you – yes, perhaps one week, but maybe less."

"That's awfully quick – my guess would have been thirty days or more."

Beiner smiled, "No sir, not with these boys. I don't know how they do it – but they are always a couple of steps ahead of whatever you are doing or thinking. I'll bet they had most of this already in the works before they even told General Powell they wanted to see him." Beiner paused before beginning again. "I think the General knew that as well. He told me I should leave immediately – not even pack. Perhaps that's the advice we should give ourselves."

Eppinger nodded silently, and then went to the office's storage closet, emerging a few seconds later with a small cloth bag containing two guns. "I've got some ammo and a couple extra pieces here," said Eppinger. "How about you?"

"Just my side-arm, sir."

"Ready?" asked Eppinger.

Exiting the Colonel's office, they passed Sergeant Harkins.

"When do you expect to return, sir?" asked Harkins.

"Tomorrow morning," lied Eppinger.

It took less than twenty minutes for Eppinger to drive home. He ran to the door, calling Lorraine's name as he entered.

"I'm here," came Lorraine's startled response.

Quickly, Eppinger introduced Beiner and told Lorraine the contents of the letter from General Powell.

The look in Lorraine Eppinger's eyes, when her husband stopped talking, was one of not being able to comprehend all that her husband had said and its implications on their lives.

"We have to leave, honey," said Eppinger, while putting his arms around his stunned wife.

"But I love Asheville," Lorraine squeaked out, "I don't want to leave. I want to have our child here. This is where we are going to raise our family. Hans, you promised."

"I know, honey, I know."

"When do we have to leave?"

"Now, Lorraine, now," said Eppinger.

Lorraine stepped back in a daze. "I'll tell Rachelle to start packing," she said in a monotone voice.

"Lorraine wait, Rachelle can't go; this is just you and me. You can put together a small bag of essentials, but no more than will fit into an overnight case."

"But, what about Rachelle? They will kill her, Hans," said Lorraine. She then stomped her foot. "No, enough is enough," she said, raising a resolute voice. "Rachelle is going. You asked me if I was a Christian, I am. I am Hans. I'm a Christian and I won't let Rachelle die for her love of Jesus while I run off!" Her tone gained timber as her protest grew.

"Christian? You are a Christian? But how? Why didn't you tell me?"

"I'm sorry Hans, I'm so sorry, but this I believe." Tears filled Lorraine's face and leaked into her voice.

Hans stood looking at his wife for a moment or two, then reached up and brushed her cheek softly. "I don't care what you are. You are my wife, the love of my life."

Lorraine suddenly pulled back. "Wait. There is more. Rachelle just found out that her children are here, in Asheville! Somehow, they were put in jail. We need to go get them, then and only then, can we all leave."

Eppinger looked at Beiner hoping for some support.

"I can prepare things here while you go get the children if you want, sir," said Beiner.

Eppinger let out a sigh of exasperation. "You people don't understand. It may already be too late for these children – and for us!" Eppinger reached over and threw the telephone against the wall while growling out, "Urgh! You are going to get us all killed!" For a moment, he stood looking at the floor with clenched fists. Finally, he turned around and growled, "Very well. This may be the end of us, but very well. Beiner, you stay here with my wife. She will show you what she needs. Just the essentials – we are not moving, we are escaping – remember that!" said Eppinger with some frustration in his voice. He then, turned to Rachelle and said, "Okay! Come with me!"

* * * * *

Though Barbara wanted to speed up as she drove back to her office, she was careful to observe the speed limit. At last, she pulled into the parking space and spotted Tim and Mary on a bench. They met her halfway to the car.

Barbara looked around to see if anyone might be within earshot. "The twins are in the jail alright," Barbara paused, "They are scheduled to be executed."

"Executed!" shouted Tim, then quickly looked around, but could see no one within earshot. "How do you know this?"

"I talked to the clerk at the adoption office. The execution order is on their chart. Seems they brought a Bible with them, and that means they don't qualify for adoption. They look on them just like any other Christian, and that means execution."

"When?"

"Don't know, but they don't wait too long once it's been determined that someone should be eliminated."

"I've got to go there," said Tim.

"What are we gonna do when we get there?" asked Mary.

"I don't know – I don't know, but I've got to do something," answered Tim, reaching for Barbara's car keys.

Barbara clenched her fingers around the keys. "No, you can't have these keys. They will want to see them after the car is gone." She thought for a second before continuing. "After I leave for that office building over there, look under the right rear fender and you will find a small metal box held by a magnet to the car. There is a spare key there. Remember, you won't have too long before I have to report the car missing. Wait for a few minutes after I go through the doors before you take the car."

Tim nodded, but was already thinking how to locate and then get the girls out. He didn't even hear Barbara's retreating footsteps. Nor did he wait until Barbara was through the doors before he went to the rear wheel well, and began searching for the metal box. Locating it, he brought it out and quickly got into the car with Mary.

"Tim, please drive slow," cautioned Mary. "We don't want to get stopped for speeding."

Tim nodded, then backed out and headed up the street toward the large building in the distance where Barbara said the girls were located. It only took a few minutes to arrive and locate a vacant parking space. Carefully, he backed into the parking space in case they might have to leave in a big hurry.

Tim shut off the car and sat quietly staring at the building. There was a section of lawn, measuring about twenty feet in depth, which surrounded the tall structure. Walkways traversed the lawn at different angles, some lined with hedges that once upon a time, were neatly trimmed.

"Now what?" asked Mary softly.

Tim shook his head again. "I don't know. I'm thinking. I guess the thing I should do is go in and play it by ear." He looked at his wife and with a small smile said, "This is a real fix, isn't it, honey?"

"Well, I got some good news – 'real fixes' are the specialty of Jesus. I have been praying about this since we left camp. I think Jesus knew the answer before we even left," she said, but did not smile.

Tim squeezed his wife's hand and smiled, "Keep praying," he said.

Mary felt him squeeze her hand tighter, so tight it began to hurt.

"Tim," she said with her discomfort evident in her voice. "You're hurting my..."

"It's her!" said Tim with wonder. "Mary, it's her!"

"Who?"

"That's the twins' mother, Rachelle Myers – the one in the blue smock walking with that Colonel." Tim put his hand over his mouth as if the pair could hear him from this distance. Tim watched as they walked into the building. That they were in a

189

hurry was obvious, and Rachelle had trouble keeping up with the Colonel, who turned now and then to see if she was close. Tim got the impression the Colonel wasn't happy. "It looks to me like Mrs. Myers works for him. Somehow, we have to get her away from him. I wonder if she knows her daughters are inside."

"I'll bet she does," said Mary.

* * * * *

Eppinger grabbed the door handle and was about to hold it for Rachelle Myers, when he realized how ridiculous that would appear. Instead, he went inside, and heard Rachelle catch the door, then follow. Quickly locating the sign indicating the Adoption Center, Eppinger set off so quickly, it forced Rachelle to almost run in order to keep up with him.

Entering the office, Eppinger went to the counter, and began banging on the bell. He continued to bang on the bell until a woman entered from the side.

"Yes, sir," she said with some annoyance in her voice.

"I'm here to get a couple of children, and I need you to hurry as fast as you can, do you understand? Do you know who I am?" snapped Eppinger.

"Yes sir, Colonel Eppinger," said the clerk, "which children?"

Eppinger turned to Rachelle, "Which children?"

Rachelle stepped forward, giving the two numbers she had copied from the TV.

The clerk went to the computer at the end of the counter and punched in the numbers. "Oh yes, the twins – you're the second people to ask about these girls today."

"Really?" asked Rachelle in astonishment.

"Yes, in fact it was only a half-hour ago. However, I had bad news for her and bad news for you. Both of these girls are scheduled to be eliminated – turns out they're labeled as Jesus Freaks."

"Oh my God!" said Rachelle, putting both of her hands to her face.

"I don't care about any order. I want them, and I am here to take them home – get those kids up here! I'll take care of any order that's been issued about these girls!" snapped Eppinger. "On second thought, I'll go back with you and get them."

"Yes sir, I'll get the paperwork," said the clerk, clearly shaken, disappeared out the side door.

Eppinger turned to Rachelle. "When I bring the children up here, you cannot show any sign that you know these girls. You are just here to help me bring them home, understood? If this girl suspects you are the Mother, as soon as we leave out the door, she will make a call. Even though this girl is a Jesus Freak herself, don't count on her looking the other way. She's got family somewhere too, and if they find out she let this happen, she and her family will pay the price." Eppinger looked up to see if the girl had returned yet with the paperwork. "When I see the girls, I'll tell them not to recognize you. Do you understand?"

Rachelle nodded silently.

The clerk opened the door carrying in her hand a sheet of papers. "I will need your signature on these papers, Colonel, to authorize me to release the twin girls into your custody.

"Of course," snapped Eppinger, grabbing and quickly scratching his signature on the indicated line.

"Follow me, sir," said the clerk opening the door that led to the retention area. Passing the photo station, she used her pass card, to open the door leading to the cells. At the next door, she had to buzz for the guard, who came quickly and, after checking the release paper that was held up, unlocked the metal door.

They followed him down a row of cells. All the faces were pressed against the bars. The usual catcalls were silent, as the sight of a Colonel struck some fear in them. Finally, the guard stopped, and the woman called out to the twins, "Would Alison and Katie Myers come here?" she said in a sweet voice.

Within a few minutes the two girls came, holding each other's hands. "Today is a wonderful day for you girls," smiled the clerk as the guard unlocked the cell. "You are going to a very, very nice home with the Colonel here."

Slowly the girls came out. It was obvious by their expression they were petrified. Eppinger took their hands as they followed the clerk and the guard. Allowing the two jailers to get ahead, Colonel Eppinger turned and motioned for the girls to stop. As they did, he knelt down in front of them. "Now, girls it's very important you listen to what I say, and not make a sound. I am taking you to meet your mother."

Katie squealed and then slapped her hand to her mouth.

"She is waiting for you in the office. Now, when you see her, don't pay any attention to her – do you understand?"

Both girls nodded with tears in their eyes.

"This is very important, girls. If they know she's your Mother, they will throw all of you back in jail."

"Colonel?" came the voice from behind him. Turning he waved at the two escorts now waiting for them at the gate. Eppinger stood up and took one girl in each hand, and squeezed their hands while giving them a smile.

A minute later, they opened the office door. Eppinger thought Rachelle was going to faint at the first sight of the girls. The twins remained silent, but tears flowed freely down their checks.

"Rachelle," snapped Eppinger, "why don't you take the girls out to the car while I finish up here?"

Silently, Rachelle reached for the hands of the twins who immediately grabbed tightly onto hers. Silently, the three

192

walked out the building and down the steps.

"Mama," sobbed Katie.

"Sssh," admonished Rachelle, "not yet sweetheart – wait 'til we are in the car."

As she opened the car door Rachelle, took a quick look around, before she followed the girls into the back seat.

"Mama, Mama!" squealed Alison, with her sister echoing her excitement.

Rachelle Myers put her arms around both girls and with tears in her voice said, "Thank you, Jesus!"

And whoso shall receive one such little child in my name receiveth me.

– Matthew 18:5

Chapter 18

"Look, the twins!" Tim shouted, his excited voice was deafening inside the car. "And, they are with their Mother! I can't believe it! She's alive!"

Mary looked where he was pointing and saw the girls holding hands with a woman walking between them.

"She was supposed to be dead!" said Tim.

"Wait, Tim, there's a man in uniform coming behind them!"

The two waited as they saw a uniformed man follow them and get into the government car. The army-brown car remained still for a few minutes, before slowly backing out of its space and heading northward.

Tim started up their car and pulled out behind them. "Mary, don't take your eyes off of them, we just can't lose them!"

Trailing the twin's vehicle by several car lengths, they shadowed it, snaking their way out of the downtown area. As the houses began to thin out, Tim allowed himself to put a little more space between them, but not much.

Finally, the lead car turned down a residential street. Tim followed, allowing now even more space between the cars. Slowly, the lead car turned into the driveway of a large home.

"Wow," said Mary, "pretty nice."

"Doesn't surprise me," answered Tim. "These officer guys always get the best houses. I heard if they see a house they want, they just kick out whatever family happens to live in it."

"Oh," replied Mary, "I don't believe that. They are still

American soldiers – I can see the Goonies doing that, but not our soldiers."

Tim shrugged. "That's just what I heard." He pulled the car to the curb while intently examining the house where the children went. "I'm going in there," he announced, as he checked that his gun was secure at his waist.

"No honey, please – there's got to be a better way. Why don't we just wait here and watch what's going to happen?"

Tim shook his head. "I can't," he said. "But, I think you should wait here."

"Wherever you're going, so am I."

Tim looked with exasperation at Mary, but did not argue. Slowly walking and then breaking into a slight jog, he approached the house, cutting across the neighbor's ample lawn. Following a neatly-trimmed hedge separating the two houses, they were able to come close to the side door while remaining partially concealed. Tim motioned toward the side door. "That's where they went in," he whispered.

Mary nodded.

Squeezing through the hedge Tim motioned Mary to follow. Crouching low they ran to the car they had been following – now parked next to the side entrance of the house. From here, he could look through the house windows to see if he could spot anyone. He did not. Again, he turned to Mary and, using hand signals, showed his intention of going inside.

Mary shook her head vigorously, clearly miming, 'No.'

Ignoring his wife's protest, Tim went around the back of the parked staff car, to the side entrance of the house and to its screen door. Within a few seconds, he felt Mary beside him. Turning, he made it very clear, though silently, that she was to go back to the car.

Mary closed her eyes and shook her head. Tim gave another exasperated sigh, noting this was becoming a habit since they married.

Gripping the screen door's handle, Tim pulled and found it unlocked. Mary then held the screen door, allowing Tim to try the doorknob of the inner wooden door. He felt the door release. Slowly, he pushed the door, while he peeked through the crack. No one was visible. He pushed the door further, and saw they were in a vacant foyer. There were four stairs to his left leading up into a kitchen.

Pushing the door further brought a squeak of protest from a hinge. Tim stopped, and listened. When he did not hear anything, he pushed the door open. Drawing the gun from his belt, Tim felt ready for any inquiring eyes. Behind him, he could hear Mary quietly enter and began to close the door. Tim quickly threw up his hand and motioned for her to leave the door open. He then motioned for Mary to stay where she was until he signaled for her to come forward. Mary nodded.

Tim slowly straightened up and silently scaled the four steps to a large kitchen. There were two refrigerators, much to Tim's surprise. He had never been in a home that had two refrigerators. There also were two sinks. A large island counter was in the center with a hood over it, from which cooking implements hung.

Ahead, was an arched doorway into a hall. Tim concluded there was no way to conceal himself until he reached it. As quietly as he could, he went to the door where he was able to look out into the hallway, which appeared to run the length of the house. Directly across from him was a room that looked like the dining room. Farther up the hall, he could see two archways on opposite sides, and surmised one led to the living room and the other possibly to either a Sitting Room or Family Room.

As he was trying to figure out the house, a uniformed man suddenly came into the hall from what Tim guessed was the living room. Tim drew back, hoping it was enough to conceal his presence. The soldier did not see him and turned left toward the front of the house. A second uniformed man, this one a Colonel, followed him into the hall, and after some nodding, returned where he had come from, while the first soldier went forward before turning right. Hoping this meant only the man in a Colonel's uniform was guarding the girls and their mother, Tim decided this might be his best chance. He gave a look back and saw Mary was now crouching behind the kitchen island. Smiling, she held up a mean-looking knife. Tim held up his hand, before indicating he was going down the hall.

Checking once more to assure himself no one was looking, he stepped out into the hall. Then, hugging the opposite wall, he slowly made his way toward the arched opening. He could clearly see the Colonel's back, and as he approached, he could hear him talking, but could not make out the words. Giving a quick look back, he almost gasped as Mary was only six inches behind him, with the large knife in her hand, still with a smile on her face. If he could have, he would have yelled at her, but under the circumstances, he only closed his eyes and exhaled.

Then, inching forward toward the arch, he could make out the words the Colonel was speaking "...I think that's the best thing we could do. It's obvious to me that General Powell felt we could face arrest any moment."

"Okay, everyone stand still!" shouted Tim as he leaped into the room behind the Colonel. "I want your hands on your head!" he shouted again, and was relieved when the Colonel slowly did it, as did the woman, and the twins.

"Tim? Tim Barter, is that you?" said Rachelle Myers.

"Yes, it's me, Mrs. Barter. Are you alright?"

"Tim!" squealed Alison as she leaped down from the couch and ran to him.

Tim held up his hand in an attempt to stop her, "Alison, don't—" he yelled.

However, Alison was already jumping toward him. Out of the corner of his eye, Tim saw the second man leap out from the other room. The gun in his hand exploded as he moved.

Alison gave a short cry then collapsed on the floor.

"Don't shoot! Don't shoot!" screamed Rachelle. "He's a friend!"

Tim was about to fire when he saw the man lower his gun. He immediately knelt down beside Alison, who lay unconscious on the floor. Rachelle Myers screamed and was about to pick up her little girl, when Tim stopped her.

"Don't move her, Mrs. Myers."

"Here," said Colonel Eppinger as he also knelt down. "Let me take a look at it." Carefully he examined the blood-soaked dress. It appeared the bullet had entered the left shoulder. Eppinger carefully lifted the garment covering Alison's shoulder. "She took the bullet just below her left shoulder," he announced. "She needs a doctor. I can't tell whether any vessels have been hit, although it seems there's more blood than there should be." Carefully the Colonel rolled her over so he could see her back. "It appears to be a through and through wound."

"Oh, my God," said Rachelle. "Is my little girl going to die?"

"We'll do whatever we can to prevent that, Rachelle. But I can't lie to you; we are in a tough situation here."

"Excuse me," said Mary. "Maybe I can help," she said. Then looking at Rachelle, she took her hand. "I can't promise anything, but maybe I can do something." She then looked at everyone gathered and instructed them to hold hands. "Once God blessed me by healing my dog after I prayed to Him."

"Your dog?" asked the Colonel.

"Yes, sir."

"Young lady, I know you are sincere, but this little girl isn't a dog!"

"Let her try, Colonel," said Tim.

The small group joined hands, one by one, including even

198

the Colonel and the Major. Mary closed her eyes for a minute or two, remaining quiet, as she appeared to gather herself. Suddenly she spoke, "Dear Jesus we come to you in this moment of need. We know that you are the author of all goodness for Your Father's glory. We ask You to have mercy upon this child and heal her body, in this her desperate hour."

"Amen," said Mary and the group stepped back while Mary put a blanket on Alison, tucking it beneath her chin. "Now, let's let Jesus love this child back to health."

Rachelle began silently weeping. "How long?" she asked.

Mary looked down at Alison, and was silent for a moment. "I don't know."

The sudden ringing of the phone caused them all to jerk.

Lorraine Eppinger answered it. "I'll get him, one moment please," she said to the caller. Quickly, she went and handed the phone to her husband announcing it was Sergeant Harkins.

Eppinger went immediately to the other room. His voice was barely audible until the last when they heard, "Thank you sergeant. I mean that."

Eppinger returned to the living room saying, "That was Sergeant Harkins from my office. Things are happening quicker than I anticipated." Eppinger gave a quick glance toward Major Beiner, and then licked his lips. "My replacement has arrived, a Lt. Colonel Decker."

"I thought he was taking the Command in the Midwest region," replied Beiner.

"It looks like they diverted him here."

"You know anything about him?" asked Beiner.

"Quite a bit, actually," said Eppinger. "He and I have been friends for many years. I can tell you this – expect no mercy. Friend or not, Decker is a by-the-book officer, and what's more, he knows they will be watching him extra closely. The fact that Decker and I are friends would not be lost on the Brothers."

Suddenly Alison moaned.

"Alison, baby," said Rachelle as she knelt down to her daughter.

"Colonel," came a shout from the front room, followed with a more urgent, "Colonel!"

Running to the front of the house, Eppinger saw Beiner peering out of the door's window. Beiner motioned him closer.

Looking out, Eppinger saw two staff cars, along with a half-ton truck, pulling up in front of the house. As they watched, soldiers dismounted from the truck and assembled next to it with their rifles. Two civilians and three officers got out of the two cars. Eppinger recognized one of the officers. It was Lt. Col Decker.

"So Decker has come himself," said Eppinger. "He certainly didn't waste any time." Turning to Beiner, he smiled, "I'll bet he's gonna try to schmooze me outside." Then, facing Beiner, "Look, you've done more than I could ever expect. You've done yourself proud for General Powell, but now is the time to save yourself, Beiner."

Eppinger removed his sidearm and checked it. "I'm not gonna let them take my wife in, or any of these people. Their going to have to kill me first. It's best you leave."

"Sir, thank you for your concern, but I've been waiting a long time to show these SOBs what I think of them, and today is a perfect time to do that. I don't wanna live forever with these jerks, sir."

Eppinger smiled and nodded. Looking out the window, he saw a delegation about to reach his front door.

"Quick, go back and get everybody out of here. My wife has a car in the garage, they can take that one – tell them not to take the staff car. I'm going to buy as much time as I can."

The urgency of his directions was magnified by the pounding at the door, followed by several rapid rings of the doorbell.

Beiner ran toward the dining room as Eppinger slowly went to the door. He waited for a minute before he addressed them through the closed door. "Who is it!" he said, in his most pleasant tone, while refusing to open the door.

"Hans," came Decker's voice, "it's me, Decker. Open the door."

Again, Eppinger waited for a minute before answering. "Can't Decker, I'm busy, busy, busy – you know how it is."

"Hans, let's not play games. You know why I am here. It's time you came out and addressed this thing like the officer I know you to be."

"Sorry Hans can't do that, my hands are full," replied Eppinger, stepping back and to the side of the door.

For a long minute, there was no reply, until he heard the front window smashed. The figure of a man was about to climb in. Eppinger took quick aim and fired two shots, and the soldier dropped without a sound.

Almost instantly, an automatic weapon fired and a series of bullets ripped through the front door. Eppinger waited at the side, then jumped in front of the door and returned fire through the door and heard someone grunt. Hans ran to the window and prepared to fire again, but saw Colonel Decker was already ducking behind one of the cars and the two men in uniform were running back to the car. The rest of the soldiers were now behind the half-ton. Eppinger knew they would instruct their men on what they wanted them to do. He figured that would take a few minutes – precious minutes that his wife and the others could use.

Beiner came up from behind him. "They are all ready to go; I told your wife you'd be right back to say goodbye."

Eppinger nodded and went to the living room. The group was waiting for him, all holding what they could carry with them. Rachelle was holding Alison in her arms.

Seeing Hans, Lorraine ran to him and began crying, while

wrapping her arms around him.

"I know, sweetheart, I know," said Eppinger softly. "It's not what we planned, but this is what we've got. You have to go. I can face this knowing you are away from here."

He looked at Tim. "Please, take care of my wife," he said with a faltering tone."

"I will, sir," answered Tim

Eppinger began pulling away, but his wife tightened her grasp. He looked up at Tim with eyes that asked him for help. Tim and Mary approached Lorraine Eppinger and placed their hands on her shoulder. Hans kissed his wife, and was about to pull away when he kissed her again. Then, giving her a final desperate look, as if trying to memorize every pore on her face, he quickly left the room and returned to the front of the house.

"Okay, let's go." said Tim as he led the small group to the back door. Reaching the door, he peeked outside, but there was no indication the soldiers had moved from the vehicles in front. Quickly, they went out the back door, and then ran to the three-car garage. Inside, was a staff car along with a four-door, silver Buick.

Without talking, everyone got into the Buick. Tim began backing out of the garage immediately. The rear seat was crowded with four people. Rachelle, Lorraine and Katie sat on the seat while they laid Alison's unconscious body across their laps.

As he exited the garage, Tim saw a row of flowers and small bushes separating this house from the rear neighbor. Dropping the shift into *drive*, he accelerated toward the back of the property. Gunfire suddenly erupted from the Eppinger house behind them. This time the shots were rapid and repeated. Hearing the gunfire, Tim did not pause, but kept the pedal floored. The car did a momentary fishtail, before heading for the rear of the yard. Tim did not slow down as they reached the dividing shrubbery between the two yards.

They heard the scraping of the small shrubs and flowers passing beneath the car, before they burst into the neighbor's backyard. Again, he didn't slow, but made for the driveway that would get them out to the road. From the corner of his eye, he saw a man emerging from the house as they flew by the side door, and out onto the street.

For a second, the car flirted with the idea of rolling as Tim yanked the wheel, trying to aim them down the street. After a brief fishtail, the Buick straightened out. It was all over in a matter of a few minutes, and the group was on their way out of the sub-division.

For several minutes no one spoke, as Tim slowed to the speed limit and tried to merge into the suburban scene. They traveled silently until finally they turned onto the main road.

Lorraine spoke-up softly. "As Hans hugged me, he asked me to say a prayer for him. I think that is the first time he ever used the word. He never thought prayer did any good before," she said quietly chocking back her emotions.

Tim took the gun from his waist and handed it to Mary. "Here," he said, "keep it handy in case we need to use it."

Mary nodded silently.

Tim looked in the rear view mirror at Lorraine. "Can you help us out here? I need some directions to get us out of town. We want to get to Route 215."

"I don't know where 215 is. I never heard of it before," replied Lorraine, her voice betraying half grief, and half fear.

"Well, it runs off of the Blue Ridge Parkway – can you get us there?" he asked.

Lorraine nodded, "Yes, I know how to get there. Up here at Cherry, take a left and it will lead right into 240 and then just follow the signs to the Blue Ridge Parkway."

"Where are we going?" asked Rachelle

"I don't know yet," answered Tim.

Chapter 19

He wasn't known around camp for being an early riser, but for some reason, this morning was an exception. Andy slipped out of bed quietly, so not to disturb his sleeping wife. Grabbing his clothes, he quietly shut the bedroom door behind him and dressed. He looked out the kitchen window to see how the day was fairing, but it was still too early for the sun, and the only thing he could determine was that it wasn't raining – a good sign.

He then checked the coffee pot to see if any was any left over from the previous day. He judged there was enough for one or two cups. His days in the service had destroyed his coffee taste buds. As long as it was black and hot, it was worth drinking.

As soon as the coffee was hot, Andy poured himself a cup and went out on the front porch. It was still half-dark. A slight morning tint in the eastern sky enabled him to see the lake and its still surface. He sat in his chair and quietly drank his coffee. He liked doing this, and wondered why he didn't do it more often. The early morning hours were so peaceful, even the birds were not yawning yet.

"The morning time is always my favorite," said a voice from behind him.

Startled, Andy whipped around and saw the Hermit standing there. "I wish you wouldn't do that," he blurted out, as he brushed spilled coffee off his leg. Then, setting his coffee cup down and regaining his composure, he smiled. "I was beginning to wonder if I'd ever see you again."

"I have come to bring you a message," said the Hermit and, as he spoke, a glow began to emanate from behind him. It grew until it encompassed his entire body. It became so bright that Andy had to shield his eyes. As the light grew, so did the

Hermit, until he was even taller than Andy's six foot two inches. Gone was the gaunt frame of the crippled Hermit, instead, a magnificent serene creature dressed in white robes stood before Andy.

Instinctively, Andy began to kneel.

"Stop that!" the angel commanded. "It is I who shall soon bow before you. Heaven is God's kingdom of authorities. Christ has given you His authority and soon you shall see its wonder. I have come to give you a message. As you read the signs of the seasons, read the signs of the time. The end of the age is upon all creation."

"I know this – how soon?"

"No man or creature of heaven and hell knows the date or hour, even our Lord Jesus knows not. I am to tell you, it is soon, and to hold on to your faith, Andy. Keep Jesus near to you, for the coming days will not be kind. You shall be taken against your will and slain for your faithful service to our Lord. Remain strong, Andy for great joy awaits all who do."

"And Stephanie?"

"Your wife shall be at your side on the appointed day. In these remaining days, you shall come to know things you should not, and in some, you shall receive great comfort, while in others, great sorrow. Your faithfulness to your beliefs shall encourage enemies and they shall plot against you. In the dark hours, they will come for you and deliver you to your enemies. However, fear not, Andy, for the Holy Spirit shall be with you. Rely not upon your own courage, but the courage that comes from Christ. Be of a peaceful heart, for all that was promised shall be fulfilled, and the fears of man shall be quieted. Lucifer, that deceiver and slayer of many, shall be finally vanquished – as it was written from the beginning, so shall it now be. Peace to you, Andy."

Suddenly the angel faded and Andy was left alone on the porch, temporarily blinded by the change from the brilliant light of the angel, to the darkness of the morning.

Andy stumbled to the chair and held onto its back while he tried to compose himself. A sense of awe, and joy, and fear bubbled up within him. Finally, he sank to his knees and gave thanks to God for His blessings. He remained on his knees for several minutes, then rose and went back into the house.

Opening the bedroom door, he slowly went over to Stephanie and placed his hand upon her shoulder. The slight motion startled Stephanie awake, but seeing Andy, she smiled.

"Good Morning," said Andy quietly.

"What time is it?" asked Stephanie looking around at the darkness.

"I don't know," replied Andy quietly as he began stroking her hair.

Stephanie suddenly sat up. "Why, Andy, you have tears in your eyes. What's wrong, honey?"

"Nothing's wrong," replied Andy. "Everything is right and I want to tell you that I'm blessed that you have been a part of my life. I want to make sure I tell you that."

Stephanie hugged her husband. "I feel the same way," she replied. "You're scaring me. Why are you saying these things?"

"I have some news I need to share with you. But, I must ask you, not to tell anyone else."

Stephanie rested her back against the headboard of the bed and held Andy's hand. "It sounds like bad news."

"Not really," answered Andy. Carefully he related to Stephanie his meeting with the Hermit, and told her how he revealed himself as an angel. Stephanie squeezed Andy's hand while holding her other hand to her mouth in awe. Then Andy told her as clearly as he could what the angel had said about his own future, and about hers.

"When? Did he say when?"

"I got the impression it was to happen very soon."

Stephanie reached out and grabbed Andy. "I won't let you leave without me. We are as one person, Andy. You don't leave without me. You understand that!"

Andy smiled. "Yes, Ma'am."

Stephanie hugged him tighter, "Don't make fun of me. I'm not going to let you go without me."

Instead of replying, Andy hugged his wife and silently thanked God again that He brought her to him.

"I think I'll go fishing," said Andy finally.

"What? Go fishing?"

"Yes, I think I will do that now. The sun is coming up, and I hear that's the best time to catch the big ones."

"But," said Stephanie, with some wonder in her voice, "you don't like fishing. I don't think you have ever been fishing."

"Even so, I think it's about time I did some. Seems to me a man should go fishing once in his life, and it looks like it's about time for me to get that done."

Stephanie shook her head. "I married a prophet and a crazy man. I can't imagine what the Lord is going to do with you in heaven."

Andy got up from the bed, kissed his wife and went out to the kitchen for some string he remembered being in one of the drawers. Fetching it, he then made his way outside. Here, the morning seemed to be getting under way just fine. The rising sun awakened a soft breeze and it was bringing freshness to the new day. He knew the breeze would chase the morning mist off the lake, as it did every morning. As he walked to the lake, he could hear the chickens complaining about the daily egg thieves. From somewhere in the distance he could hear voices chatting, spiked with occasional laughter – probably the kitchen folks on their way to the Great House to fix breakfast. Off in the distance, he heard a tractor start up and knew the lower garden was going to be tilled or harvested.

Andy breathed in deeply. It was a good morning. Even though he had just been told about his coming death, he felt fine – almost jubilant.

Andy, stopped short of the docks to size up the willow stalks growing there, before picking one about four feet long. That size looked proper, or would from the shore. After trimming the willow stick until it was fairly smooth, he withdrew the length of string from his pocket. It was some five feet long, about the right length, he thought, and attached it to the end of the pole. Andy did not know how to fish, or like to eat fish, or even touch them for that matter. In fact, he determined long ago to avoid catching fish at all costs. Catching a fish would entail grabbing hold of the fish and actually wrestling the hook out of it. To be certain this would never happen, he did not put a hook on the end of the string. After all, he thought, the real value of fishing was the solitude it afforded. At the dock, he laid his pole in one of the boats, then untied it from the dock. He was about to get in when he heard his name called. Looking up, he saw Betty Jo Kegler half-walking and half-jogging down the path toward the dock.

"Oh, Prophet Andy – Yoo-hoo!"

Andy waved, gave a smile, and waited until Betty Jo came on the dock.

"What's up Betty?"

Betty stood a minute huffing and puffing, trying to catch her breath. Finally, she took a deep breath and said, "Prophet Andy, I need to talk to you. It's about Mary."

Andy nodded. "Tell you what, Betty. Why don't you hop in this boat with me and we'll go fishing and have some time to talk."

Betty hesitated a moment, then smiled. "Alright. You know, it's been a long time since I even thought about going fishing."

"Me, too," smiled Andy.

Andy helped Betty in and waited until she was securely seated before pushing off from the dock. Then, taking the oars, he began to silently row until they reached near the center of the lake.

"I think this is about right," he said, taking the fishing pole in his hand. "Now, the first thing we gotta do is make sure you have a fishing pole too," he said. He eyeballed the middle of the pole before he snapped it in half. Then, taking the length of string in his hand, he broke it in half, and tied each of the pieces to the poles. "There, I think we are in business," he said as he handed Betty her pole and dropped his line in the water.

"But there's no hook," said Betty.

"Nope, might catch something – then what?" asked Andy, smiling. "Don't think I would like to handle fish. I don't much like eating them either, but I do now and then, if I must."

"What's the point?"

"Well, Betty, I'll tell you. I think a man should do some things at least once in his life, and so I decided to go fishing. I think I would like to come out here, just to think. In fact, I wish I had done it more often. There is nobody to bother me and it is just peaceful. Now, if I just sat out here without a pole, well, then people on shore would wonder, 'What's wrong with the Prophet? What's the Prophet doing out there, just sitting?' Or maybe, 'I wonder if God is telling him something we should know,'" smiled Andy. "Now, you know they would. I just thought it would be wise to make sure I have a pole and some string. So now they don't think I'm a nut, or a crazy man – I'm just another fisherman, a noble sportsman – nothing to worry about – 'Why, he's just fishin,' they'll say."

Betty smiled, "Well, you can count on me to keep your little secret."

Andy nodded, "Now, tell me what's on your mind?"

"I gotta tell you, I'm getting scared," said Betty. "We haven't heard anything from Mary, or about her. I was hoping you might know something."

Andy was silent for a moment and then lowered his stick to the water and tapped it several times. "It's hard, isn't it, Betty? This not knowing. That's the tough part of faith, the not knowing. It is easy to look in the rear view mirror and talk about past faith and all it has meant to your life, but when you look ahead and the night is dark, and the fog heavy – why, it gets scary. We want answers. We want signs and indications. We need God to hug us now and then, just so we know. Hmmm, that's it, isn't it? We need to know."

"Yes," agreed Betty.

For a few moments they were both silent. Andy quietly pointed to the water where they could see a fish was investigating the string.

"Lucky for both him and me there isn't a hook," smiled Andy.

"How soon, Andy? I heard you told someone that we won't see another winter."

Andy nodded slowly, "I don't believe we will – the gathering of God's creatures is near."

"I hope that it is," said Betty in a low voice. "I saw what they did with that ugly creature on TV the other day. I think that's evil."

Andy smiled slightly, "You are right." Then, dropping his stick-pole to the bottom of the boat, announced, "I think it's time to get in now."

Betty smiled, "That wasn't a very long fishing time, if you ask me."

"No, Betty, they aren't biting today – you have to be a good fisherman to know when you're wasting your time and when you aren't," he smiled. "But, before we go, let me say something to you about Mary."

Betty's eyes fastened upon Andy's face, as though she might miss something he was about to say.

"Mary is coming home."

Betty gasped, "You know this?"

Andy smiled, "I do. Believe this – Mary is coming home and she is bringing your grandchild."

Betty let out a scream of excitement "She is? When?"

Andy began rowing back to the dock, and saw Stephanie waiting for them on the dock. "That – I don't know," he said "but I believe it will be soon."

When the boat was tied to the dock, Betty reached over and hugged Andy so tight he thought his oxygen would be cut off.

"Thank you! Thank you!" said Betty before she jumped on the dock and began running.

At the end of the dock she ran by Stephanie shouting, "Baby! Baby!"

Andy was grinning as he approached his wife, "I think Betty wants to be a Grandma," he said.

Stephanie laughed, "I think you're right. So, you told her. Why?"

Andy shrugged, "Don't know, just seemed she needed to know."

"All these things you tell me Andy, I don't know if you should."

"Really?"

"Well, it's hard to keep straight what I should say and what I shouldn't."

Andy nodded, "Yep, I agree, but there are some things that are meant to be known at certain times, and not at others. I wish I could be sure which was which myself."

For a few minutes, they walked in silence holding hands.

"I heard you told Roy we wouldn't see another winter," said Stephanie. "It's all over camp now, you know."

Andy nodded.

"When are you going to tell them the rest?"

"I suppose I will, but not until I know I should. I had a dream the other night, Stephanie. At first, I didn't think I should mention it, but now I do."

"Oh, no, I can't take any more of your dreams. Tell me it was about us having a picnic or something."

Andy led her to a bench that faced the water. "Wish it was. Yes, wish it was." Andy sighed bending down and gathering up a handful of stones. He picked out the flatter ones and threw them at the water, one by one.

"I never was able to get the trick of making these things skip," he said with some dejection. Sitting down on the bench, Andy was quiet for a second before speaking. "Now, about the dream: it's about these so-called Visitors. Would you say that they are beautiful, honey?"

Stephanie nodded, "Without a doubt. I guess that's how they want everyone to think they will become when they speed with them off to the stars."

"Well, I don't think they are truly beautiful – certainly not like the images we see of them. In my dream a man was standing. He was as tall, and as good-looking as any of these creatures we have seen. Then, slowly, he began to transform into some kind of beast. His skin turned a dark green, and his head was the head of a pre-historic animal."

"Wow, so what happened?"

"Nothing really, but as I saw him standing there looking like this ancient beast, it leaned forward towards me, and spoke!"

"In English?"

"Well, sorta. I mean, I heard it in English, but his lips didn't seem to be moving – 'course he really didn't have lips that I could see. But he spoke my name – actually what he said was, 'Andrew, I see you.'" Andy paused. "It was one of those dreams where everything feels so real. When he spoke to me, I could even smell the stench of his breath."

"What do you think it means?"

"At first, I kept thinking it was just some kinda nightmare, and it didn't mean anything, really. Then I talked to the old guy who keeps going around camp preaching."

"You mean, Mr. Dorby?"

"Yeah, Elmer Dorby. He stopped me, all upset. He said he had a dream about dinosaurs and the Aliens.

Stephanie smiled. "That's ridiculous," she said with a slight laugh. Then seeing Andy's face, she asked, "Isn't it?"

"Probably. But, do you remember when we were aboard ship, and you were investigating the disappearance of TJ Jenkins?"

Stephanie nodded. "That seems like years ago now."

"I remember when you were talking to me about finding the remains of TJ, you said something like, 'They think it was a shark. The bites didn't seem like a shark, just almost like a shark.' You specifically said 'almost', like maybe you didn't believe they were."

Stephanie thought a moment and then nodded. "Well, it wasn't so much I didn't believe it, but the doctors who did the autopsy were divided on how he met his death. The one I spoke with, I don't recall his name, told me he didn't think the bite marks were consistent with a shark, that they more closely resembled those of a lion or tiger."

"Yes, that's what you told me," said Andy.

"Oh, now Andy – you don't think it was some kinda pre-historic beast. Don't tell me that. I'd be worried you were going nuts."

"Well, how about half-nuts? Let's not say it was a pre-historic beast, let's say it is a modern being that resembled a pre-historic beast."

"What are you talking about? You think these Visitors have animals that are like the dinosaurs?"

"Not at all. I'm saying these so-called visitors from space

213

are actually demons, which could resemble those beasts of the ancient world. In fact," said Andy standing up and beginning to pace, "they may have created those ancient beasts in their own image."

"You're talking crazy, Andy."

"Probably. However, let's just play with the notion of being crazy. We saw two of them come to our camp, and when Mary detected they were not human, they up and disappeared – now that is crazy – yet we all saw it. I'm convinced that the spiritual world can reveal itself in our natural world appearing different than they really are – whenever they want. Didn't Satan become a snake for Eve and seduce her into sin?"

"So, I take it, you're saying these creatures are beast-like, and are able to change their appearances for our sake."

"Exactly."

"Honey, let's stop this. I don't like where this is going and I don't like you being there. Besides, we have to go up to the Great House for something to eat before they close the lines down."

"Okay, okay," said Andy.

"Let's at least start to walk to the House."

Andy nodded and got up with Stephanie. At this hour, many were making their journey to the House for breakfast. There were three sittings for each meal: Early, Middle, and Late. Stephanie and Andy had chosen Middle seating long ago. Arriving late for your seating was considered rude as it delayed someone else from eating who had arrived on time for his seating.

Stephanie tried to hurry Andy by walking a little faster than he did, but to no avail.

"Let's say that holy is beautiful, but sin is ugly, just for arguments sake. When we submit and follow sinful ways we actually become ugly in the sight of God, and that it's through the sinless nature of Christ that beauty is restored to our souls.

However, when Lucifer sinned, he became a new creature – an ugly, deformed creature, losing the beauty of his holy nature and was cast down to Earth. He became a new creature – unholy in appearance and purpose – named Satan."

Stephanie remained silent.

"And now, as we approach the End Times, he wants to reveal himself, but can't, because of his appearance – he knows we would immediately reject his appearance as appearing evil. Our natural instincts are that beauty is good, while ugly is not. So, what does he do? Well, perhaps he decides to change our perception of what is beauty and what is not."

"Have you figured that out?"

"Well, suppose he made ugly prehistoric creatures in his own image, and claimed, through evolution, they are natural creatures of Earth – the natural evolutionary creatures of Earth – the first earthlings, if you will. Maybe in the present times, he makes these creatures cute. Perhaps he puts them in comic books so children can color them. Maybe he puts them on television as adorable and funny animals that love children – how about as fuzzy toys made for the children to snuggle up to at night? And then, ugly is not so ugly anymore; in fact, maybe they're considered cute – or, maybe beautiful, perhaps, even loveable."

They turned in front of the Great House and walked toward the door.

"Honey, please don't talk like this anymore, especially to anyone else," said Stephanie. "Andy, it sounds crazy. You talk like that and everyone is going to question whether you are fit to lead. They need someone to lead whose judgment they can trust, and look to for guidance. If you talk like this, everyone is going to think you're crazy."

Andy nodded. He knew she was right. It was a nutty idea anyway and everyone would agree with him on that – everyone but Elmer.

215

Take heed that ye despise not one of these little ones; for I say unto you, That in heaven their angels do always behold the face of my Father which is in heaven.

— Matthew 18:10

Chapter 20

"Is she breathing?" asked Tim over his shoulder, as he drove down the North Carolina highway.

"Yes," answered Rachelle, from the back seat. "God is going to save my baby," she added quietly.

Tim looked at Mary next to him in the front seat. "Your prayer didn't do much good," he whispered with a sneer.

"Yes it did. Why don't you just leave us and God alone?" she hissed.

"Then why isn't Alison alright? Why didn't he bring Mickey back to life? You said that Prophet guy brought his wife, Stephanie, back from the dead – healing a little girl should be no problem at all, right? Or, does he just do those things for his favorites?" snapped Tim.

"What are you two whispering about up there?" challenged Lorraine Eppinger.

"Nothing," answered Tim. "Just nothing."

"Is this man a Christian?" asked Rachelle, nodding toward Tim.

"He used to be, now he's just being a jerk," replied Mary.

"Young man," said Rachelle, "I thank you for all you're doing here, but I'm going to ask you to not say negative things about God or our Lord Jesus."

"Yes, ma'am, sorry," answered Tim. He felt anger growing within him. He needed to stretch his legs, take a deep breath, and regain his composure. He took the next road off to the right.

216

"Where are you going?" asked Mary. "I don't think this is the correct turnoff."

"I think we need to stop for a minute and relax – try to get ourselves together. I know I do. I think we need to take a deep breath before we go on making decisions on the spur of the moment."

"You're probably right," answered Mary. Looking at the back seat she saw they had joined hands, and were praying silently.

It wasn't long before Tim spotted the kind of country road he wanted, and turned onto it. Then, pulling the car off the gravel and under a large tree, he sat back and rubbed his head. Giving the praying women in back a glance, he got out of the car and Mary followed.

Walking over to a large tree, he stretched his arms out under its welcome shade. Leaning against the tree, Tim closed his eyes. "Sorry about what I said, honey."

"I'm sorry too," answered Mary beside him, grasping his arm with both hands. "I think we are getting weary – you know, I mean, emotionally worn out."

"I guess. We just seem to go from one mess to another."

"Does all this talk about God, and what Mrs. Myers said, bother you a lot?"

"Oh it's not that, it's sorta everything." Tim paused for a moment and then added, "You know, Mary, I think Alison is going to die."

"Don't say that!"

"Sorry. I didn't mean to upset you, but, she hasn't improved… and from what I see and hear – are you listening to her breathing? There's a rasp to it that wasn't there before."

"That's why they're praying."

"Praying, praying and praying. That's what gets me – we need a doctor, not prayer. I need another gun and some ammunition. We need a new vehicle – it's only a matter of

217

time 'til they figure out how we got away and put out an APB on us. We need some food, and place to rest. We need a plan – I keep asking myself, 'what should we do'?" Tim paused and took a deep breath. "Right now, I guess we're running back to Camp Noah, but should we? Do we know how to get there, even if that's the best choice? We're just guessing here, just guessing. The worst part of it is you all are looking to me to solve these problems. I can't! I want to. I'm trying to, but I can't honey, I just can't."

Mary reached her arms around her husband and drew him to her. "We're with you, Tim, we're all with you," she said softly. "I think it would be easier for you if you weren't so mad at God. I can't imagine how it must be to face all this, not knowing that God loves you. He does Tim; believe me, He does."

Tim stroked Mary's hair and kissed her on the forehead. Then stretching his arms, he did a couple of knee bends followed by two deep breaths.

"Okay. I'm ready to go."

Mary kissed him softly and smiled, "Come on," she said, "I'll race ya!"

Tim shook his head slowly, "Oh, I just don't feel like running," he said as he watched her closely; then, seeing her relax, suddenly began running to the car.

Caught by surprise, Mary tried to catch up, but the race was over before it began.

"Cheater," she said without smiling as she got in the car.

"You're easy," replied Tim with a grin.

Tim retraced the path they had taken from the expressway. The day was growing older, and the sun was beginning to disappear on the western horizon, as he turned onto the expressway and got back up to speed. Soon darkness closed in, and Tim was relieved when he saw the exit for Route 215. Finally, he knew where they were, and turned onto it.

However, as he did, he glanced down at the gas gage and gasped.

"What's the matter?" asked Mary, alarmed.

"We need gas," he announced, shaking his head. How could he have been so stupid as to let the gas get so low? He replied, trying not to betray the panic he was feeling, "I have no idea where we can get some. Not around here. None of the gas stations are going to sell to us without a card or The Mark."

"I have both," replied Lorraine. Her voice sounded monotone, as though in a daze from the events of the day. Her tone reflected a weary heart from certain knowledge that her husband was now dead. She heard the gunfire, and knew what it meant. Silent tears had flowed down her cheeks over the past hours; their dried trails were still visible on her cheeks. She had not bothered to wipe them away. Except for the children, it did not matter to her whether they escaped or not. She should have stayed with Hans. What life could she have now without her sweet Hans to hold her at night and stroke her hair, or kiss her on the neck, and nibble on her ear; to tell her everything was going to be all right, or hold her hand during their evening walks? It was all gone. No more dreams of spending the rest of her life with the one she loved, or having a child they could cherish. There would be no more laughter at the dinner table, or feeling his arm around her at sad movies. She should have stayed. She should have stayed.

The car began to slow as Tim spotted a promising place just off the expressway exit. He pulled into a combination gas station and store. For a minute, no one moved as they looked around the station. At last, Tim got out of the car, while he continued to survey the scene, examining all he could for signs of anything that might warn him that they should leave.

Inside the car, the women gently repositioned Alison, allowing Lorraine to exit the car with her card. Mary got out of the front seat, and with Lorraine, went in the store while Tim waited by the pumps, unwilling to allow his guard down. The girls were in the convenience store longer than made Tim comfortable, yet finally emerged carrying two sacks of grocery items. A nod from Rachelle told Tim he could start pumping.

He kept a watchful eye as he put the nozzle in the car's side and waited as the gas began to flow in the tank. Suddenly, a voice spoke to him from behind.

"Traveling far?" it asked.

Tim whipped around to find a tall man standing no more than three feet from him. Where he came from Tim could not imagine. Adding to his fear was his recognition of the man's features: he was tall, with crystal blue eyes. He knew from the talk around camp, and on television, this probably was not a human.

"Uh, no – not at all," answered Tim, fumbling for words. As he spoke, his mind was racing. What should he say, or not say? Where was his gun? Why hadn't he left the car running?

"You seem nervous, young man. You have no need to be, you know. You haven't done anything wrong today, have you?"

"No sir – of course not. I'm just out driving with my friends," smiled Tim.

The man looked in the back window of the car. "I see you have a sick little girl there," he said with a deep, calm voice.

"She's just tired," answered Tim. "We had a big day, you know – all the driving and stuff."

"She's just sleeping?"

"Yes, of course," answered Tim. "Well, there that ought to do it," he said, pulling the nozzle out of the gas tank. The gas had only flowed a couple of minutes, hardly enough to help; but it was clear to Tim they had to leave, and right now. He did not want to continue this conversation another moment.

"Why, young man, you just started pumping – I doubt you got more than a gallon or two."

It was obvious to Tim this whole scene was not going to end nicely. He could tackle this creep and yell for Mary to go, but would she? He could run to the driver's door and try to get his gun; but was it in the console, or under the seat – or did he give it to Mary?

The tall stranger walked slowly to the opposite rear door, then, bending his tall body almost in half, peered through the window.

"Yes, I believe this little girl is sick," he said. "That's right isn't it?" he said without looking up at Tim. Without waiting for a reply, he reached for the handle, and opened the door.

Tim could wait no longer and sprang for the driver's door. Reaching inside he tried to grab the gun from the console, but it was not there. He made a desperate grab for the gun under the driver's seat and felt his hands grasp the cold metal. Quickly he drew it out and pointed at the man.

"Okay, that's enough! Back away!" he shouted. "Mary, slide over and start the car. Start it now!"

Keeping his gun trained on the stranger, Tim walked around the front of the car to the passenger side.

Mary turned the key in the ignition, but though the starter whirred, the car did not start. She tried the key again, but to no avail.

Paying no attention to Tim, the man reached into the car focusing his eyes on Lorraine Eppinger. "You've been crying, Lorraine, but there is no need for tears," he said, holding her right hand with both of his own. "He's going to come home soon. He'll be waiting for you and he rejoices as we speak," he said quietly.

Then, laying both hands on the shoulders of the unconscious Alison, he smiled and looked back at Rachelle. "Your prayers have been heard, Mother. Rejoice, for your daughter, my charge, lives to love the Lord."

Finally, he backed out and looked at Tim standing with his

gun pointed at him. "Your journey is not over, young Tim. There is trouble ahead, but I tell you to trust – learn to trust. It is your faith, not deeds, which shall serve you well. Now start the car, and leave."

The man turned, and walked several steps away before looking over his shoulder. "I think you better go quickly, they know you are here," he said.

Mary tried to start the car again, and this time it roared to life.

Quickly Tim jumped in the passenger seat, and slammed the door shut.

Mary dropped the shift into *drive* and floored the pedal. The tires spun briefly before grabbing hold, and the car jumped as if excited to get going again. Immediately Mary applied the brakes.

"I can't drive!" she exclaimed. Then turning to Tim, "I never learned how."

Tim jumped out of the passenger side and traded places with his wife.

"I forgot," he said sheepishly. "I never think of you having been blind, sorry."

Tim looked back to see if he could spot the stranger, but there was no sign of him. "He's gone," said Tim meekly. Then he bent to see how much gas he had been able to pump. The gage read *full*.

"Look Honey! The gas tank is full!"

Before Mary could reply, he heard, Alison yawn, as if awakening from a sleep.

"Alison? Alison? Can you hear me?" her Mother exclaimed.

Alison rubbed her eyes, as she yawned again and then stretched. "Hi Mommy," she said.

Suddenly, Lorraine said "Oh, my God!"

"What is it!" shouted Tim.

"My hand," exclaimed Lorraine. "The Mark is gone!"

* * * * *

Lt. Colonel Decker burst into the outer office from the hallway, startling the three soldiers at their desks. All three men jumped to their feet, but Decker ignored them as he stormed past them into his office and slammed the door behind him.

Sgt Harkins looked around at the others, while raising his eyebrows. Slowly, he sat down again, while giving Lt Colonel Decker's door one last glance.

The sudden ringing of the telephone made him jump. Quickly he answered it and heard the familiar voice of his friend, Sergeant Doyle Brunswick. Before Harkins could speak, Brunswick blurted out, "Did you hear? Eppinger is dead."

"What? How do you know?"

"I know a Corporal who went on the squad to arrest him."

"I can't believe it! How'd it happen?"

"Big gun fight is what he told me. Eppinger started shooting and everyone ran for cover, and then I guess rounds were flying all over."

"So, where is he now?"

"He and another man that was with him, I don't know him – he was a Major – were transported to the Asheville morgue. Don't know what they'll do with them after that.

"Does his wife know?"

"Don't know anything about his wife, she was with him, though. Some say she ran."

Harkins was stunned. Rather than replying, Harkins simply hung the phone up while staring ahead. Finally focusing, he saw the other two were looking at him.

"He's dead. Colonel Eppinger's dead," he said, without

expression.

He felt sick to his stomach, not only at the Eppinger news, but also from a growing ball of fear. Did Decker know he had called and warned Eppinger? Harkins dismissed the thought. If Decker knew, he wouldn't still be sitting as this desk – more likely he'd be in a cell somewhere. Would Decker find out? Again, he doubted that – as far as he could figure, only Colonel Eppinger knew he called – and now he was dead.

Suddenly, the door to Decker's office flew open. "Harkins! Get in here!" shouted Lt. Colonel Decker.

Sergeant Harkins jumped and went into the office, closing the door behind him. The ball of fear in his stomach grew.

"Yes, sir?"

Decker was facing away from him, looking out the window. Suddenly without a word, Decker kicked the wastebasket next to him sending it across the office, dumping its contents on the floor.

"Eppinger, that fool. He's dead; you know that, Harkins?"

"I'd heard, sir."

Decker went to his chair and slumped down, resting his chin on his chest. "He was a friend of mine – did you know that?"

"Yes sir. Colonel Eppinger had mentioned your name a few times, and it was always very complementary."

"So, tell me Sergeant. Why did he do it? I could have worked something out. I might even have talked the brass into dismissing the charges," he said, then remained quiet for a couple of minutes. "Nah, they wouldn't allow that. He was a goner, but he was a good officer; I don't care what they say. He was a good officer, and he was my friend."

"Yes, sir, and I liked him too."

Decker looked up at him, and nodded. "I know you did, son. I know you did. And," he said, allowing his eyes to search the room, "I know you called and warned him I that was coming."

"But sir, I–"

"Oh, don't worry about it. I only wished you'd called him sooner so he had a chance to disappear," said Decker. "But we have our duty, don't we Harkins? We are soldiers, and we have our duty. So they say, 'kill your friend' and so, you go out and kill your friend."

"Well sir, you didn't want to kill him, you just said that."

"But he's dead isn't he? Like they say, 'he's dead as a door nail'; 'he's history', 'his card has been punched.' Isn't that what they say Harkins – make little jokes like that, and go on with their miserable lives?"

"I guess, sir."

"You're a good soldier, Harkins, and I'll tell you why; you called the Colonel and warned him. Yes, you saw the crap the army has become, and you wanted to save a good man – a loyal man. Isn't that right Harkins, he was a loyal man?"

"Yes, sir. He always tried to do his best."

"Absolutely. Now we go around like some puppets whose strings are pulled by jerks that call themselves 'Visitors'. Isn't that a crappy name – Visitors? And you know what?" asked Decker standing up. "We do their little dance," said Decker, as he began to prance, "like little ignorant puppets. They pull the strings and say, 'kill your friend' and we do it – like good little puppets."

Decker went over to the liquor cabinet. "You want a drink, Sergeant?"

"A drink? Uh, no, sir. Thank you, but no, sir."

"Get over here and have a drink. That's an order. If I can order men to kill my friend, I can order someone to have a drink. Here," he said, handing a glass to Harkins, "we'll salute a man we both admired, then we'll have another drink. Maybe we'll drink to us, The Royal Order of Puppets; and maybe another to this stinking war, and maybe we'll have a few more toasts, and maybe just get drunk as skunks. What do you say?"

Harkins raised his glass to the Lt Colonel, "I haven't been drunk in ten years, but I think today would be a good day to change that."

Chapter 21

Everyone in the car was silent as Tim drove away from the gas station. Even the twins seemed meditative as they lay back in the arms of their Mother, while Loraine Eppinger stared out the window at something only she could see.

Tim, too, found himself reflecting back upon recent events – the horror of losing his parents, suddenly not having a home, and then the responsibility of the children. Yet, juxtaposed to these memories was the realization that the children were safe and so was he. He had met and married the most wonderful woman, and the twins found their Mother. Perhaps he had been wrong. Maybe the Lord was caring for them. Perhaps it was God who had blessed them in the midst of their troubles. Suddenly it all seemed to fit together for Tim. The pieces he had been unable to match suddenly melted into one cohesive, glorious picture. He felt a joyous glow emerging from the dark spaces within him.

"Honey," he said smiling, "I owe you an apology. I owe God an apology and," he said, looking at the rear view mirror, "I owe all of you an apology too." He paused, trying to maintain his composure. "I finally see how Jesus has loved me all this time, helping me to care for these children, leading me to the camp, and showing me the love of a wonderful woman. Before, I was...was thinking He didn't care."

Mary reached over and squeezed his arm, but did not speak.

"Mary," he said, "How you came to love me, I'll never know. I'm so ashamed at how I acted toward the Lord."

"I think I fell in love with the man Jesus showed me you were going to become, but you didn't know," she smiled.

"I have a lot to learn, I know. Will God forgive me for doubting Him and speaking against Him?"

"Of course!" remarked Rachelle Myers from the back seat. "God forgives all who confess their sins and come to Him. He greets them with open arms. I think there would be few, if any, in heaven if our past sins counted against us. He accepted me and gave His forgiveness when I thought no one could. I am a new creature in Christ, and so are you."

"I went to Sunday school and my parents were very religious," said Tim. "We used to take turns reading the Bible after dinner."

"It has nothing to do with what you did or didn't do with your parents. This is a personal embracing of Jesus as your Lord and Savior. Let me ask you this, do you believe that Jesus Christ is the Son of God?" asked Rachelle.

"I do."

"Do you believe He died for your sins?"

"Yes, I do – I really do."

"Then pray with me, Tim," said Rachelle, "Father, I accept Your Son, Jesus Christ, as my personal savior. I believe He died for the remission of my sins. I accept Jesus into my life and ask for Your forgiveness of my sins in His name. Amen."

Tim repeated the words, meaning every one.

Rachelle leaned back and smiled, "You are a new man in Christ, do not let your old self rule you anymore, accept now the fact that you're a new creature in the Eyes of Christ."

Mary reached over and squeezed Tim's arm. "I can't tell you how happy you've made me," she smiled.

"I don't feel much different," confessed Tim. "I mean, I feel happy and relieved, but I feel like I'm still the same old jerk. Aren't we supposed to do this with water?"

"Water baptism is an important ceremony, but in and of itself, does not convey anything. It is the commitment of the mind and soul. The water is a ritual we use to show others and ourselves that commitment.

"What if I sin again? Am I not suppose to sin anymore?"

228

Rachelle laughed. "No, no – not by a long shot. You are going to sin everyday – I sin more times a day than I care to count. That's the point – Jesus doesn't count. Each day I ask for His forgiveness, and each day He is faithful to me, and to God's Word to forgive me."

Rachelle smiled, "Don't let your feelings trouble you. Different people come into Christianity in many different ways. Some start jumping around and dancing. I didn't do that. Others feel a quiet but deep confidence build within them. Still, with others, it takes a little while. I suppose they have a lot of stuff that has to empty out before they can be filled up with the new stuff of Christ. Be patient. In the right time you will rejoice, believe me."

Through all of this, Lorraine Eppinger remained silent, staring out the car window as it traveled through the dark. She was lost in her own battle.

They continued for the better part of an hour until Mary said, "Uh, Oh." She saw two sets of headlights coming toward them down the previously empty highway. As the approaching vehicles got closer, they began flashing their headlights.

"Goonies," said Mary quietly.

Tim asked the car for more speed, and though it came, it was sluggish. They watched the cars flash past them.

"Tim," said Mary with an anguished voice, "they're turning around."

Tim floored the accelerator, but the car did not respond; it was already giving everything it had.

Behind them, the trailing headlights began steadily gaining. Soon, they got so near their front bumper was almost touching them. They began flashing their lights. Tim searched for the gun he had laid down. Locating it, he glanced down to see if the chambers were full. He held the gun just below the side window, ready for whatever might happen.

Suddenly, the car behind them pulled out into the left lane

and accelerated. They began to gain on them until they pulled even.

Tim rolled down his window; grasped the gun and was prepared to fire.

The passenger window of the pursuing car rolled down and a hand came out along with a face yelling some words. What the words were, Tim couldn't hear, but the face he knew – Roy Kegler.

"It's your Dad, Mary – it's your Dad!" he yelled with relief.

Immediately, Tim took his foot off the accelerator and allowed the car to slow. He finally pulled to the side of the road. The two other cars did the same, and stopped. Mary jumped out and ran toward her father. Roy Kegler met her half way, embracing her.

"You've come home! Praise God, you're here!" he shouted.

Tim and the others followed Mary and, for a few minutes, the group did everything but dance on the highway.

Finally gaining his composure, Tim asked, "So how did you know it was us? Why are you out here away from the camp?"

"The Prophet," answered Roy Kegler.

Tim laughed, "I should have known."

"Yes, he came to me and said he saw you coming down this road and that we were to go out and bring you home. Good thing we did too, about five miles up ahead was a roadblock. Some Goonies had set it up – like they knew something was coming. We got rid of them quick, but I don't think we should hang around here long. Never know when they'll decide to come back with some friends."

With their two escorts in the lead, Tim pulled out and followed. The highway remained deserted for the next thirty miles as they neared the camp. He was never so happy to see the old sign and welcome lights of Ken Johnstone's country store. As they pulled in, Roy motioned for Tim to continue toward the rear of the store while the other cars hung back to make sure no one was following.

As Tim passed the store, they saw Johnstone greet them by holding up his prosthetic arm. Tim waved back, while the twins rolled down the rear window and yelled out a greeting. It felt wonderful to be back again, and he was certain both Rachelle and Lorraine would love the camp as much as he did.

He followed the makeshift trail, which ran from the back of the country store, down to the river embankment. Driving next to the river, he saw the water move in its quiet journey, quite different from the times he had seen the angry waters charge downstream after a storm. Suddenly he stopped the car, and turned to Rachelle.

"I think I would like to be baptized," Tim said quietly. "Can you do that that?"

Rachelle smiled. "Any Christian can baptize when necessary."

Tim got out of the car and walked slowly down the embankment to the quiet river. He didn't understand what was happening, but he felt a strange excitement deep within him. The realization that he was going to participate in an action shared by millions upon millions of Christians since Christ was born gave it a meaning and import far beyond that which he could explain.

Reaching the riverbank, he removed his shoes, stepped into the water, and waited for the others to meet up with him. Mary was the first to come to the river; she also removed her shoes and joined Tim, giving him a kiss. "I can't tell you how wonderful I feel right now," she said.

Rachelle, with her Bible in hand and her children at her side, joined Tim and Mary. For a moment, all stood silent then Rachelle smiled, "This is a wonderful moment, Tim. You will remember this time for the rest of your life, and celebrate it for all eternity in heaven."

"I can feel how right you are, Rachelle."

Rachelle expertly thumbed through her Bible, finally stopping in the book of Acts. "I think the story of the eunuch is an appropriate one. She began to read... *Now, the eunuch had accepted Christ as his Savior and wanted to be baptized. Philip was traveling with the eunuch and, as they traveled, they came upon some water, and the eunuch said. 'See, here is water. What hinders me from being baptized?'*

"*Then Philip said, 'If you believe with all your heart, you may.'*

"*The eunuch answered and said, 'I believe that Jesus Christ is the Son Of God.'*

"*He commanded the chariot to stand still. And both Philip and the eunuch went down into the water, and he baptized him.*"

Rachelle handed her Bible to Allison and put her hand on Tim's shoulder. "Tim, do you believe that Jesus Christ is the Son of God? Do you believe He came for the remissions of your sins? Do you accept Jesus as your personal Savior?"

"I do."

"Kneel down, Tim," instructed Rachelle. When he had, she, along with Mary, leaned Tim back until his whole head was under water.

"I baptize you in the name of the Father, the Son and the Holy Spirit."

Tim rose up, coughing. "I think I swallowed a lot of the holy water!" he said smiling, and coughed a couple more times.

"Well?" asked Mary. "How do you feel?"

Tim stood up, allowing the water to drain back into the river while he squeezed his hair to drain the water from it. Finally, he stood still for a moment, considering Mary's question. "I feel great – I mean that. I feel like I am fresh."

The small group made their way back to the vehicle, laughing with joy. They continued to laugh as they dragged their soaked bodies into it. At last, Tim drove back up the riverbank and through the gap between the hills to where lights from the village came into view.

Tim felt their wheels come on to the hard packed camp road called Forest Trail. A few minutes later, they pulled on to Grand Circle Drive, and stopped. A crowd of camp residents was there to greet them, alerted by Ken Johnstone's phone call. It took several minutes before they were given enough room to exit the car, only to be immediately surrounded again with handshakes and hugs, accompanied by surprised yelps as their friends embraced the soaked bodies. Someone started singing, and soon everyone joined. If there was anyone in camp trying to sleep, Tim was sure their homecoming wasn't looked upon with equal enthusiasm.

Soon the crowd moved the party to the Great House.

Tim put his arm around Mary. "It's wonderful to be home, Mary."

Mary smiled as she kissed him on the cheek.

"Welcome back," said a familiar voice from behind.

Turning they saw Major Charles Essex smiling at them.

"It's great to be back," smiled Mary.

"I understand a lot of changes are out there now. I'll want to talk to you about them when you get a chance," said the Major.

Inside the Great Hall, the party seemed to grow, not diminish. Someone began playing the piano and was joined by a guitar and finally by a bass player.

Betty Jo and Roy Kegler sat with Rachelle Myers and the twins. They encouraged Lorraine Eppinger to sit with them, but she declined, preferring one of the small tables against the wall. Tim and Mary joined the Keglers and joined in the singing.

Finally, Betty Jo leaned over, "Mary," she said. "The

233

Prophet told me that you were going to have a baby. Is that true?" Betty Jo's eyebrows rose, anticipating of the answer.

"Yes!" squealed Mary with a smile, "I was going to wait for a neat moment to tell you and Dad – isn't it wonderful?"

The two women hugged one another as the men shook hands.

"Always wanted to be a grandpa," said Roy Kegler smiling.

Tim shook his head. "That Prophet, he is really something," he smiled. "By the way, where is he?"

"Oh, he's been acting a little strange the past couple of days," said Roy Kegler. "In fact, both he and Stephanie have been mostly keeping to themselves. I see them going up to the gardens in the evening a lot. During the day, they just hang around their cabin. Frankly, I'm a bit concerned."

"Oh Roy," said his wife, "Now, there's nothing to be concerned about. They just need time alone – you know it hasn't been that long since they were married. I don't wanna hear no talk from you like I hear from some others. The Prophet and his wife just need some alone time, that's all."

Roy nodded, but Tim sensed maybe that wasn't the reason.

* * * * *

Stephanie lay on her back staring up at the stars that were peeking down upon them through the wispy clouds. Lately, the clouds over the mountain hadn't been as thick as usual – a clear sign things were indeed changing for the camp. No one had noticed it yet, except Andy… and Stephanie.

"Clouds are still thinning out, Andy," said Stephanie.

"It's time," replied Andy, lying down next to his wife.

"What about the other signs – the crops and the water? Are they signs that's it's soon, too?"

"Yes," replied Andy softly.

"I'll miss this place, Andy," said Stephanie wistfully.

Andy squeezed her hand gently.

"Will we remember this place, this time – will you remember me? Will you hold my hand again in heaven?" asked Stephanie.

Andy rolled onto his side and looked at his wife. "I will never forget you. Although heaven lasts a million years, I will always love you; and, I promise, I'll hold your hand."

"I guess it was foolish of me not to go down and greet her when they arrived," said Stephanie. "I just wasn't ready to see her. That sounds un-Christian, doesn't it?"

"It sounds human. She is not a bad person, you know. She is struggling in her walk with Christ. We should not hold her responsible for what Satan is leading her to do. She has been deceived, as we all have been, from time to time. In her mind, she'll be doing what's best for the camp, for the children."

"The children – what's she doing?"

"She's trying to save them. She is intent on saving their lives, this I know, and that's all I know.

"I love you too much to see you hurt," said Stephanie. She was silent a moment, then asked, "What's her last name?"

"I only know that her first name is Lorraine."

Stephanie got on her feet. "I think it's time I started acting like a responsible Christian. I'm ready to go down and greet her now – besides, I can't wait to see the twins again!" she smiled.

They made their way down from the garden to the cart, and then to the Great House, where they were greeted by smiling faces who had been celebrating the return of the group to camp. Some insisted on shaking Andy's hand, as though this joyous occasion was because of him. Andy knew that clearly it was not.

When finally they reached the building, the celebration seemed over. Andy suggested they make a special trip to see

Tim and Mary, and Stephanie enthusiastically agreed. A few minutes later, they pulled up to the cabin, and saw the young couple sitting on the front steps.

"Welcome back!" said Andy smiling. Stephanie jumped out, and ran over to the couple where hugs and handshakes were enthusiastically exchanged.

"We worried about you all the time, though we knew we shouldn't – God was with you every step of the way," said Stephanie, smiling.

"Yes, He was – He certainly was," agreed Tim. "I want to tell you that this experience has been so wonderful. I have been led back to Christ. I owe you an apology, sir."

"You owe me nothing," smiled Andy. "We all rejoice that you are again in love with Christ."

"And now," said Andy, "I suspect your Mother has asked you about the coming child!"

Mary laughed, "Yes, I don't know who's more excited she or us!"

"Prophet Andy," said Tim, his tone sounding suddenly serious, "We have a question to ask you."

"Okay. Shoot."

"We're very concerned about having a baby during these times. We wonder what will happen to the baby's soul if the end should come before the baby is born, or just after. We were going to come to you tomorrow to talk about it."

Andy nodded silently, "We live in tough times, and I wish I could tell you that what lies ahead is filled with wonderful days that any newborn would love. Let me bring up three things you might think about and see if maybe, they ease your minds."

Andy rested one hand on the railing of the cabin. "First, how big do you think a soul is?" he asked.

"Big?" asked Tim, and then looked at Mary. "I don't think it gets big. It just is."

"Yes, I agree. If your soul doesn't get bigger, then it was just the right size when you were born to get you into heaven. In other words, it doesn't grow as you get older. It's the same size for old people as babies – sorta like, 'One size fits all', whether in a womb or in a coffin," Andy smiled. "Trouble is, once we're born, life starts to fill our mind and body with all sorts of things it shouldn't until the soul gets covered up with a bunch of junk. And what we have to do is uncover it so we can be free to enter God's kingdom, and that's what Jesus helps us do."

"Now, the second question is: how much junk do you think is on top of a baby's soul?"

Mary smiled, "None. I don't think there's any."

"I agree. I think whatever is over its soul, Jesus brushes away without even being asked. I believe He died, not only for our sins, but for the sins of all souls, even those not born."

"Now, the final question: when do babies get their souls – their tickets to heaven?"

For a moment, the young couple looked at each other before Tim ventured as answer. "I suppose they get it when they are born."

Andy was silent for a moment before speaking. "Well, I have to disagree. I believe we can find the answer to that question by looking at Jesus. He came into this world as a child, just as we did. God knew Jesus before He was even born, before He was even in Mary's womb. He knew His name, His purpose and loved Him before He took the first breath. I believe Jesus' soul was His before He was physically born; if so, we received our soul before we were born. In fact, there are several places in the Bible that alludes to the fact that God knew individuals before they were born."

"So, I think my answer to your original question is this: if Jesus was given a soul before birth, then He gave us one too. Because Jesus was born as a human, lived as a human, died as a human and was brought into heaven with His divine soul to sit at the right hand of our Father. We should expect no less. Your baby, Mary, will sing the songs of angels, even if his earthly life ends before breathing even once, his eternal soul lives on. Those unborn souls do not bear the price of original sin are perfect. The souls of the unborn shall rejoice, as we all shall be united in our heavenly home, as promised so long ago."

*For mine enemies speak against me; and they that lay wait for
my soul take counsel together, Saying, God hath forsaken him;
persecute and take him; for there is none to deliver him.*
– Psalm 71:10-11

Chapter 22

"Harkins!" Lt. Col. Decker's voice came through the doorway. Why the Colonel didn't use the intercom was an amusing mystery to Sergeant Harkins and the others. Harkins got up from his desk and opened the door to the Colonel's office.

"Ah, there you are," said the Colonel sitting behind his desk. "I just got off the phone with Headquarters. They are giving out the word that General Powell has retired, which is probably a bunch of crap. However, the real news is that none other than Prefect Arthur Ramon is now heading the entire Southeastern Regional offices.

"Who?" asked Harkins.

"Ramon, surely you know his name."

Harkins thought a moment then shook his head. "I don't believe I do, sir."

"Ramon is the very first person to receive the full benefit of accepting the authority of the Ancestral Brothers!"

"Oh, now I remember. I think I saw him on television going up and being cured – he is the one who started dancing around on the stage."

"Exactly," said Colonel Decker. "Well, they made that goof-ball Prefect of this region – and he's going to come here for an inspection!" The Colonel was obviously distraught at the thought. "We aren't ready for an inspection, you know that Harkins! I haven't had time to whip this place into shape!"

Decker got up out of his chair and began pacing behind his

desk. "Get out a memo to all Commanding Officers – I mean all, even those pipsqueak Lieutenants. I want them all to hear my instructions to prepare for the Prefect's visit."

"When is he coming?"

"I don't know, but I know he will be coming. I do not believe for a second that General Powell retired on his own initiative; no sir – not for a second. He has been relieved of duty, probably even lost some of his pension, because of this area. Now I am here – you know, Harkins, I shouldn't be here. This is not my mess!"

"No sir."

"I got stuck here, I got dumped here!" said Decker as he began to pace again. "It's those Christians up on that mountain – that's the source of it all, you know. And now added to that is this crazy program Eppinger started about adopting Christian children under seven, not to mention making those Jesus Freaks workers and letting them walk around as free as you please. I know the Ancestral Brothers don't like it. I should have told Eppinger to get rid of them the first minute I set foot here! Well, I'm not going to let those programs give them a reason to take my pension away, no sir!"

"But they seem to be working so well, sir."

"That's not the point – that's NOT the point!" ranted Decker. "The Brothers don't like them – that's the point. Yes sir, that's the point." Decker stopped pacing, then swung around and pointed his finger at Sergeant Harkins. "Well, we'll do something about that right now. At least I can show the pipsqueak Prefect that we are making some progress here. Get me Major Zerski. He worked with Eppinger on that stupid adoption program; he is the perfect one to clean up both that and the Christian Worker mess up. I'm sure he's looking for a way to make a name for himself."

"Yes sir," replied Harkins as he exited the room. In the outer office, he immediately instructed one of his men to contact Zerski. Harkins then returned to the Colonel's office.

Decker had resumed his pacing, stopping now and then to look out his window. "Yes sir, the real problem is that Christian camp. Yes, that is the problem – it is what brought my predecessors down, but I am not going to let it bring me down, Harkins. No sir, not me." Decker leaned on his desk. "Yes, sir, a real problem – lot's of stories about what happened when Lt. Colonel Syme tried to assault the place."

"Yes, sir," said Harkins.

"You were there," remembered Decker, "What did happen?"

"Well sir, what I saw, and what's the official version, is quite different. I wouldn't want to contradict the printed version."

"Forget that, tell me what you saw. I assure you, Harkins, I will not be offended. I just want the truth so I can plan how to eliminate them. I do not want a repeat of the first debacle."

"Well sir, from my vantage point – and that was at the bottom of the mountain – I stayed with Lt. Colonel Syme, the events unfolded this way. The men went up in squads first, followed by the main force. At first there didn't seem to be any resistance and it looked like they were going to surprise the people at the camp."

"No gunfire?"

"No sir."

"Any lights or flares?"

"None. So, the advance parties got about half way up, and suddenly they started screaming – I could hear them all the way down at the bottom. Then we started getting radio traffic about tanks coming, and thousands of soldiers – a lot of them were saying they were outnumbered."

"What did you see?"

"Nothing. Not one thing."

"Nothing? Then what?"

"They started breaking ranks and running down the mountain. It was a rout, sir. Some of the Officers and Sergeants tried to get the men back, but it was no use. They were all running, and when they reached the bottom, I saw such fear in those men's faces like I had never seen before. I saw a few run, jump into the trucks, and hide in their beds. Can you imagine that? Sir, I know these men – they are good men. They are all battle tested in the Middle East; but, on that day, they were a pitiful group of soldiers."

"I hear the Lt. Colonel executed some Officers for dereliction of duty."

"Yes, sir, he had them shot that night. Then, the next morning, he ordered all the troops back in the trucks and we left."

"Amazing," said Decker.

Two crisp knocks came at the door. Harkins barked to enter, and Major Curt Zerski entered. Immediately the Major saluted the Lt. Colonel, "Sir. You sent for me?"

Decker came to the Major and shook his hand.

"Major," said Decker. "I've got a special job for you. I believe Prefect Ramon, who has assumed the duties of the Director of the Southeast Region, will be paying us a visit soon. By the way, are you familiar with him? His name is Arthur Ramon."

"I recognize the name, sir. I don't believe I've ever met him."

"Well, as I said, I believe he'll be coming here. I have not been informed of the time of his arrival, but I am sure he will arrive soon. When he does, he is going to be breathing fire. With the screw-ups of the last three Commanding Officers, I am sure he is not going to give us any leeway. We have to show him that we are ahead of the game."

"Yes sir, I agree," said Zerski.

"Now, I also want to eliminate the way Eppinger got these

Christians into the work camps – and that includes this stupid adoption program that he had you working."

"Yes sir, I never agreed with it."

"Of course you didn't; now, this is your chance to show the Prefect how much you didn't agree with it. I want both programs eliminated immediately after we take care of Cloud Mountain."

"Yes sir, of course."

"That's the spirit."

"Now by elimination," asked Zerski, "exactly what do you mean?"

"Just what the word means. I want the programs eliminated," said Decker. "I want every Christian associated with the program eliminated. I want every sniveling baby in the program eliminated." said Decker. Then, seeing the look on Zerski's face, Decker put his hand on his shoulder. "I know. This is a terrible business, but Major, let me put it another way; either they are eliminated, or you and I will be. Believe me Zerski, I know how these Brothers work, there's no middle ground."

"I understand," said Zerski. "You can count on me."

* * * * *

Sergeant Curt Evans walked to the vegetable garden by the lake. It was larger than the one up on the mountain where the Prophet had his garden. Lately though, it wasn't looking so good. Some said they had had too much rain, others said, not enough rain. Some said it needed more fertilizer, while others said that the fertilizer was killing the plants. No one seemed to know the answer, but the gardeners kept trying. At any time of the day, various groups of workers could be seen working in the gardens. The gardens were pressed to their limits. Not only were they were slowly failing, but also the population of the camp seemed always to be increasing. There was growing concern among the camp leaders, as well as the population in general, that soon they would not have enough to feed everyone.

The sun was setting as Evans picked out a hoe and made his way toward the back of the garden. Passing the corn, red peppers, and cabbage areas until he reached the cucumber patch, where he saw the three waiting for him: David Jones, Lorraine Eppinger, and David Leitz. All were leaning on their own hoes as he approached.

"Anybody pay any attention to you coming here?" asked Jones.

Sergeant Evans shook his head. "No, everyone's too busy doing their own thing." he said, then added, "I don't like this. I feel like a traitor."

"None of us likes it Curt, but it is what it is," replied Jones.

"So, what's the plan?" asked Curt.

Lorraine Eppinger looked around at the others. "I think you all agree the Prophet isn't up to the job anymore. I mean the stuff about dinosaurs and all. He's losing his grip on reality. I think God brought me here to protect these precious children here in camp, and that's exactly what I am going to do."

"I was there too," added David Jones. "He supports that Elmer fellow and his talk about dinosaurs being demons and stuff. It's just obvious the pressure has got to him, or he's just getting old. Plus, I heard he's now saying that everyone is going to heaven. And, I mean everyone."

"I hadn't heard that. You mean even the men who kill Christians?"

Jones shrugged his shoulders. "That's what he says."

"When did he say that – are you sure?" asked Sergeant Evans.

"I wasn't actually there either, but the people I heard it from are reliable."

"Who ever heard of a jerk theory like that?" scoffed Leitz.

"But, why do we have to get rid of him?" asked Jones. "Maybe he's going nuts. I have known Andy now for quite awhile, and he's a good decent man – wouldn't hurt a flea. We could just ask him to step aside and let others take over his responsibilities."

"My question is what will the others say? I can't imagine the rest of the camp telling the Prophet to sit down and shut up," said Leitz.

"Well now," began Evans, "I know the military. Remove the head and the body is yours. The Prophet is the head man here – once he's gone I think the place is ripe for a new leader to step forward."

"I've been thinking about that," said Jones. "All we have to do is sit back and wait for the right time. The Prophet is his own worst enemy. He keeps saying crazy stuff and soon everyone will begin having their own doubts. The problem is who will we put forward as the new leader?"

The group was silent for a moment, and then Eppinger spoke up. "Well, if it were my choice, I would say Sergeant Evans here would be the right choice. He's been here a long time, people respect him, and he's already in the army here."

The others mumbled their agreement.

"Maybe, but how much time do we have?" asked Leitz.

"From what I hear, not too much," said Evans. "The latest I hear is there are big things stirring with the troops in Asheville."

"Yes, my husband ended up being killed by some of those troops. That got me thinking about this. I have come to think he died so that I could come here and save these children. In a way, I think all these children are my babies. I am going to do whatever it takes to keep them safe. I can assure you, it is only a matter of time until they assault this location again. I understand the last time they attacked and failed; but whatever mistakes they made then, they will not make the same ones again. My husband was already making plans for additional troops and vehicles for the assault. The only chance to save the children, and the rest, is to negotiate."

"If that's the case, seems we need the Prophet more, not less. He's helped us keep safe thus far," ventured Dave Leitz.

"Believe me, Dave," said Lorraine Eppinger, "when they come again, it will be to wipe this place out. I've been living with the army for almost thirty years. That is exactly what they will do."

"She's right," chimed in Evans.

"Besides," said Jones, "the Prophet all along has been talking about the day they will come – he expects it. I don't think he plans on doing anything about it, either."

"Exactly," said Lorraine Eppinger. "But I think I have a suggestion for us to consider. It's one that will not only spare this camp, but assure the safety of the children and our safety too."

Sergeant Evans shook his head, "And that is?"

"Before he died, my husband started a Christian Workers Program," said Lorraine. Briefly she explained the program to the others concluding, "The Christians live in their assigned areas in complete peace and security. Everything that a normal city has, they provide," she said smiling. "Now, here is the great part for us: We already have our own community. We could go to them and propose that Camp Noah and the other small camps just become part of the program!" she concluded with excitement.

"I don't know," said Jones. "Would they really go for it? Even if they did, how do we know they would leave us alone? And, what would the Prophet say?"

"I've seen it work!" replied Lorraine. "We all would be given normal jobs – we could even begin to eat food we haven't had around here for awhile!"

"I don't know," mumbled Jones. "Why would they want to give us a break like that?"

"Because we have a bargaining chip which also solves our Prophet problem, too."

"What are you talking about?" asked Jones.

"We negotiate with them. We have something they want – the Prophet and his wife."

"What? You want us to give them the Prophet? Are you crazy?" exclaimed Jones.

"Wait a minute, let's just think about this for a minute" cautioned Leitz. "If we agree the Prophet is starting to lose it, then maybe he becomes valuable in another way. He might even agree to it himself, if he could look at it logically. Would he trade himself for the lives of thousands? I think he would."

"Another thing I think may be in our favor," added Eppinger. "I know the Commanding Officer. His name is Decker – I even had dinner with him and his wife. I think I could reason with him. I think this is a good solution for several problems."

"Why don't each of us search out some people we think might feel the same way? I don't mean we start making speeches, but maybe we'll find that some of our closest friends might just feel the same way about the Prophet as we do," suggested Jones.

"And his wife too," added Lorraine. "I think she's about as bossy a woman as I've ever seen. I think she has a Joan of Arc complex with her ordering our soldiers around. I would ask that we keep in mind the lives of the precious children. To me, that's what it is all about."

For a moment, the group was silent. Finally, Sergeant Evans broke the silence.

"Well, if we are going to do anything, it better be soon."

Chapter 23

Sergeant Harkins asked for a Humvee, but was told they were all out. In fact, the only vehicles left were M923 five-ton trucks. Harkins shook his head, and reluctantly signed the five-ton out. Trucks were in short supply since those crazy Jesus Freak soldiers had commandeered them in their flight out of the city. After a quick safety check, he drove out of the Motor Pool. It had been awhile since he had driven a 923, and he was embarrassed by more than a few grinding gears as he headed toward Asheville. He was nervous about this trip, which was not that unusual. He was always nervous when he knew his actions could see him shot.

As he drove into the downtown area, it was immediately obvious the quakes had their effect on the town. A number of the taller buildings were missing portions of their upper floors, or sections of walls. All of the rubble lay in mounds at their bases. It was also a safe bet the rubble would stay there long after the Elect had left this Earth. There simply were no longer people available or willing to clean up the mess.

Yet, despite the rubble, the town still showed activity. The streets were reasonably busy with cars and people walking about, although not nearly in the numbers they were before the Visitors came. Driving was more difficult, not because of the traffic, but because now many sections of the street had piles of bricks and garbage. Harkins easily found a parking space on Patton road, near the center of town. Parking such a big truck would have been a problem in the past, but now with so few vehicles on the road, the task was simple.

Leaving the truck, he began walking east to Biltmore; there he paused to casually look around and see if anyone was following. Satisfied, he turned north on Biltmore for two blocks until he arrived at a squat, two-story building sandwiched between two larger buildings.

The sign that hung above the display window read *Randy's Thrift Shop*. Below, in smaller letters, the sign read *Discovered Treasures*. As he approached the building, Harkins slowed his pace until it became an almost casual walk. Then, slowly turning for another check around, he opened the door and went inside.

The unlit interior was dark, as usual. Ransacked shelves lined the walls while display cases, most with broken glass, were almost empty. What treasures may have been held by the store, were long gone. There were only bits and pieces on the shelves, and empty cases on the floor. Once inside, Harkins turned around and watched to see if anyone outside was showing interest in his coming through the door. Satisfied his entrance had gone unnoticed, he searched the darkened interior for any sign of movement.

"You here?" he said in a loud voice, finally.

From the back of the store, he heard some movement followed by a voice. "Back here, Scott – I'm in the office."

Harkins made his way to the back of the store, carefully stepping over the broken glass as well as the worthless items strewn about the floor. Arriving at the back, he found the Reverend in a small office illuminated by a lantern on an old wooden desk.

"Hey, how are you?" greeted Reverend McDee, shaking his hand. "I got your message – I still check the website daily and look for that flat tire," he smiled, referring to the website established some time ago, and used by several as their means of communicating

Harkins shook his hand enthusiastically. "Time doesn't do you any harm, Reverend – you just get prettier as the days go by," he smiled.

"Now don't go trying to get me to put in a good word for you with the Lord, young man," smiled McDee."

Harkins smiled. It had become a common exchange between them. The Reverend was always trying to convert Harkins to the Christian path, but to no avail thus far.

"So, what's up?" asked Reverend McDee.

Harkin's face became serious. "We got a new Commander. His name is Decker and he is determined to see an end to your camp – and I mean soon. Then, as soon as he wipes the camp out, he's going after all the Christian workers that Eppinger set up."

McDee was silent for a few moments. "Bad times just seem to get worse; but it's expected. I have been talking to the Prophet and he told me much the same thing. It was going to happen sooner or later – and I guess this is more sooner than later," smiled McDee.

"Yes, now the one you call, the Prophet – the Colonel has heard of him, and he's after him most of all. I think getting him would be a real feather in his cap to the Ancestral Brothers." Harkins leaned back out of the doorway so he could see the front of the store. Satisfied no one was coming, he continued. "So, what are you going to do?"

"I suppose it seems strange to you, but I don't think we'll do much at all – oh, I'm sure we'll have some prayer sessions going – more than usual. You see, young man, we have always known this day was coming. Now it is here. The real question is – what are you going to do?"

"You mean – am I going to become a Christian? Oh, Reverend McDee, I guess I am just not into that – you know, not my thing. Still, I can't stand by and see you all treated like this. It's not right."

"You've been a great help to us, Scott. I want you to know we all appreciate it. I think this might be the last time we'll meet, so I'm going to ask you one last time: come, give yourself to Jesus."

"Thanks, but I…"

Suddenly McDee held up his hand for silence. Quietly, Harkins turned and peered into the store. Four men were inside the store, standing near the front door. They appeared to be listening also.

Harkins carefully unbuttoned his sidearm, but did not remove it. He motioned to McDee that the men were there as he mouthed the word, 'Goonies'. McDee nodded while pointing to a door at the back of the office and motioned Harkins to follow. Carefully and slowly, McDee put one foot in front of the other, making his way toward the outside door. Harkins waited until the preacher had successfully opened the door then, taking one last peek toward the front of the store, slowly followed the Reverend.

He only made a couple steps, when something on the floor caught his foot, and he went crashing down. He jumped up immediately. He could hear shouts and running footsteps approaching. Dashing through the door, he found himself on a small, elevated loading platform. He attempted to bar the door, but was unable to do so. He leaped to the alleyway and began chasing after the Reverend, who was attempting to run, but without much success.

Behind, he heard the men burst through the door. Immediately he dropped to one knee and grabbed his forty-five sidearm.

Before their pursuers could aim their weapons, Harkins began firing.

The first Goonie never knew what hit him, while the next two, though firing their weapons in return, did not get a second shot, as they dropped off the loading dock onto the alleyway and lay inert.

Harkins jumped to his feet. As he turned, he saw Reverend McDee standing about fifteen feet away from him looking at his shoulder where a red circle was beginning to spread. He looked up at Harkins with an expression of astonishment.

Harkins arrived just in time to grab him as the Minister began to sink to the ground. Gently he lowered the Reverend to sit on the alley asphalt.

"Go on," said McDee. "Don't worry about me, son."

"Think you could make it over to those steps?" asked Harkins, referring to three steps leading to the back door of another store.

McDee nodded. The two stumbled over and Harkins set McDee on the bottom step. Leaning back, McDee said, "Now, you go. I'm just fine."

"Oh, I don't think so. Listen, you rest here, I'm gonna run and get the truck."

McDee nodded weakly.

"Now, don't go running off with any young ladies," smiled Harkins.

"I will if they're prettier than you," replied the Reverend, punctuated with a cough.

Harkins was about to run when he noticed his uniform jacket was soaked with the Reverend's blood. Taking off his blood soaked jacket, he threw it down and began running. He raced up Biltmore, back to Patton and finally, to the truck. He did not hesitate in getting the big rig started and out on the street. A couple of turns and he drove down the alley until he saw McDee still leaning against the steps. The Reverend, seeing him too, gave a little wave.

It didn't take long for Harkins to install the Reverend in the passenger's seat after making a makeshift bandage by ripping off parts of his discarded jacket. Finally, he got in the truck himself, and made their way out onto Patton Street, then turned on Biltmore.

"Where we going?" asked the Reverend, his voice betraying weakness.

It was a good question – just where was he going? He hadn't thought about it, really. Up 'til now the only concern he had was getting the Reverend out of the city. Now that Harkins thought about it, there was only one place he could take him – Cloud Mountain.

"I'm taking you home."

"To the camp? What if they see you go there?"

"We'll cross that bridge when we get there. I want you to lay back here and try to rest."

Reverend McDee smiled, "Yes, Mother," he said with a feeble grin.

The highway was mainly deserted, as usual. Turning on to Highway 215, he could see Cloud Mountain in the distance. The clouds over the top were not as thick as he remembered them when he was here with Lt Col. Syme, during his ill-fated attempt to capture the village on top.

As they rounded a curve in the road, he saw two pickups on the road. One truck was on either side, allowing only enough room for a single vehicle to pass. Two men with rifles stood by the vehicles. Goonies.

"What's up?" asked McDee, struggling to open his eyes as he felt the truck slow.

"Roadblock, don't worry, I can handle it," replied Harkins.

Slowly the military truck approached the two, armed men and stopped next to them.

"Army, eh?" ventured the one Goonie next to the driver's door.

"Yep," replied Harkins producing his military ID.

After a cursory look, he stepped back, motioned the truck through, and saluted as it passed him.

"The idiot saluted me, Reverend," said Harkins as they left them behind.

"I think he was saluting me," smiled McDee weakly as he began coughing and did not stop for a minute or two.

"You're sounding worse," stated Harkins.

McDee nodded, but did not reply. Within a few minutes,

Harkins saw the road that led to the camp. He remembered it from standing at it with Syme. It looked different in the daylight; in fact, he almost passed it because of the overgrown weeds. He turned onto the road and began driving slowly up the side of the hill. He had not gone more than a hundred yards when two pickups came over the ridge at a high rate of speed. Standing in the back of the first truck was an individual manning a fifty caliber machine gun. In the second truck were two other men holding AK 47s.

Harkins brought the truck to a halt. Opening the door, he stepped down and raised his hands above his head. In response, three men jumped to the ground as soon as their pickups stopped, and approached him warily. The lead man was dressed in a well-worn army uniform.

"Who are you and what d'ya want?" barked Essex at Harkins.

"Harkins is my name – Sergeant Harkins U.S. Army. I brought you one of your own, Reverend McDee. He's been shot and needs some medical attention, immediately."

"Watch him," the leader snapped at the others as he rushed to the passenger side of the truck.

"It is Reverend McDee!" shouted Essex back to the others. "He says this guy is alright. We gotta hurry." Then, motioning Harkins back into the truck, Essex climbed on the running board, and instructed Harkins to follow the two pickups.

The three-vehicle convoy started down the incline into the camp. Harkins was surprised at the size of the village. The camp was larger than he thought, and there seemed to be quite a few people everywhere.

The two pickups turned into a large parking area; however, Essex directed Harkins to continue driving until they arrived at a small building bordering Circle Drive.

Waiting for them were several people, already alerted, who immediately helped bring the unconscious Minister into the building. Inside, there was a small clinic. They passed through the waiting room to one of two examination rooms. They laid Reverend McDee on a table. He was immediately attended by those in charge.

"If you both would wait in the other room, I would appreciate it," said one of the men attending the Minister. "Just for your information, this isn't as serious as it looks. Sometimes this type of wound gets rid of a lot of blood, but heals pretty quickly; just thought you'd like to know."

Both Harkins and Essex thanked the doctor and left for the front office to wait. In the waiting room, each took a seat at opposite ends of the rectangular room. After several minutes, Essex spoke up.

"So, exactly who are you and how do you come to know the Reverend?"

* * * * *

"Harkins!" shouted Lt. Col. Decker.

The soldiers in the office looked at one another, as if one were going to volunteer. At that moment, the outer office door opened and Major Zerski entered.

"Is he in?" asked Zerski.

"Yes, sir," answered Sgt. Ingram. "Sir, may I ask if you've heard about Sgt Harkins?"

"What do you mean?"

"About the fact that he has disappeared, and why."

"Disappeared? Harkins? What are you talking about?"

"Well sir, we were wondering if you would tell the Colonel what we have learned."

"Which is?"

Ingram glanced at the two men. "Well, the report is that he took a five-ton from the motor pool and went into town to meet with some Jesus Freak."

"What? Do you know what you're saying?" challenged Zerski.

"Yes sir, we wouldn't tell you this unless we already had confirmation. I heard it directly from MP investigations. They asked us to inform Colonel Decker, and we were hoping you might do that. I think he would take it better coming from an Officer."

"What else have you heard that's been confirmed – don't tell me any rumors. I want facts," snarled Zerski. Then, in a low voice, as if meant only for himself said, "Harkins – I can't believe it. He seemed such a by-the-book guy."

"Yes sir, we were shocked too. What I have told you are the only facts we know. " Again, the Sergeants exchanged glances. "Well sir, we were wondering if you would tell the Colonel what we have learned."

An astute smile played on Zerski's face. "I get it, afraid to tell him? Very well, I'll inform the Colonel," said Zerski, and then paused. "Well, go ahead, might as well tell me any rumors, too."

"Yes sir, they say he went out to that camp where that so-called Prophet is, and he might be there now."

"Unbelievable," said Zerski, shaking his head as he turned and approached Decker's office door. Knocking twice first, he went through the double doors. Zerski found the Colonel looking at a wall map of the area. Outlined on the map was an area around Cloud Mountain.

"Hi Curt," said Decker. "Say, when you came through the office, did you see Sergeant Harkins out there?"

"Well sir, that's one of the things I want to talk to you about. The men in the office were going to tell you, but I think they were a little tentative about it – seems Harkins is gone. Rumor has it, he's turned into one those Jesus Freaks."

"What! Harkins?"

"Yes sir, that's what it looks like." Briefly, Zerski relayed the information regarding Harkins taking the truck.

"I don't believe it," said Decker quietly. "No, I don't believe it. I know Harkins pretty well, and I don't believe it." Decker sat down in his chair. "So, where is he now?"

"I don't think they know for sure, although there's a report that he might be at that camp on Cloud Mountain with the one they call the Prophet."

"Just doesn't make sense," said Decker. He was silent for a moment, and then he slammed his fist on top of the desk. "We've got to get rid of every last one on top of that filthy mountain! They are seducing our finest men! They're a cancer and the sooner we get rid of it, the better!"

"Yes sir, I agree," echoed Zerski, "The sooner the better."

"When we get into that camp I want special attention paid to getting Harkins alive. I want to make an example of him to the other men. First, he deserts his command, and then he joins up with the Jesus Freaks. If I could have him executed twice, I would – in fact, maybe I will anyway," thundered Decker.

Jumping up from his chair, Decker went to the map on the wall, slamming his open hand over the area where Camp Noah was.

"I want this place obliterated! I do not want anyone but Harkins coming out of there alive! I want everyone there executed. I want every structure burned to the ground, and then the remains of both bulldozed into the soil! Do I make myself clear, Major?"

"Yes sir!"

And he shall send his angels with a great sound of a trumpet, and they shall gather together his elect from the four winds, from one end of heaven to the other.

– Matthew 24:31

Chapter 24

The early shift for breakfast was in full swing with only a few empty seats in the large dining room. The air was alive with hundreds of conversations.

As Stephanie entered the room, she began searching tables for the face she knew was there. She was so intent in her search that, at first, she did not hear her name called.

"Hey, Stephanie – over here," came the voice a second time.

This time she followed the voice to the smiling face of Reverend McDee. Quickly, she made her way over, gave him a partial hug while being careful to spare his wounded shoulder, now in a sling.

"So, how is the shoulder doing?" she asked.

"Oh, me – I'm doing great. That young man got me to the witchdoctors just in time. I only had to spend a day in there. I'm a little weak, from losing so much blood, but other than that, I'm fit as a fiddle. How about you? Haven't seen you or the Prophet around here lately. Are you hiding out?" he smiled.

"No, just getting in some alone time, that's all."

Reverend McDee looked around first to see if there were any interested ears, and then leaned closer to Stephanie. "There's some crazy talk going around I'd like to speak with you about," he said.

"Can you walk alright?"

"There is nothing wrong with my legs that youth wouldn't cure."

"Well good, maybe later you could come over to our cabin. I think Andy would like to talk with you, too," Stephanie said. "If you excuse me right now, I have to find someone. Why don't you come over tonight, if you've nothing to do?"

"I'll be there," smiled Reverend McDee. "Make sure the coffee is on."

Stephanie smiled while patting the Reverend on his good shoulder. "I will," she said before walking away, again searching for the face.

Finally, she saw her sitting at a small table against the far wall. Lorraine Eppinger was eating alone. Slowly, Stephanie made her way over while framing out what she wanted to say. If Andy knew she was doing this, he would be more than a little upset.

At last, she stood silently beside the table looking down at Eppinger who, at first, didn't realize her presence. When she did, she was a little startled. "Yes?" she said, almost timidly.

"Good morning," replied Stephanie. "May I sit with you a moment?"

"Uh, why certainly."

Stephanie sat down and, for a moment, both women silently looked at each other. Finally, Stephanie asked, "So, what do you think of our camp?"

"I like it. I think there are a lot of wonderful people here who have made me feel at home, especially the children. My husband and I always wanted children, and now at the Care Center, I have over a hundred that I can devote every day caring for."

Stephanie nodded. "That's wonderful. I am happy you've found some peace. Have you met my husband yet?"

"No, but I'm looking forward to it – in fact, I received a message this morning saying he wants to meet me by the lake this morning. I guess he does that with everyone, right?"

"Yes, Andy has always wanted to spend some alone time

with all new arrivals."

The conversation died for an uncomfortable moment before Stephanie spoke again. "Don't do anything to hurt my husband, Mrs. Eppinger. A lot of good people live here, and raise children here. They look to Andy to lead them. Don't do anything to hurt him," said Stephanie. The tone of her voice carried an edge with it emphasizing the weight of her request.

"I would not do that, I assure you," answered Eppinger a little startled. "I will do everything I can to make sure the families of this camp are safe, especially the children. I lost my husband; I know what it feels like to lose a member of your family."

Stephanie stood up, trying to feel comforted by Eppinger's assurances. However, she was not. What was to be would be – that's what Andy would say. It was just that Stephanie needed to confront this woman, who would kill her husband, and yet she wasn't able to say all she knew.

For a moment, she stared at Eppinger. She could kill the woman, but that was not the answer. If it wasn't this woman, it would be someone else. This had to take place. She knew it, and Andy knew it. Without saying goodbye, Stephanie slowly turned and walked to the door, feeling she had failed, and yet knowing it was for the best that she had.

Lorraine Eppinger watched Rachelle leave. She was more than ever convinced this woman was dangerous. Although she had only been there a few days, it was clear to her what was happening. Perhaps it was because she was so new to the camp that she was able to see this so clearly. Andy Moore was a danger to these people. Clearly, he did not realize what the Brothers would do. She did. She had seen it take place; they would show no mercy. All in camp were in mortal danger, especially the children. Yet, this so-called Prophet was doing nothing to save them. She was convinced he was trying to turn this place from a Christian retreat into a personal cult. Perhaps he had a martyr complex. Could she stand by and let all these wonderful people, and their children, perish because of one egomaniac? If there ever was going to be a false prophet, this Andy fellow could well be the one. Moreover, she wasn't the only one who saw this about Andy Moore – there were others. Perhaps, she thought, God had sent her here for this very reason. Maybe her husband did have to die so that she could come here, and save these wonderful people, and their precious children.

It was becoming plain to her that the Lord no longer favored this camp. There was clear evidence God was removing His protection from the mountain: the waters were becoming too warm for the fish to live. In fact, she had seen teams of men scooping up the dead fish floating on the surface of the lake, and then they buried them on the far shore. The streams were beginning to dry up – they all could see this. These very streams were providing the camp electricity. Several steps had already been taken to reduce the electric consumption, including no streetlights at night. Furthermore, she heard the man, who was in charge of camp agriculture say the crops in the two gardens were beginning to fail.

If this kept up, soon there would be no fish or crops to feed them, and no electricity. God was clearly angry with this Andy fellow. Did this Andy Moore character expect them all to simply wait here until there was nothing for the children to eat or drink? On the other hand, did he expect them to wait here until the soldiers came and killed them all?

Lorraine couldn't finish her breakfast, instead she made her way outside. Though she was supposed to meet the Prophet down by the lake docks, she considered not going at all. She was too upset to treat him nicely; however, after giving an exasperated sigh, she began walking toward the lake. Whatever plans might develop in the future, best she not give any hint now as to her attitude. There was plenty of time for that later.

Perhaps, she could meet with the people again who felt as she did, and they could come up with some course of action to save this camp and the people in it.

Today was warmer than the past few days and Lorraine's walk down to the water was a pleasant one – as long as she didn't run into that Stephanie woman again. The warm sun and a pleasant breeze softened her mood. It was hard to be angry on such a nice day. By the time she arrived at the lake, her demeanor had changed, and she felt almost happy.

She saw him sitting on one of the benches facing the lake. For an instant, she felt hesitant, but quickly dismissed it. She could stand up to anything he said, she was sure of it.

There were three boats out on the lake and the figures inside them appeared to be fishing – but probably not successfully. She saw the Prophet reach down, now and then, and throw a stone out on the water. Occasionally, one of the stones would skip a time or two before diving below the surface.

Lorraine came around the bench and greeted Andy. "Hi," she said pleasantly. "I'm Lorraine Eppinger, it's nice to meet you at last," she said with a smile.

Andy stood up and shook her hand while returning her smile. He motioned for Lorraine to take a seat beside him "Yes, thank you for coming," he said as he dropped the few stones left in his hand. "I'm trying to teach myself how to skip these things. There must be a trick to it that I'm not getting," he said, wiping his hands on his jeans.

"I used to be able to do that when I was a kid," replied Lorraine.

Andy smiled, letting the silence hang heavy for a moment before resuming.

"I want to tell you how sorry I was to learn that your husband was killed," he said.

Lorraine nodded. "Thank you."

"I know it concerns you that he died before you were able to talk to him about being a Christian; and that weighs heavy upon your heart. Am I right?"

Lorraine nodded, somewhat taken back, but did not speak.

"Well, I want to take this opportunity to talk to you about that. I'm going to tell you something, with which a lot of people don't agree." Andy paused before continuing. He could see the woman's eyes were not filled with kindness. There was some distrust there, perhaps even resentment. "Lorraine, I believe your husband will rejoice with you in heaven."

Lorraine's eyebrows crawled together. "That can't be, it says so in the Bible."

"Does it?"

"Yes, it does. It says unless you believe Jesus was your Savior before you die, well, then you go to hell."

Andy nodded slowly. But, it also says, 'For God sent not his Son into the world to condemn the world; but that the world through Him might be saved.' In addition, in Second Peter it says, 'The Lord is not slack concerning His promise, and not willing that any should perish, but that all should come to repentance.' It also says He has chosen His people 'from before the foundation of the world'."

"Well, yes, but it also says that unless you are born again, you will go to hell."

"But Lorraine, if I accept that as the final end, then I must also accept the implication that God chose some people, before the foundation of the world, to go to hell. Because, I believe you are saying, only those who, while they are alive upon the Earth, and give their souls to Christ, will be saved."

"Of course I do, and so should you, if you are a true Christian," answered Eppinger defiantly.

"Well, let's say you are right. That means, I think, that Jesus is running a giant lottery of salvation. I would have to be lucky: lucky enough to have met someone who told me about

Jesus; or perhaps, lucky to be raised by parents who showed me the way; or lucky to be born in a location where Christianity was known, or lucky to be born at a time in history when there was knowledge of Christ – if I'm that lucky then, I have a chance to know, and accept, Jesus as my personal Savior."

"Well, you make it sound bad, but I don't think it is."

"What about all the people who lived in the South Pacific, or Asia, or the Arctic Circle, or the Americas – or anywhere else – that died before Yahweh was even known by them? Or perhaps died before ever hearing the name of Jesus in their entire life, regardless of when or where they were born? What happens to their souls? Were they just unlucky?"

"All I know is if you don't accept Jesus, you are destined for hell."

"I agree with that. The question is: when is that allowed to happen? If it must occur before we die, who wins this great contest between good and evil? It is obvious that only a fortunate portion of the people, who have ever lived, have accepted Christ. If, when it is all over, and we line up and count the souls garnered by each, how do you think God would fare? Personally, I think God could show His millions and millions, but Lucifer could show his billions and billions. By any measure, it would appear Lucifer had won, don't you agree?"

"Why are you asking me all these stupid questions?" snapped Eppinger.

"Because I want to show you something I believe," answered Andy. "I want you to see the greatness of God's mercy, of His plan, of His victory. Now I admit, not many people believe as I do – that I grant you. Moreover, if you choose not to be persuaded, how could I hold you at fault? For in the end, only God knows the truth. But just give me a chance and then see if it rests well with your soul."

Andy got up from the bench, and looked out over the waters for a moment before slowly turning back to Eppinger.

"Scripture says He knew my name before I was even born. He knew me personally. He loved me as an individual before I was even born. It also says He wants everyone to have life and not perish with death. It has been my experience, and my belief, that whatever God wants, He gets – sooner, or later. He is God. He neither bends nor bows to anyone else's desires, which are not in the best interest of His beloved creations. We are the brothers and sisters of Christ, whether we like it or not. One has to come to that conclusion, if you believe the Bible, which I do. God sent Jesus, His only Son, our earthly brother, and personal, Heavenly Savior to rescue us. If I were to accept that death is the end of the Salvation line, then I would have to accept the conclusion that Christ failed – in fact, that God failed. Because God did not rescue all His children whose names he knew and treasured; nor did Christ. No, not by a long shot. In fact, of all that were born, only a few were rescued. But, I don't believe that will be the case."

"What's this got to do with my husband?"

"I believe, from what I have been told, that your husband was not a Christian. Is that right?"

Eppinger hesitated. She felt her face flush and pent up tears rushing to escape. She shook her head, forcing her emotions back. "So?" she said with some defiance.

"So, I believe your husband, along with all unsaved souls will be given a last opportunity to accept or reject Jesus."

"That's crazy. There is no 'second chance', every Christian knows that – every true Christian."

"Oh, I think God is a big believer in Second Chances. I screw up all the time, I get second, third and fourth chances every day of my life, and Christ says 'that's okay, I understand, I still love you'."

Eppinger got up from the bench. "I was taught that we

265

should accept Christ when we are alive in order to go to heaven. I think the overwhelming number of Christians – and Christian leaders, believe that also. I don't know why some didn't accept Christ or why they couldn't – all I know is that they didn't, and therefore they are going to spend eternity in hell."

Andy nodded. "Yes, many people believe just as you do – in fact, I would say the majority of Christians have been taught this and accept it as part of their faith. The religion they practice doesn't really deal with all the dead souls. Most of the sermons are about how we should live our lives as Christians, or why we should save all the people we can before they or we die. And, if they aren't saved, hell awaits those souls – we call them, lost souls, don't we?"

"And they are," said Lorraine, with an edge to her voice.

"Are they? I think there is something else we should consider. In Revelations, we are told that before the gates of the New Jerusalem are closed, locking all others out, there is a period of one thousand years in which Satan, the devil, is bound. In other words, we have a thousand years of peace and an absence of temptation and evil ways. A thousand years, that is a long time. Why is it necessary for the thousand years? What is the point? The souls of the saved are abiding in the New Jerusalem, their salvation assured. Christ knows that, and Satan knows that. These souls are no longer up for grabs. They already belong to Jesus, forever."

"Look Andy, I think this is all nice and everything, but I really don't feel like discussing this. There is no point. The Bible says what the Bible says and anything else isn't right to discuss."

Lorraine stood up as though to leave.

"I am asking these questions because I hope you will possibly find some truth in what I'm saying. If you do not, so be it. You can label me a nut."

Lorraine smiled, "You know, some already do."

Andy smiled. "Yes, I know – and from time to time, they include my wife."

Lorraine sat down. "Okay, what else do you want to say? Andy, I really don't want to spend any more time on this."

"Fair enough," he answered. "I will give you the short version. I believe that the final score in this contest for the souls of man will be: Satan: 0, and God: Everyone."

"You're saying that no one goes to hell?"

"Well, it won't be exactly zero because there are some, such as Satan and the False Prophet – perhaps there will even be some who still refuse God. However, I do not think any of God's created people will be in hell. They were created with heavenly souls, in susceptible bodies, and deceived by Satan. It is Satan's sin, not theirs. To believe otherwise, I would have to be convinced that I, a mere mortal, went into battle, toe to toe, with the second most powerful creature in the entire creation of heaven and Earth. And, that God expected me to win. Do I believe that human beings with all their weaknesses could out maneuver, out think, the second most powerful creature in all of heaven and Earth? A creature so influential, he is able to deceive and subjugate even the angels?" Andy paused for a moment, before continuing. "No, I don't believe that. We were, and are, sitting ducks. We were sent to lure Lucifer, who is Satan, into breaking his covenant with God, and thereby condemning himself to hell. We were sent here to acquire and teach Faith to each other and to the angels. The Law has failed, as God knew it would, and Faith is our doorway to eternity. However, Satan has held our souls in bondage from the beginning with Adam and Eve's sin. The souls of those who Satan has lured away are held captive against Satan being sent forthwith to hell. Because if God executes his sentence upon Satan, then He must also execute it upon His beloved children, for the law is the law.

"But, we have a 'get-out-of-jail' card free. We have Jesus Christ. He has been given the authority obtain our forgiveness. And I believe God's love, through His Son, is so intense that He will not allow Lucifer to capture our innocent souls, which are upon this Earth, without a clue, until it is too late for many."

"How can you say that? I'm not a theologian but I'm not aware of anyone I know who believes that. Is this what you are trying to get the camp to believe?"

"I'm stating what I believe and nothing more."

"So, you're saying my husband, though he wasn't a Christian, is going to be in heaven? That is a wonderful thought, and I wish it were true. But I think it is a deception away from the truth."

"I'm saying, through the mercy of Jesus Christ, and the Will of our God, he will get a second opportunity, as will all unsaved humanity, to accept or reject Christ. Only this time, he will make the choice in full knowledge of the truth, which is, Christ. It will not be an easy choice, for Satan is the master of deception. He has already deceived or kept the truth from these people in the past, and there is every chance that he can do it again after the thousand years. How long after the thousand years will Satan have to persecute, deceive, and mislead all the people outside the new City of Jerusalem, I don't know. They will have come to know the power and authority that comes with faith in Christ, yet the deceptions of Satan are many and powerful. Even though accepting salvation in this time will be many times more difficult than it would have been originally, they will continue, in faith, to believe. For, if these new brothers and sisters of Christ are able to resist the deceptions of Satan, the city's gates shall open for them. Remember, it is not by logic, but by faith that we come to Christ. Faith is the key to Heaven's door, which is Jesus. It is through this door of faith, after the millennium, which I believe your husband will come."

268

For a moment it was silent as each looked at the other. Then Lorraine spoke. "I wish what you're saying was true, I truly do, but it isn't. The only thing I can do now is try to save as many innocent people, and especially the children, from the same fate as my husband. That means doing all I can to protect and provide for them." Eppinger stood up, "No, Andy. I have heard enough. I loved my husband more than you could ever imagine, but I've been told what the Bible says, and it doesn't say he will ever be in heaven." Lorraine stood up and glared at Andy "Is this why you dragged me out here; to torture me with fantasies about seeing my husband again?" Eppinger's voice rose until she was nearly shouting.

"I thought you might be comforted."

"Some say you are losing it. Do you know that?"

"I do." replied Andy. "And, you are among them," replied Andy, with a soft tone. "We all have our role to play in these last days. I just wanted you to know that I believe great joy awaits you in God's kingdom."

Lorraine took a deep breath. "I know that you are trying to comfort me, and I appreciate that, I do; however, I believe you are stepping outside of God's Word. I haven't been around here long, I understand that, and perhaps that's why I can see more clearly than others how you've drifted from God's Word. You are creating your own word, Andy. And, in all honesty, I must say, I think God will spill His anger out upon you, and in so doing, may cause many in camp to suffer."

"I understand, Lorraine. You must do what you must do."

Lorraine stood still for a second examining Andy, then without a word turned and began walking back to the Great House.

Andy watched her go. It was done. It would not be long now.

Chapter 25

Without benefit of streetlights, it was a dark walk to the Prophet's cabin. Even when they were kept on, it was a dark walk – but now, Reverend McDee had to be doubly careful he did not stumble. It was a little sad walking at night. The cabins used to have their lights on, looking like bright snakes, bordering the many twisting streets and paths. It had always struck him as being cheery, and full of life. In fact, he had occasionally climbed to the upper gardens to look down on the village at night. It was a beautiful sight – but now, it was mostly dark.

Eventually, arriving at Prophet Andy's cabin, McDee knocked, and almost immediately, Stephanie opened the door and invited him in with a smile. Andy was at the kitchen table eating a bowl of something McDee could not identify. Seeing the bowl, McDee raised his eyebrows and smiled.

Andy saw him and grumbled, "God loves fat angels, too."

"I certainly hope so," responded Reverend McDee rubbing his own belly.

"So," said Andy motioning for McDee to have a seat at the table, "what's on your mind?"

Reverend McDee sat down as Stephanie brought him a cup of coffee. Thanking her, he took a welcome sip, as much to buy time as to taste the brew.

"There's some talk around camp, Andy," began McDee.

"Yes, I know," answered Andy, pushing his bowl away.

"They're saying maybe you've strayed away from the purpose of the camp. You know, maybe trying to write your own rules instead of sticking to what God wants."

"What do you think?"

"Me? What do I know? I'm just an old country preacher that some say should'a been put out to pasture a long time ago." McDee, allowed a small smile, "but I think they're nuts. Now, that's what I think."

Andy laughed softly, glancing at his wife, who smiled back. "Well, maybe not nuts. Maybe they are just a little scared. You know things are not going well with the camp lately. The crops in both the upper and lower gardens are looking like they might fail this year. Fishing is terrible, certainly nowhere near the quantity we used to get – and the weather, it's getting colder. I suppose it is only natural they look around for somebody to hold responsible. So they are looking at me – well, I expect that, since I have been saying some stuff lately that they probably never heard before. But it's just stuff I need to get off my chest before it's too late."

"What stuff? And what do you mean 'too late'."

"Well, Reverend, I think the time grows short. Actually, we should be jumping up and down with joy. But, here we are fighting and fuming trying to hang on, not willing to see the signs of the times, or the clues of the day." Andy smiled, leaning back in his chair. "But let me ask you a favor; council them not to punish those who persecute me in the days ahead. We are all subject to the deceptions of Satan, and some are more vulnerable than others. Even those who call Christ their Lord are able to be deceived. They think they do God's work, but it is the Devil's tools they use. They are deceived. Ask them to be merciful."

"You're talking about all the stuff that's going on about this camp?"

Andy nodded. "I think we all see it; but some just ignore it, hoping it'll go away; others see it and look for ways to change it; but then some do see the joy in it."

"So, you're saying the end is coming soon."

Andy smiled. "I believe so, Reverend. I believe so."

"It's said that no man knows the hour or the day," responded McDee.

271

"That's very true, and neither do I; however, that doesn't mean we can't see the signs of the time as foretold to us all those many years ago. For instance, there was a spot on the news a day or so ago that said the last piece of the pyramids was not going to be in the Antarctic, after all. That in order to secure a lasting peace in the Middle East, Abdon was going to author a peace treaty and that he would enforce it by locating the last pyramid piece in the Mediterranean Sea. Now, is that plain enough for us? Can you beat that? Yet, the outside world applauds this announcement and heralds it as another step in their journey to Never-Never Land, and Utopia."

"That's true," said McDee.

"No, as I said, I don't know when, I just have this certain feeling we are near – I mean, very soon."

Reverend McDee smiled. "I hope you're right, Andy. When I was a young man and first heard about the End Times, I thought it would be neat to be there when it happened. I mean I was sorta envious of the apostles: them being there, seeing Him, walking and talking with Jesus – how wonderful that must have been. I hoped maybe I could be at the end, and see Him coming. The thought now, that it may be very near, excites these old bones. For these thousands of years so many have read about the end, that it is the doorway back to our heavenly home where we will see Jesus Christ, hob-knob with the angels. But, on the other hand, I gotta say, it scares me to death."

Stephanie came around and collected Andy's and McDee's empty cups. "I must confess, I'm scared, too," she said as she took the dishes to the sink.

"I must confess as well, I have a bit of fear mixed in with my excitement."

"There's something else I want to say to you," said Andy, stealing a glance toward Stephanie who was rinsing the dishes. "The time is coming when they'll come for me, I mean the people in the camp. They will take me into custody and turn me over to the Brothers. Do not worry about me, I will be singing His praises until I die. Do you understand? Do not let them do anything foolish, like try to rescue me. The time for guns has past now. I want everyone in camp to throw down their guns. Today is the day of faith. I once saw a woman, named Sarah, stand with some Christians and face the Brothers without guns. It was a demonstration of faith in God, a willingness to sacrifice their lives rather than take the life of another needlessly. I saw them stand, the whole camp with Sarah out front. Facing them were the soldiers with their guns, yet none wavered."

"What are you talking about?" asked McDee, suddenly concerned.

"Oh, I'm just talking about some time in the future, when I hope I can stand as Sarah did – could be years away, or could be now. Only God knows. It is just that, when it comes, I do not want any foolishness to take place over me, Reverend. I mean no guns. This isn't our battle – not this time." smiled Andy. "Remember, all things are in the hands of our Lord. Let's not waste our time on instances between now and forever."

McDee nodded silently, then got up from his chair and reached his hand out to Andy. "Son, it's been an honor to know you. You deny being a prophet, won't accept any kudos for anything that's been done, and get angry when anyone tries. But let me tell you, if Jesus tells me we should honor those who have followed His directions, and have taken care of His people, I will add your name to the list."

Andy looked down at the floor. "Well, thank you. Coming from you, I consider that a real compliment."

"And young lady," said Reverend McDee walking over to Stephanie, "It's been an honor to know you, as well. I can't tell you how much I admire how you've taken care of this camp, nor could God have picked a better mate for Andy."

Stephanie smiled, unable to speak. Instead, she reached over and gave him a hug.

"Okay, guess I should get on my way. I'll see you both tomorrow," he said as he reached for the door, then turning said, "Well, don't hold me to that," he smiled.

Andy put his arm around his wife as they watched Reverend McDee fade into the dark night.

Stephanie turned toward her husband. "Andy, today I was sorta thinking back when I was a child. You know what I wanted to be?"

"No clue."

"A cowboy."

"Really? I'd like to see how that could be done."

"Okay, a cowgirl. Now, don't be funny, I'm serious."

"Can you ride a horse?"

"Yes, in fact I was very good at it. My horse's name was Jeremy. He would rear up when I wanted, gallop when I asked, or just walk – a wonderful horse, he was a stick."

"And, I'm sure, a very good stick."

"I wanted to ride along a mountain ridge and look down on all the people. I wanted to rope cattle, and have barbeques at night."

"They called them campfires."

"Quiet. Then, later, I wanted to be a movie star, well actually, a television star in a soap program."

"And now, you're here with me," said Andy. "Something obviously went wrong."

"No, something went very right. I didn't get to do all that I dreamed about or planned; but, meeting you, living here, seeing how God's hand has been upon us, and upon you, has been better than anything I could have imagined. I just wanted to tell you what a privilege it has been to be your wife. God has blessed me so much, Andy, and I thank Him for it. But I want to thank you for being such a wonderful husband."

Andy hugged her. "I feel the same way about you. When we first met I didn't know what to make of you; one minute you were a very by-the-book, stern officer, yet the next moment, an engaging, almost innocent woman." Andy put his arm around her shoulder. "I didn't think I would ever meet someone who could put up with me, but you did. In fact, you did more than that – you led me to Christ, and you helped me believe in me. Because of you, I accepted God's whispers and here we are at this camp, with all these people who have been safe all this time. I credit you, because you believed in me. Stephanie, it's been a privilege to be your husband, truly."

Stephanie turned and buried her face in his shoulder. The two stood there for several minutes, slowly rocking back and forth. Finally, Stephanie said, in a muffled voice, "Remember what you promised."

A New Song

(1)
Angels sing, as the hour draws near,
No sweeter words could we hear.
Gone all sorrows and their tears,
For in clouds He shall soon appear.
Come now sweet revelation,
End this long, sad tribulation.

(Chorus)
A new song the Angels sing,
'Comes at last the King of Kings.'
Proclaim now, oh Promised One,
"It is over! Now it's done!"

Then we sing the sweet, Amen.
Sing we all, the sweet Amen.
(2)
All in heaven hold their breath,
As this hour He conquers death.
Now the promised time is near,
His holy shout we all shall hear,
angels and men loudly cheer,
"The Day of Days, at last is here!"

(Chorus)
A new song the Angels sing,
'Comes at last the King of Kings.'
Proclaim now, oh Promised One,
"It is over! Now it's done!"
Then we sing the sweet, Amen.
Sing we all, the sweet Amen.

(3)
We gather for the wedding feast,
Satan locked up with his Beast.
A thousand days we'll sing His praise,
For lost souls Christ shall raise,
The Lamb shall now all unbind,
No, not one is left behind.

(Chorus)
A new song the Angels sing,
'Comes at last the King of Kings.'
Proclaim now, oh Promised One,
'It is over! Now it's done!'
Then we sing the sweet, Amen.
Sing we all, the sweet Amen.

(4)
Trembling in the land of Gog
By he who claims to be like God.
That Dragon, and deceiver,
Of the Christ's true believers.
To hell he'll go, that evil one.
So it's written; so now be done!

(Chorus)
A new song the Angels sing,
'Comes at last the King of Kings.'
Proclaim now, oh Promised One,
"It is over! Now it's done!"
Then we sing the sweet, Amen.
Sing we all, the sweet Amen.

Chapter 26

Headlights from the passing convoy fell upon Lt. Colonel Decker, illuminating his breath in the cool morning air. He rubbed his hands together. It was obviously Fall but it seemed early this year. In fact, everything seemed out of whack. The seasons were different, the Earth had rumblings all the time, scientists studied the changing sea currents, even more scientists up at the poles watched the ice melt. Everything was screwed up, but Decker did not care. He was a soldier. He had a mission and he was going to accomplish it, come hell or high water.

Today the mission was Cloud Mountain, and its vexing nest of Christians. It was a dirty business they were in today, but when wasn't it? However, there was an upside to the day. There was Harkins. Today he would get to wring his neck, or shoot him, or both. He had trusted that boy, and how had he repaid him? Why, by becoming one of those Jesus Freaks. Well, today he, and everyone else in his Command, would see what happened to people who betray Lieutenant Colonel Decker's trust.

Decker exercised his arms, trying to push out the cold that was beginning to creep into his body. Then, he walked to the waiting Humvee. He got in and pointed his finger forward. The driver responded, driving the Humvee parallel to the convoy, passing the many trucks until they reached the front, where the driver pulled into the lead position.

Decker was confident he had left no stone unturned. Not only did he have three times the troops Syme had, but he had also arranged for air strikes in the morning. Decker didn't want to bomb the camp out of existence, not at all. That would be too easy. The bombing would simply disrupt any troop organization they might have while his forces were assaulting.

No, what he wanted was most of the people in camp to survive, and be waiting for him when he arrived. He wanted to see them beg for their lives. He wanted to have television cameras there to record their panic, their screams, their misery, and finally, their deaths. He was certain the Brothers would be impressed with how completely he had cured the problem of these Jesus Freaks. It brought a rare smile to his face.

As the convoy came within sight of Cloud Mountain, Decker signaled a halt and requested all Senior Officers meet him at the front. He waited patiently until they arrived.

"Now Gentlemen, we are about to embark on an operation, at which, one of my predecessors failed miserably. To this day, his name is used as a mark of derision. I do not intend this operation to end in such a way. I want to make it very clear to all of you that I expect my orders to be executed to their fullest, or I will see some of you in front of a firing squad. Do I make myself clear, Gentlemen?"

Mumblings with a few clear, "yes sirs" came in response.

"I want the circle around this so-called mountain to be tight – no one escapes – no one! For now, the circle is to be one mile out to allow for the bombing runs, which begin at dawn, but after the bombing raid, have your men ready to tighten the circle to five hundred feet. One last thing, I have instructed the Air Force that this is a minimal target – the bombs are really for disorientation as much as anything. I want as many captured alive as possible – pay particular attention to the so-called Prophet, I want him alive; and I want Sergeant Harkins brought to me. Understood?"

Again, a low chorus of "yes sirs."

"Very well, deploy your men and wait for the Air Force to come," said Decker as he checked his watch. "The scheduled jump-off time is 0500. Be alert!"

Returning to his Humvee, Decker watched as the convoy began splitting up. They each went to their assigned areas as they began to encircle the camp. By 0430, all were in place, and waiting.

* * * * *

Andy woke with a jolt, hearing frantic pounding on the front door. Jumping out of bed, he heard Stephanie stir behind him, as he threw on his robe and ran to the front door.

"Andy!" shouted Roy Kegler, as he saw Andy. "Big trouble! They're coming! They're coming now!" shouted Roy in a frantic voice.

Already Andy could see lights coming on all over the camp, accompanied by distant shouts and the sound of people rushing.

"Slow down, Roy; tell me what's going on."

"The lookouts on the ridge saw a long, long line of headlights coming down the road. Andy, they say there are thousands of them. Then, they started surrounding the mountain, but they are not doing anything, just sitting there. We are in the middle, Andy. They are coming for us. I just know it! What are we gonna do? I got my gun with me. Shouldn't we make sure everyone has one?"

"Now, Roy, calm down. Let's keep a cool head. I will get dressed and meet you along with the senior members of the council, at the Great House in fifteen minutes. "Roy," said Andy putting his hand on the older man's shoulder, "don't lose your cool. A lot of people look up to the council for answers, and this is no exception. One last thing, there are to be no guns. Tell everyone, there are to be no guns!"

Roy nodded. "I'll see you at the Great House." Roy turned and began running toward the center of the camp.

Andy watched him go and shook his head. Then, turning to Stephanie said, "Looks like it's nearer than I thought, honey."

Unable to speak, Stephanie nodded with tears in her eyes.

"Now, honey, let's not make this a time of tears. We should be rejoicing. Soon we shall see the Christ. Soon we shall sing a new song."

Stephanie nodded, with tears in her voice, "Remember, you promised to hold my hand."

* * * * *

Lorraine Eppinger ran into the motor pool and was surprised to see at least fifty people there along with the original three. Even as she arrived, others were following her inside.

"So," said Dave Leitz, "looks like this is it. They say they got thousands of troops with them," His voice betraying some fear.

Lorraine Eppinger motioned for the original four to follow her as she made her way to a pickup truck and climbed on to its bed. Standing up, she held her hands up, trying to quiet the growing crowd.

"I'm sure we all know by now that today is the day they are coming to murder us, and our families, including the children," she shouted.

A few women began crying, but eventually the crowd quieted down with only an occasional sob escaping.

"Now," said Lorraine, surprising herself with the note of authority in her voice. "I believe I have a plan that could save us, and the children."

The crowd became so still, the only sounds were those seeping in from outside the barn.

"A lot of you don't know me because I'm new here, but I am very concerned about you and the children – I've already lost my husband, and I don't want that sorrow to come to you. I know how the Brothers think. My husband was once the

Commander of the forces that now surround us."

There was a great murmuring of the people around her.

"So, why should we listen to you?" yelled Thomas Iley's voice, recognizable from the rasp it always carried. Some said his voice came from his smoking too much when he was younger.

"Because I am a Christian, and I have a plan, and I know these troops very well. Now, hear me out." Eppinger paused while the crowd became quiet again. "We have someone else here to our advantage. This here is Sergeant Harkins," she said pointing him out. "Sergeant Harkins was the Administrative Assistant to Lieutenant Colonel Decker, who replaced my husband, and is in all likelihood, at the foot of the mountain now. We know this man, and I believe we can reason with him – that is, if we have something to bargain with."

"Like what?" asked Marcia Jacobs, a volunteer at the children's camp.

"We have two things. First, we have ourselves – a ready-made workforce for Decker to use in improving this area. With our efforts, he could make this a showplace for others to follow. My husband started the worker program, and those Christians who are part of it, lead peaceful, secure lives, free of harassment. Decker would declare this camp off-limits. We all would be assigned jobs in the surrounding area and come home each night. Then, each morning, much as we did before this big trouble, we would go to work. It may not be the job we like, but it keeps us and our families alive."

"They aren't going to do that," sneered Thomas.

"They're already doing it. There are a number of camps doing exactly that!" replied Eppinger.

"She's right," chimed in Harkins. "I've seen them myself. The residents of the camps come into town each morning and run the town. In the evening they return home and are free of any interference."

"Secondly," said Eppinger. "We have something I know Colonel Decker wants very much."

"And what's that?" asked Thomas.

"The Prophet."

There was murmuring in the crowd. Finally, an older woman toward the back spoke up. "You aren't saying we should give them the Prophet, are you?" This time it was Helen Yeager, one of the camp schoolteachers.

"Yes," said Eppinger holding up her hands to quiet the expected protest. "But hear me out. The Prophet is not as he used to be... I'm sure you will all agree. If you did not, you wouldn't be here now."

"That doesn't mean we want to give him to the Brothers!" said one unidentified man to Eppinger's right.

"Many of us believe the Prophet is now holding himself above all of us," responded Eppinger. "That he has become enamored of his own position, and is spouting things that are not Christian. Have you not heard his proclamation that everyone on Earth goes to heaven? Now, I heard that one myself!"

"I heard something else many of you may not be aware of yet," began Sergeant Evans. He told me that when the Brothers come, he is going to ask that everyone bring their guns and stack them up by the Great House. He then plans to burn them all. He told me it will be an offering of faith that we give ourselves over to God's Will."

This time there was a great murmuring in the crowd, until Jim Graff spoke up. "You make him sound like he's the devil himself; maybe he's just becoming senile. I don't think we should throw him away because of that."

"Let me ask you this," said Lorraine. "Are your lives, your husbands and wives lives, and especially your children lives, worth one man who may be senile – or possibly self-infatuated? Someone with whom God himself is now probably angry for His misleading words. It is possibly the reason why the troops have come. I think God might be angry with Andy, and we are all going to pay the price. I leave the decision to you. If you decide to give Andy over, Sergeant Harkins and myself, along with Sergeant Evans, Dave Leitz, and Dave Jones will comprise a delegation to speak with the Colonel and bring the Prophet to him." Eppinger looked slowly around the quiet room. "You decide, but we haven't much time."

The voices grew louder as those gathered there began to argue the merits of the plan. Their emotions and their voices ran equally high. Finally, the crowd quieted.

Lorraine looked over the people for a moment; then said, "All in favor, raise your hand."

For a moment, no hands rose, then one by one, timid hands came up, followed by others, until nearly all their hands were in the air.

"Very well, go now – do not tell anyone what has gone on here. They will find out soon enough, and let's pray they will also see the wisdom of our decision," said Lorraine.

The group silently filed out of the barn and made their way toward their home.

"Let's take the van," said Eppinger, when almost all had left. "Dave, you drive. I will ride up front with you and point out the Colonel. The rest stay with the Prophet in back – and, by the way, we should take his wife too. Leaving her is asking for trouble."

The others nodded their agreement and began walking toward the van. Suddenly, Sgt. Harkins stopped.

"Quiet!" he commanded. For a several moments, they stood quietly, and then Harkins said, "Do you hear it?"

For a second no one said anything, until Sgt. Evans spoke up. "Jets! It's jets! They are coming here! Seek cover!" he shouted. No sooner had he spoken than a large explosion came from somewhere in the camp. The noise of the unseen jet was deafening, screaming in protest as the pilot pulled hard to gain altitude. A second one instantly followed it. Again, they heard an explosion, this one louder, closer.

People were falling flat on the ground or running for shelter. In the northern part of the camp, flames began growing. Several screams pierced the air as the Great House disappeared in a ball of flame. Then, with a last explosion falling in the travel trailer area, the runs stopped. For a few moments, no one moved and an almost eerie silence fell upon the camp. The silence was interrupted by a growing number of cries for help, and voices yelling for their loved ones. Flames crackled everywhere, including the Great House.

Lorraine Eppinger jumped up. "We've got to hurry!" she yelled as they got in the van and drove towards the Prophet's house.

As the van pulled out onto the Circle Drive, they could see the smoke rising from several homes. Jones wanted to drive faster, but was afraid he might hit one of the many people who were running in all directions accompanied by various shouts and screams.

"Wait – look," shouted Lorraine while grabbing Jones' shoulder. Ahead they could see the Prophet and Stephanie trotting toward the Great House.

Dave pulled up in front of them and blocked their path. Eppinger, Sergeant Evans, Leitz and Harkins jumped out of the van waving the two toward them. "Here!" shouted Lorraine.

Andy and Stephanie jumped in the van with Andy shouting, "The Great House, fast!"

Without warning, the three men in the back grabbed Stephanie and Andy, pinning their arms behind them while Lorraine produced two pieces of rope. Within seconds, both were tied up.

"So," said Andy in a subdued voice, "You are the ones. I knew about Eppinger, but I didn't know about you."

"There are many of us, Andy – more than you can imagine," said Lorraine in a low voice.

"What now?" asked David Jones from the driver's seat.

"Take us to the main gate, but don't drive fast. We don't want any attention drawn to us right now."

Turning the van, Dave began driving toward the main gate as another jet screamed overhead. There was a large explosion somewhere to their rear.

"Keep going," said Eppinger softly.

Finally, arriving at the overhead gate, they stopped. Eppinger got out and tied a white T-shirt to the van's antenna. Getting back into the van, no one spoke including Andy and Stephanie. For a few moments, all were quiet as they stared at the soldiers at the foot of the mountain. From their number, it was obvious they intended to take the camp by force, and soon.

Jones turned to Lorraine Eppinger. "Well?" he asked.

Eppinger nodded silently, and Jones took his foot off the brake.

Chapter 27

The radioman looked up at Colonel Decker. "Sir, the Fly Boys are asking if you have reconsidered and want a second strike."

"No, I think that one was just about right," he smiled. "Thank the Air Force for its service. If we need any more help, we'll be sure to call them," said Decker. Above, he could see the top of Cloud Mountain glowing from the flames within the camp concealed by the rim of the mountain.

"Private," said Decker to the radioman, wearing the name of Private Ward, "Inform the Commanders to move up."

Ward, with one earphone lifted to hear the Colonel's words, nodded.

Decker's attention was caught by the sound of an approaching vehicle. It stopped a few feet from where the Colonel was standing, and, as a black robed man got out, Decker felt his heart sink. It was Arthur Ramon. Decker gave a silent curse. Ramon was here without giving the courtesy of even notifying Decker. The sight of this man struck fear into the hearts of all Commanding Officers, if not everyone else. A flick of his finger could spell the end of a life, and he was known for his ruthless and capricious decisions. If ever there was a man hated by all men, Ramon had to be a candidate.

Ramon climbed out of the Humvee, pulling his back robe tight around his waist to prevent it catching on the Humvee. The hood of the robe was pulled over his head. It was rumored he wore the hood up to hide his partially-bald head. It had been some time since Decker had seen Ramon in person, and he was surprised by his gaunt appearance. The last time he had seen him, Ramon had on a red robe, but his new position of Supreme Prefect, gave him the authority to wear black. His eyes seemed sunken even deeper and the circles under them more pronounced while his large nose emphasized the face's gaunt appearance. He was not smiling, nor could Decker remember ever seeing him when he did.

Ramon approached Decker, who gave a crisp salute. Ramon nodded acknowledgement with a stern face. "So, what's the situation?" he asked curtly.

"Sir, we are about to launch our attack on the home of these fanatics."

Ramon nodded. "I expect, Colonel, that your operation today will meet with much greater success than your predecessor's."

"Absolutely, sir. We have just concluded our initial action, the planned air strike. The smoke you see coming over the ridge is the result."

Ramon nodded, "Carry on," he said quietly.

"Sir," shouted a captain coming towards them. "There's someone on the side of the hill, and they're headed toward us!"

"Let me see," snarled Dexter, grabbing his aide's binoculars. He fastened them to his eyes and after a moment of silence, he said, "Yes, I see them. They have a white flag. Maybe they want to surrender."

"There will be no surrenders, Colonel!" snapped Ramon.

"No sir – of course not. Shall I have the vehicle destroyed?" Decker felt his anger rise with his voice. This was what he hated about Ramon being there; suddenly, he felt robbed of initiative and professional judgment, both usurped by this creep. He felt in the position of a child having to ask his father could he do this, or that.

Ramon shook his head. "No, let's see what they want."

The van came closer until it was approximately one hundred yards from them before it slowed, and then stopped.

"See what they want Decker," commanded Ramon in a monotone voice. "Here, give me your gun. Your empty holster will show them we want to hear what they have to say."

Decker grunted, handing Ramon his forty-five; then signaled his driver to the Humvee. The Humvee came to life and headed for the van waiting on the hillside with its white flag visible in the semi light of the morning. As they neared the van, the Humvee slowed, and then stopped twenty yards short. Decker got out and walked toward the van a few yards, before halting. A woman opened the van's passenger door, got out, and began walking toward him. She stopped a few feet short of Decker.

"Well, I must say I'm surprised, Lorraine," said Decker. "I'd heard you were at the camp, but didn't expect to see you."

"Yes, Richard, I'm here," she said as she closely watched Decker for any sign of what he was thinking. Their previous meeting had been friendly, though strained. She never trusted him as much as her husband did. However, the few times she had met him at social occasions, he had been courteous toward her. She was counting on this civil behavior to help her now.

"So, why are we here?" he asked in a low voice.

"Well, Richard, I've come to bargain."

"Bargain? Now what in the world would you have that would make me want to bargain?" he smiled, seemingly genuinely amused by the thought.

"I bring you the Prophet."

For a moment, Decker was silent, "The Prophet? The one everyone talks about?"

"Yes – and, I also bring to you his wife, who was once in charge of the camp's security."

Decker was silent for a moment as he looked at Lorraine, then shifted his gaze to the van.

Seeing him shift his gaze to the van, Lorraine gave a signal with her hand. Immediately, the side door of the van slid opened revealing the Prophet, bound and sitting on the floor, with his wife. Next to them was Sergeant Harkins.

"Well, I'll be. You surprise me, Lorraine. I couldn't think

of any reason I would want to talk to anyone from this camp when I came up here, but now I'm glad I did. Not only do you give me the gift of the Prophet and his wife, but I see Sergeant Harkins is here also. I was looking forward to seeing Harkins."

Lorraine smiled. "I'd say your smile's a good sign."

"So, you said you wanted to negotiate. So, negotiate."

Eppinger outlined her idea of the work camp, stressing to Decker the many talents of people in the camp, and the assets they would be in accomplishing the many tasks needed to operate the town and surrounding area. "I think with the help of all those in camp, your Command could become a shining example for the whole country."

Decker nodded silently, allowing a small smile to creep on his face. "Okay," he said, "Now, there's someone here who could grant you what you want, but you will have to talk to him yourself. I want you, Sergeant Harkins, the Prophet, and his wife to get into my Humvee and we will take you to him. I think I can guarantee you he will be very interested."

"Will we be under the protection of the white flag?"

"Of course, everyone will be safe. After all, we are just negotiating."

Decker turned and climbed into the Humvee as Eppinger returned to the van, to tell the others what they had agreed. Decker could tell what she was saying by the men looking up and staring at him from time to time. Finally, he saw Harkins got out of the van, turn and help the Prophet and his wife out.

Decker smiled as he saw them begin to walk toward him. He maintained the smile until they were within talking distance. "So, Sergeant Harkins," said Decker as they neared. "It's good to see you again."

"Thank you sir, it's good to see you too."

Decker watched the Prophet and his wife get into the back seat of the Humvee. It was crowded as the four visitors scrunched together. Decker continued to stare at the Prophet as they all were seated.

"So, you are the great Prophet, the one everyone talks about."

Andy remained stoic. Next to him, Stephanie sat quietly. Andy wished his hands were not tied. He wanted to put his arm around his wife and comfort her.

"And now your people turned you over to me, that must be quite a surprise to you," smiled Decker, as Andy continued to stare straight ahead.

"Well, sir," said Harkins, "we haven't done that yet. We are still negotiating."

"Yes, yes, of course," said Decker, as he signaled his driver to go.

It only took a few moments to retrace their track to the foot of the mountain. On the hill above, the remaining two men in the van watched the proceedings below as their white flag waved fitfully in the morning air.

As the Humvee drove up to where Ramon was waiting, Decker smiled. "You won't believe what they wanted to talk about," he said to Ramon. "Look who I have here, none other than the great Prophet!" laughed Decker. "I think they want to trade him for their lives." He motioned for them all of them to get out of the Humvee.

Ramon came forward while looking silently but intently at the three prisoners. "Who is this?" asked Ramon, looking at Stephanie.

"This is his wife – and here," he said, "is Sergeant Harkins, who deserted a few days ago. I could not have asked for better!"

"Harkins, you come over here. I'm not through with you," snarled Decker. Then turning his attention back to the prisoners, said, "This is Lorraine Eppinger."

"Yes," said Ramon. "I know Mrs. Eppinger."

"Yes sir," smiled Lorraine. "I think we met briefly last

291

year."

Ramon nodded, but did not smile.

* * * * *

Roy Kegler paced as he waited for Andy outside the burning Great House. The flames seem to grow by the minute, spewing out a cloud of mixed white and black smoke rising and mingling with the smoke from other burning buildings. He could not imagine why the Prophet was taking so long to join them. Time was of the essence. Shortly, Ken Johnstone and Reverend McDee joined him

A confused crowd was gathered on the Circle drive. They wandered back and forth, most with guns in their hands. Some watched the Great House burn, some shed tears, and some just wandered in a confused state waiting for someone to tell them what to do.

"So, where is he?" asked Johnstone.

"Have we sent someone to get him?" asked McDee.

Kegler turned as he heard his name called from the back of the crowd. The crowd parted and allowed a man to run through to get to Kegler. "Roy, Roy!" he gasped as he arrived. "They got the Prophet!"

"What! Who's got what?"

"The Prophet," he gasped again. "The soldiers got the Prophet; we saw it from the ridge of the mountain."

"How did that happen?" demanded Johnstone.

"There was this van that came down from the camp. We couldn't believe it when we saw it – who would be leaving the camp at this time? It was stupid," he said, looking around for some agreement, but met with icy gazes. "So, then the van stopped and a Humvee came up and they talked for a minute then they both go down. Then, outta the van they bring the Prophet and his wife with their hands tied behind them, along with another guy I didn't recognize. You can see it all from the ridge."

Suddenly the crowd began running for the mountain ridge.

Roy, using the cart, was among the first to reach the crest and looked down upon the valley beneath. Army trucks were all around the mountain, in some places four deep. Soldiers were in relaxed formation around the trucks as if waiting for a Command.

Near the entrance road to the camp were some trucks and in front of them a small group of men. Putting the binoculars to his face Roy could see the Prophet and his wife with their hands tied behind them standing in front of the men.

"They got him, alright," said Roy, his voice evidencing despair and sorrow

* * * * *

Decker looked at Ramon. "Mrs. Eppinger here has come with an interesting proposal," he said. "She wants to trade the Prophet, and his wife for the safety of those in camp. She also says those in camp will lay down their arms and go to work for us in whatever jobs need to be done."

"We don't negotiate with filthy Jesus Freaks," said Ramon in a low voice, filled with contempt. "Haven't you wasted enough time on this fool?" he shouted. "Every time you have him in your grasp all you do is talk, talk, talk!"

Andy felt Stephanie moved close to him as if trying to burrow into him. He looked at her and softly began to sing, "Jesus loves me this I know..."

Stephanie looked up and smiled, and began singing with him. "...because the Bible tells me so."

Ramon walked toward Andy and Stephanie, until he was within a couple of feet. He stood silently for a moment before withdrawing Decker's gun from beneath his robe. Quickly putting it to Andy's head, he pulled the trigger.

Bam!

The bullet snapped Andy's head back as he fell soundlessly to the ground.

Stephanie screamed.

Ramon, redirected his gun toward her, pulled the trigger again.

Bam!

Stephanie's scream was cut short as she dropped, landing on top of her dead husband.

"That's how we negotiate with Jesus Freaks," said Ramon quietly.

"Oh, my God!" screamed Lorraine Eppinger.

* * * * *

From their vantage point on top of the hill, it was difficult to make out individual faces. However, Roy and McDee could figure out the individuals from their general motions and dress. A few of the other people from camp had binoculars also glued to their faces.

"It's obvious the one with the black robe is from the Brothers," said Kegler. "And it looks like the one in brown there is the leader of the military."

Johnstone, continuing to look through his binoculars, nodded. "Andy and Stephanie are just standing there – looks like their hands are tied behind their backs."

"Isn't that the Eppinger woman talking with the Brother there?"

Johnstone paused before nodding, "I think you're right. I never did trust that woman. The one who's standing next to the Colonel is that army fellow who brought in McDee. I didn't trust him either."

Kegler pointed to the van that was displaying the white

flag. "Whatever is going on looks like they expect somebody to return. I don't get it, what could they be negotiating?"

"From the look of it, I'd say the Prophet was on the auction bl. . . Oh, My God!" exclaimed Johnstone, as the echo of the gunshots reached them. "They just shot Andy and Stephanie!"

There were scattered screams from others seeing what had just happened.

* * * * *

"You," said Ramon, looking at Eppinger with hatred in his eyes, "I spare you only to go back to that camp and tell them what has happened. Tell them we are coming. Tell them to prepare to die."

Eppinger staggered back, her hand to her mouth as if holding her screams inside. Reaching the Humvee, she climbed in, and the driver quickly drove her back to the waiting men by the van.

As they saw the van coming, both men raised their AK-47s, prepared for anything that might occur. The Humvee stopped fifty yards short of their van and Lorraine got out. Immediately the Humvee turned and started back.

"What happened?" shouted Jones.

"They shot them!" sobbed Lorraine, unable to hold her emotions in any longer.

Sergeant Evans helped her to get in the van. Then turning to the other two, he asked, "Now what?"

"What did they do to Harkins?" asked Leitz.

For a moment, Lorraine said nothing, and then gathered herself. "They put him under arrest. I think the guy in charge, Ramon, is gonna execute him."

"No one answered my question – what do we do now?" demanded Evans. "If we go back to camp, they'll shoot us! We can't stay here, and we can't go down."

Dave Jones took a deep breath. "We go back to the camp. We tried to do what we thought was right for the camp, and we failed. It is time to face the music. If they shoot us, so be it."

For a moment no one moved or said anything; then, slowly, Evans got into the back of the van, followed by Leitz while Jones climbed in the driver's seat and started the van. No one spoke a word as the vehicle retraced the worn path to the camp.

At the top of Cloud Mountain, a group, made up of those who had supported the idea, waited for the van to return. There were many tears, for Andy and Stephanie, and for themselves. Advancing toward this group was the rest of the camp, and it was clear they were not happy. A few of the men of those who waited checked their guns and faced the advancing crowd coming toward them.

The van reached the group before those coming from the camp did. It took only a few moments to relate what had happened with the Prophet and his wife. Eppinger finished telling them just as the advancing group reached them. The advancing group stopped just short. A few of the men, on both sides, raised their weapons, yet did not point them at the other side.

For a few moments, both sides stared at the other, as if sizing up one another. Finally, Tim Barter, arrived with Mary, and Roy Kegler, made their way to the front.

"What's going on here!" demanded Kegler.

Instinctively, the men of Lorraine's group drew their guns higher, an action which prompted a similar response from Kegler's group, which continued to grow.

"You are the people who had the Prophet shot! Who do you think you are?" shouted a man's voice in the crowd.

Sergeant Evans, along with Dave Jones and Dave Leitz, pushed their way to the front. "We were trying to help," shouted Jones. "Believe me; we just wanted to save the children and all of you from the soldiers below!"

"You mean you just wanted to save yourselves!" The words came again from a nameless voice in the crowd and were accompanied by sounds of agreement from others.

"Wait a minute – hold on here!" shouted Roy Kegler.

Lorraine Eppinger came to the front. "It's me, Roy, I'm to blame," she sobbed. "I'm so sorry. Jesus forgive me. I'm so sorry."

"What were you thinking?" demanded Roy.

"The children, Roy, the children. I was thinking of the children."

Kegler faced Lorraine, "I'm not going to say what you did was right or wrong, but…"

He had to stop as a chorus of protests came from the camp crowd.

"Hear me out!" he shouted. "That's something between them and God!" he shouted. Then, turning around said, "But I know this – here we are fighting among ourselves. Do you think Andy would want this? Does this honor his name? Is this what our Christianity has come to be at the last hour?"

McDee stepped forward. "Andy knew this was coming. He knew." said McDee in as loud a voice as he could muster. "It's now clear to me that he knew all of this. We talked, and he told me that we should not punish the deceived. He asked that we should be merciful. I didn't know what he meant at the time, even tried to get him to explain it, but he said I'd know when the time was right. I know now. He was speaking of now. He's telling us that the way of Christianity is confession, and forgiveness."

Kegler stepped forward to Lorraine. "He's right, Lorraine. No one here will say what you did was right, it certainly brings us a great deal of grief, but I feel, in my heart, that you were trying to do what you thought was best."

Eppinger burst into tears, "I was – God knows I was. Oh, Jesus, forgive me."

Reverend McDee held up his uninjured arm. "Let us all pray that in this final hour we shall not fail our Lord, or Prophet Andy. Let us forgive each other and ask that Jesus forgive us as well." He then knelt down. One by one, others of both groups joined him on their knees. A few minutes of silence followed as the entire camp struggled with the moment of their private thoughts and prayers.

At last, Reverend McDee got up, and held his hand high. "Andy told me about a time when he was at another camp, with the Prophet Sarah. They knew the Goonies were coming, but they did not take up arms, instead they met their attackers as defenseless followers of Christ. They trusted in God to deliver them. Before he went down the hill he asked me that there be no guns."

Kegler spoke up, "He told me no guns also, just before he was taken away. Andy knew, and he wanted no guns."

The group was still on their knees and were silent.

McDee looked slowly around the kneeling group. "I'm asking you now to follow Andy's wishes. Throw down your weapons. Let us meet our fate as souls trusting in the salvation of Jesus. Will our lives be gained if we kill a hundred of them, or a thousand, or even ten thousand? No. However, even if such was the case, could we face tomorrow knowing such was on our heads? What then would separate us from those who persecute us? Today is the day we have known would come. Let's not meet Jesus with blood on our hands."

"He's right, said Sergeant Evans, lifting his AK-47 over his head, and throwing it aside.

Soon, one by one, then by the tens and finally by the hundreds, weapons were tossed aside. Then slowly, in small groups, they began walking silently toward the center of the camp, and the smoking ruins of the Great House. As they walked, meditating, and in silent prayer, some woman began singing 'Amazing Grace." One by one, thousands of camp voices joined her. Arriving back on Grand Circle Drive, the people encircled the embers of the Great House. Joining hands they sang the song over and over, swaying, many with eyes closed, in a slow rhythm, lost in the beauty and comfort of the words.

"This," said Reverend McDee, "is the hour for which we have waited."

For the Son of man shall come in the glory of his Father with his angels; and then he shall reward every man according to his works. Verily I say unto you, There be some standing here, which shall not taste of death, till they see the Son of man coming in his kingdom.

– Matthew 16:27

Chapter 28

"Harkins, I ought to shoot you right here," growled Decker at the sergeant. "Since when did you become a Jesus Freak?"

"I wasn't sir," said Harkins. "I just didn't like all the killing, but then something began happening to me – I feel like I'm changing."

Decker snorted. "Well, you sure ain't gonna like one more killing that's gonna happen," he said, allowing a small smile to cross his face. "When we get back to camp, I'm gonna make you an example, but I'm gonna do it by the book. Maybe I'll hang you, and before you die, I'll shoot you too," he chuckled.

Harkins remained silent as he stood with his hands tied behind his back.

"Perhaps, Colonel, this man has information about the camp that would be useful," suggested Ramon.

Decker thought for a moment, then smiled. "That's very true. Yes, now that's interesting," he said as he took a couple of paces to Sergeant Harkins' left, then turned back. "Here's the part I like – Harkins here doesn't want me to know what he knows. So, it means I'll just have some unpleasant persuasion applied," Decker smiled as he warmed to the idea. "Yes, that's exactly what we'll do. Now Harkins don't disappoint me and tell us the answers we want right away. I want to play awhile, do you understand?"

Harkins, visibly shaken, stammered, "But I don't know

much, sir. They didn't tell me anything. I don't think they trusted me."

"Perfect. Exactly what I hoped you would say." Decker held up his hand and snapped his fingers.

Sergeant Brunswick came to him, and saluted. "Yes, sir," he said crisply.

"I want you to take a couple of men and Sergeant Harkins here to the Command Station. I believe you will have some privacy there. Now, I want you to interrogate Sergeant Harkins thoroughly. Do you know what I'm saying, Sergeant?"

"I think so, sir," responded Brunswick, some doubt showing in his voice.

"Let me make it very clear, Sergeant. I want you to break every bone in his body, one at a time, 'til he tells you everything we need to know about that camp. I wanna know how many people are up there; how many weapons they have; how much artillery; I want to know the names of everyone in that camp. Do I make myself clear now?"

"Does he know the names of everyone, sir?"

"I hope not, but I guess you'll just have to keep breaking bones 'til he remembers, won't you? And when you run outta bones, you can start pulling teeth, understand?"

"Yes sir," answered Brunswick, with a note of fear, and clearly disturbed.

"I hope so, Sergeant – because if he doesn't give me everything I want to know, you'll be next – now, do you understand?"

"Yes, sir!" said Brunswick, snapping a salute. He motioned to two other men to take Harkins. They each grabbed an arm and began walking toward the Command tent.

Decker watched him go with a smile growing on his face. "You know, Prefect Ramon, that was a wonderful suggestion," he smiled.

"Do you think he knows anything?" asked Ramon.

"I hope not," smiled Decker. "Besides, what do I need to know? I have the force here to defeat them. By evening, every last bugger will be dead." Decker paused then smiled again, "I promise you."

A Private came running up. "Sir, the scouts have reached the ridge and are reporting no resistance."

Decker nodded, "Very well," he said, then turning to Ramon. "That surprises me a little. I would have thought we would meet stiff resistance. Ah, well, these Christians – who can ever figure them out, completely?"

A few minutes later, the radioman approached. "Sir, Major Zerski reports his scouts have gained the ridge and can look down upon the camp. He says he can see the entire population. They are all standing around a burned-up building, and they are singing, sir."

"Singing?" snapped Decker. "Idiots! Tell him to pull back his scouts and wait for the advance teams. Tell him they are pulling out now and should be at his position in a few minutes. I am starting the main assault behind them in ten minutes, as planned. Is that clear, soldier?"

"Yes sir!" was the practiced response.

Decker rubbed his chin. "I don't like this. It's too easy." He paused for a moment, then yelled to have Sergeant Harkins brought back.

Within a few minutes, Harkins arrived, limping between two soldiers. His face was bloodied, and he walked in a semi-crouch, hinting a rib or two were broken.

Decker ignored Harkins appearance. "Harkins," he snapped. "What's going on up there – why are they just standing around? Do they have some secret weapon I don't know about? You better tell me, and tell me now – or I swear your Mother will hear your screams!"

"They are waiting," coughed Harkins.

"Waiting for what?"

302

"Jesus."

"Waiting for Jesus? To do what?"

"Save them, sir."

"So, they think all they have to do is wait and they'll be rescued, is that correct? Is there another force around here I don't know about? Speak up!"

"No sir. They are waiting to be taken away in spirit; they called it 'snatched' – raptured away."

"What did I tell you," he said, turning to Ramon. "A bunch of crazies, they're all like that."

Ramon did not return the smile instead, he addressed Harkins. "Sergeant," he began, his voice was deep, as though it was scrapping the bottom of something. "Do you mean they are waiting to be saved from this life to the next – is that what you mean?"

Harkins nodded, "Yes, sir."

Again, the Radioman approached the group. "Sir, I have a report from the advance troops. It's sounds screwy sir."

"Well? What is it?"

"Major Zerski says they're gone."

"Who's gone?"

"All those crazy Christians, sir. They don't see any of them."

Decker looked first at Ramon and then at Harkins. "So, where did they go, Harkins? Do they have a secret hiding place? I swear Harkins, if they have a secret place, you better tell me right now – I mean this instant or your life is gonna be a living hell!" screamed Decker.

"No sir, no secret place. They are gone. It's the snatching, what they call The Rapture. They talk about it all the time."

Decker reached over and slapped Harkins hard across the face. "Don't toy with me, Harkins."

Harkins coughed three times as some red spittle dripped from his lips. "They are gone." He repeated, managing a smile,

"It's what they've been waiting for. You lose, Colonel." Harkens then dropped to his knees "Jesus, I've been so wrong, save me!"

"Shut up!" shouted Decker, looking first at Harkins then at Ramon. "You ever hear of anything so stupid?" he asked Ramon. "Harkins, you sound like one of those Jesus Freaks!"

The Radioman spoke up. "Sir, all hell is breaking loose. There are reports coming in from all over that the Jesus Freaks have escaped!"

"Escaped?" yelled Decker. "To where? What's going on here?"

"Don't you get it, you ignorant jerk?" snarled Harkins from his knees. "They were right. They're gone!"

"I can't believe that!" said Decker.

Suddenly the rumbling beneath them began to move throwing many of the soldiers to the ground. Arthur Ramon grabbed hold of the truck to prevent being thrown down, while Decker grabbed the radioman.

The motion stopped, and they all regained their composure. Standing up, Decker turned to Harkins, lying on the ground, his hands tied behind his back, but before he could speak, the ground moved again. From the top of the mountain, came a loud high pitched and intense scream as superheated gas shot skyward in a fountain reaching thousands of feet within moments. The sound of the escaping steam grew in intensity, its piercing wail so loud many covered their ears. The white steam continued to shoot straight up until it encountered currents of the upper atmosphere, which flattened it out. The anvil shaped cloud began covering the entire area.

* * * * *

It was night over the pyramids, but no one was sleeping inside. Men and women were running to their workstations, something was seriously wrong. Even the Visitors seemed unsure of what to do as evidenced by the looks they shared between them as they too rushed to their assigned stations.

Reports were coming in from all around the world of natural disturbances; earthquakes and eruptions that were turning rock to soil, then to quicksand. The heavens had suddenly came alive with fierce storms, the like of which men had never seen. The lightning bolts were like explosives destroying mile-wide areas when they struck. Everyone's fear grew as the day progressed into night and the conditions around the world worsened.

However, General York was not fearful, worried, or nervous. General York, Four Star General York, was the happiest he had been since before the Academy Days. His old nemesis, General Brian Powell had screwed up. Yes, royally screwed up, and York knew he would. He did not know the nature of his screw-up, but the General had been removed from Command, and now it was his – as it always should have been.

York ordered another glass of wine from the nervous waiter, then reached into his pant pocket and retrieved the four star insignia. Each gold star nestled next to one another and all fastened securely to the pin that would affix them to his shoulder. Tomorrow he would put them on for the first time.

Suddenly he felt the room tremble. He sat up and looked around as though expecting an explanation. He saw was his waiter run from the kitchen and escape the restaurant through the entrance door. Again, he felt a shaking, but this time it was more violent. York rose from his chair and made his way to the window. Outside, the sea was in great turmoil. The waters, already under assault from some storm, seemed to be erupting and boiling from the depths. The action was so violent he saw three freighters capsize before his eyes, with two of them disappearing suddenly beneath the water as if the three hundred foot behemoths had been sucked whole beneath the waves.

Fear, for the first time, began to grow within him. He realized something was happening that was life threatening in nature. He could hear the screams of people coming through the doors of the restaurant. Through the window, he watched in horror as the other pyramids began to collapse. He realized he had to get out. As York ran toward the door, the entire room leaned further to his left and dropped several feet. The sudden action caught him off balance and he fell, sliding to the exterior wall.

He struggled to get up, but was prevented as the pyramid tipped even further to the left, steadied, then fell, under its weight, into the boiling sea carrying with it all the inhabitants of the structure, including the General and his four shiny stars.

* * * * *

As Decker watched, the Earth moved again, along with a deafening explosion from the top of Cloud Mountain. The sound was so loud and forceful, that the car windows exploded and human eardrums burst. Men screamed in pain and fell to the ground holding their heads. In an instant, the mountain's top disappeared in a fiery conflagration of smoke, ash, molten lava and flame. Liquefied rock, released from the bowels of the Earth, burst free along with a pyroclastic flow of superheated gas reaching temperatures over a thousand degrees. The pyroclastic gas flow came over the top of the shattered mountaintop, and began racing down the hill at over four hundred miles an hour. Men in cars and trucks tried to escape but the flow easily overtook them. When the flow hit the vehicles, they instantly burst into flames, incinerating all of them.

All the children of Christ, throughout the world, gave thanks to God who rescued them in this last hour, and they sang praises to Christ as He prepared to welcome His brothers and sisters.

Arthur Ramon, shouted with fear and began to run, yet was only able to take a step or two before he was blown away by the fast moving super-heated gas flow, and consumed by the flames as was Colonel Decker, the radioman, soldiers, and all the surrounding life. Cries for mercy, and the screams of pain, were cut short, swept away by the gas, red molten rock, and flame. The fiery flow showed no mercy, devouring everything and everyone in sight for several miles, until its appetite finally cooled.

Those who saw the inferno from miles away fell to their knees in terror, crying out in fear; yet, they were not spared the horrors of that day. All the Earth saw mountains turn red with fire, and the Earth shake, and its seas boil. The Pyramids, in the southern ocean, were devoured by the raging sea, as was the one in the Mediterranean. Men and women cried out around the Earth for mercy. The whole world moved in a Biblical dance of death. All of humanity cried out in fear and pain, for the end of days had come.

* * * * *

Then the angels sang their new song, at last. All the Christians from years gone before shouted with joy as they and the angels gathered. They rejoiced for those they were there to greet, who Satan had deceived; for now, the love of Christ would be revealed, including Major Frost, and Colonel Syme, and Major Eppinger, and so many, many others.

All joyfully shouted, "Today, at last,
Our Father's Kingdom's come to past."
The sisters and brothers of Christ rejoice.
Following Christ, their heaven bound choice.
Reverend McDee and Tilly danced as they sang,

As did Armando, Mickey and Jeffry Lange.
The Myers family shouted with joy.
Betty Jo joined them, and so did Roy.
Ken Johnstone waved arms in jubilation.
Ned Padilla thanked Christ for salvation.
Tim and Mary danced as they praised.
Elmer thanked Jesus he was raised.
Dave Clawson embraced his wife.
Sarah and TJ danced for their new life.
Jed Drexton and his wife cried as one,
Larry Evans shouted, "It has now begun!"
Charles Essex cried, "Our Lord has come!"
Lorraine thanked Christ for mercies given,
Scott Harkins praised, his sins forgiven.
Jerry Grabner joined the celebration.
Robert shouted praises for salvation.
Andy held hands with Stephanie, and then,
all God's people shouted, "Amen!"
Now bring forth lost souls of the past,
Freed and to love their Christ at last.
All creation in joyful celebrations,
Of God's long awaited revelations!

And I saw heaven opened, and behold a white horse; and he that sat upon him was called Faithful and True, and in righteousness he doth judge and make war. His eyes were as a flame of fire, and on his head were many crowns; and he had a name written, that no man knew, but he himself.

And the Spirit and the bride say, Come. And let him that heareth say, Come. And let him that is athirst come. And whosoever will, let him take the water of life freely.

The End, and The Beginning